D0895501

THE STEWARDSHIP OF PRIVATE WEALTH

Managing Personal & Family Financial Assets

THE STEWARDSHIP OF PRIVATE WEALTH

Managing Personal & Family Financial Assets

SALLY S. KLEBERG

McGraw-Hill

New York San Francisco Washington, D.C. Auckland Bogotá
Caracas Lisbon London Madrid Mexico City Milan
Montreal New Delhi San Juan Singapore
Sydney Tokyo Toronto

Library of Congress Cataloging-in-Publication Data
Kleberg, Sally S.
  The stewardship of private wealth : managing personal & family
financial assets / by Sally S. Kleberg.
    p.   cm.
  Includes bibliographical references (p. 291) and index.
  ISBN 0-7863-1032-4
  1. Finance, Personal– –United States.   2. Inheritance and
succession– –United States.   3. Rich– –United States.   I. Title.
HG179.K567   1997
332.024—dc21   96–29708

McGraw-Hill

A Division of The *McGraw·Hill* Companies

Copyright © 1997 by The McGraw-Hill Companies, Inc. All rights reserved. Printed in the United States of America. Except as permitted under the United States Copyright Act of 1976, no part of this publication may be reproduced or distributed in any form or by any means, or stored in a data base or retrieval system, without the prior written permission of the publisher.

1 2 3 4 5 6 7 8 9 0 DOC/DOC 9 0 9 8 7

ISBN 0-7863-1032-4

Printed and bound by R. R. Donnelley & Sons Company.

This publication is designed to provide accurate and authoritative information in regard to the subject matter covered. It is sold with the understanding that neither the author or the publisher is engaged in rendering legal, accounting, or other professional service. If legal advice or other expert assistance is required, the services of a competent professional person should be sought.
    —From a Declaration of Principles jointly adopted by a committee of the American Bar Association and a Committee of Publishers.

McGraw-Hill books are available at special quantity discounts to use as premiums and sales promotions, or for use in corporate training programs. For more information, please write to the Director of Special Sales, McGraw-Hill, 11 West 19th Street, New York, NY 10011. Or contact your local bookstore.

Ghandi's Seven Blunders Plus One

Wealth without Work
Pleasure without Conscience
Knowledge without Character
Commerce without Morality
Science without Humanity
Worship without Sacrifice
Politics without Principles
and
Rights without Responsibilities

To Thomas, Benjamin, and Shannon,
who inspire and inform my work,
who teach me the most,
who matter the most,
who are my best friends.

PREFACE

The genesis of this book lies several generations behind me when my ancestors made a commitment to build a community deep in the "Wild Horse Desert" of the Texas coastal plains, near the border with Mexico. I grew up in a five generation-long tradition of stewardship of resources—human, natural, material, and financial—that binds my family in a unique culture and perspective. The desert was good to us, paying us back for tending it; farming and ranching it; managing its abundant wildlife; scientifically researching better ways to make a desert productive; and giving back to its people with employment, with educational resources, by embracing their culture and language in a township built for them, and with an implicit agreement that our family would work with them, side by side. The individual, family, and corporate philanthropic actions flow from this same business mission yet move beyond it to other interests such as social service, medical and veterinary research and cultural programming.

Four generations after my family settled in South Texas, oil and gas were discovered under that desert. The company, thus the family, were the beneficiaries of that blind luck. Being a member of the King Ranch family has been a challenge and a wonder. Being in a business (with over 100 shareholding family members) that has successfully operated for so many generations, has taught us all many lessons about the law; accounting; the oil and gas, ranching, and farming businesses; philanthropy; the real estate and commodities businesses; and only very recently, in the ancestral scheme of things, the challenge of financial resource management.

In 1977, after having all the assets managed within the company, a source of liquidity was distributed out of the family corporation to the individual family shareholders. When this distribution of wealth occurred, I was not prepared or trained to manage my share. The road to my self-styled financial education for the ensuing years has been a long and bumpy one. Teaching stewardship comes naturally because it has been modeled and practiced by my family for generations. My goal to broaden that understanding of stewardship to include financial literacy derives from the lack of easily understood, available reference sources I needed for my own financial education. I didn't have the language with which to make decisions. Thus, after 20 years of seat-of-the pants training, I developed this guide to the exercise of wealth management and stewardship for the "newcomers" who want clear and basic information on this subject.

The book is written with the women, the rising generation, and the newly wealthy in mind; for anyone unclear about the issues and responsibilities of stewardship of your (or someone else's) good fortune. If you are a marriage partner, widow, divorcee, a member of the next generation just testing the waters, a successful professional, a rock star, a star athlete, an inheritor in a long line of inheritors, or even a highly compensated CEO supremely at home managing public corporations but uncertain of how to manage personal wealth, you are the most vulnerable to inappropriate, insufficient, wasteful, or untrustworthy advice and advisors. As is often the case, this new responsibility you face may come at a time of a crisis or major transition, the impact of which heightens your sense of confusion, naïveté, uncertainty, fear, and vulnerability. Taking charge of your own education and beginning a stewardship process can embolden you to wise and gratifying action over time. At times such as these, people can make snap decisions that have lifelong effects, without thinking.

People of extraordinary privilege have complex challenges to define, accept, and meet. The purpose of this book is to bring individuals and/or families to a level of understanding and knowledge that enables them to act on these challenges calmly, wisely, and with careful planning. The idea of managing new wealth often causes people to panic and turn everything over to someone they barely know or to an unprepared or inadequate advisor to manage it for them. Abdication is a dangerous thing.

I encourage you to see challenges and changes as uncommon opportunities rather than as reasons to shy away from the complex nature of the excitement and fear, and hope and isolation that often accompanies wealth ownership, stewardship, and administration. Acquaint yourselves with the basic information contained here before rushing into complex decisions you may have little or no foundation to make.

Myriad opportunities exist to dissipate or dismiss the value of your resources for faulty, naïve, or ignorant reasons. The greatest single cause of bad judgment in wealth management is the failure to admit or realize that decisions around money (especially in families) are primarily emotional. Only secondarily are these decisions practical, educated, or studied, however much we convince ourselves otherwise. The most successful advisors to the wealthy instinctively know how to tap into the clients' needs to gain their trust because they understand this psychology so well. Without the fundamentals at hand, you may erroneously abdicate your power to one of these advisors, relying too heavily on someone who might not be trained to guide you in the many areas affecting you and your family.

To make this knowledge work for you rather than against you, and to empower you rather than handicap you, this toolbox of information, resources, and useful governance structures is arranged in building-block fashion (with many useful appendixes) to get you started in your education and planning. This format provides a simple, straightforward approach to getting your arms around the challenge, so that, individually or as a group, you can manage what Pogo calls the obstacle of "insurmountable opportunity."

Making dispassionate, wise decisions about allocating and deploying all of your resources for yourself and others will make you a successful and satisfied wealth steward and provide personal gratification for you. By these actions, you can serve as a model for those who follow you. After all, who cares more for your well-being and that of your family than you?

ACKNOWLEDGMENTS

The Seven Blunders Plus One are a gift to us from Arun Ghandi, who received the first seven blunders as tenets for world citizenship from the Mahatma Ghandi. Arun was sent by his parents from South Africa to India when he was 13 years old to live with and learn from his grandfather. Now living with his family in Mississippi, Arun is director of the M.K. Ghandi Institute for Nonviolence. He has added his own eighth blunder to the list.

The compendium of contributors to *The Stewardship of Private Wealth* have been carefully chosen for their understanding of wealth stewardship as a process, not as a series of qualitatively balanced quantitative decisions. They espouse the imperatives and value of planning. Many self-styled educators approach the private wealth marketplace as sellers of singly focused products and services. A minuscule number come as listener–educator–advisors. The book's professional contributors believe in the importance of team management, and none hold themselves out as experts in areas outside their domain. Yet, without exception, they understand the other issues outside their expertise with which families and individuals must wrestle. They are wise enough to admit when they don't know something, and they are willing to find and work with trustworthy and knowledgeable sources. The experts in some key result areas such as various investments and philanthropy are experience-taught wealth managers themselves.

It is our goal to provide simple, straightforward tools to help you and your family to dynamically plan, ensuring good decisions now and in the future. This book is a guide to help wealth stewards take charge of their lives from a foundation of personal confidence, without abdicating their personal responsibility or using advisors inappropriate for this work.

Unless otherwise noted, Ms. Kleberg is the chapter author. In all other instances, where another contributor is the author, it is clearly indicated at the beginning of the chapter or chapter section. Major chapter collaborations are credited as they occur.

In addition to my collaborators, there have been others whose substantial guidance and challenge contributed to the project, and who deserve special notice for their inspiration, advice, mentoring, and availability, including Bryant Cushing, father of the project; Nanny, Thomas, and Benjamin; Judy Kenney; Eileen Hackim; Nancy Busch; Joan Thorne; Susan Russell; Malcolm Bessent; Greg Blasko; Dan Fleming; Peter White; Mayra Woo; Tony Kaufmann; Robert Baensch; Don Trone; Bill Clawson; Adrian, Stephen, and Ruxandra; Lee Hennessee; Amy Ost; Ralph Rieves; New Horizons Group; Charlotte Beyer; Alex and Grace; and The Strickland Group, especially Don Monaco.

CONTENTS

Chapter 9

Money Management: Take Time and Trust Yourself— It's Your Money   165

Chapter 10

Venture Capital: Investing in New Ideas   189

Chapter 11

Real Estate: The American Dream   207

Chapter 12

Oil and Gas: The Oil Patch   227

1

INTRODUCTION AND BACKGROUND
Private Wealth Stewardship

> I repeated my concern for the quality and value of Rockefeller Center. . . . the financial advice given my grandfather by Frederick Gates, who counseled John D. Rockefeller 'to make final disposition of this great fortune...for the good of mankind' [that resulted in] the Rockefeller Foundation, and assistance to a legion of other institutions and individuals both here and around the world. My brother Laurance and I are proud of how younger members of our family are continuing this stewardship in ways that reflect their own interests, beliefs and hopes for a better world.
>
> *David Rockefeller, Sr.*[1]

Rt. Rev. John H. MacNaughton, retired bishop of West Texas, suggests that stewardship is what we do with what we have, all of the time. Stewardship is not an action of dissipation or hoarding. Stewardship is an act of tending or enhancing with care the value of something you have influence over and passing it on to those who succeed you.

Private wealth is an inclusive term, referring to human (physical, psychological, and personal talents and interests), monetary, real property, operating business, career, professional, environmental, educational, and philanthropic resources. Preparing you to make good stewardship decisions is the goal of this book. If a collector of fine art is truly a steward, she or he serves as a conservator, not a hoarder, enjoying the art and minding the asset while it is held so that those who follow will have their turn at conservatorship, sharing, enhancement, and enjoyment. As long as they are tended and cultivated, families, fine art, and enterprises can outlive even the hardiest human being.

Private wealth is better served by stewardship than by a detached management of things. Whether an individual or family comes to their fortune by lottery, inheritance, fame, earnings, invention, or entrepreneurship, effective stewardship and management of personal fortunes and lives very seldom come naturally or without plenty of help along the way. With every conceivable hand extending to "help" you, sell you on something, or receive something from you, you, as the ultimate decisionmaker, will need a keen, deep understanding and the motivation to take control of your family's lives and assets.

The basic assumption of this book is that managing wealth is a new subject to you. Even if you have wealth around you, you will not have had direct responsibility for making major management decisions about it. Perhaps you just had your 21st birthday and were put on the board of the family foundation, but you can't read a balance sheet or don't know in what to invest the foundation's capital for the next year. If so, this primer has tools you can use to familiarize yourself with terminology and with financial planning in order to help make you an effective wealth management student and board participant. But you are going to have to crawl before you can walk. Just because you happen to have great resources, the outside perception is that you are a genius. How else could you have the wealth? The world often equates wealth with wisdom. Not so. You need a vocabulary and a context in which to begin to do all that will be asked of you and your family over the next years and generations as you develop your stewardship skills and style.

Each of the following chapters is a compressed book of knowledge. Consider it a starting place—a primer. Experience, involvement, and further study will take you the rest of the way. The information is not meant to tell you how to manage money, what insurance to buy, what bank or venture capital fund to choose, or what philanthropic structure to adopt. This book tells you where and how to start, what the language is, and what tools are available; it sets a framework for your planning, gives you a sense of where to look for advice and ideas, tells you how to ask questions, and identifies the fundamentals for getting on the road to whatever objectives you set. The book does have a healthy bias; it encourages you to take the reins to the extent that you are willing. Anyone is able. It does encourage you to incorporate philanthropy in all that you do. Private wealth stewardship is private wealth management with responsibility, with a conscience, and with a heart. Now, let's talk about how to learn the fundamentals.

Historical modeling generated from an operating family business experience over five generations, good and bad advice, personal trial and error, mentoring the sixth generation, and advising other families and individuals has helped me develop the following construct for managing the many disciplines involved in the stewardship of wealth.

Private wealth stewardship is three dimensional, dynamic, and complex. The following Figure 1.1 illustrates the three areas about which you will learn in your role as a steward. It is through this three-part construct that your family will experience and manage its wealth over the generations.

A represents the driving forces in the stewarding of private wealth—you and your family group and the attendant emotional or psychological dynamics of the individuals and family. From this position, the group defines the mission, goals, and objectives for *A*, *B*, and *C*, as well as their flow and direction in the future. This important task should never be left to someone else without your involvement.

B represents the key result areas your group will address on a regular and ongoing basis. You will define the areas and be responsible for keeping them current.

C represents the flexible but firm foundation you will need in order to meet the mission of *A* while doing the work in *B* and *C*.

None of these components operates independently of the other. I have organized this book in such a way that you are introduced to the personal information first, then the planning and key result areas, followed by the foundation governance structures, and finishing with the specific investment areas. This is the ideal learning process: moving from the general to the specific. However, don't be deceived into believing that this is a one time string of actions, or that it is a straight line to learning and managing the work you will

FIGURE 1.1

Wealth Stewardship Construct

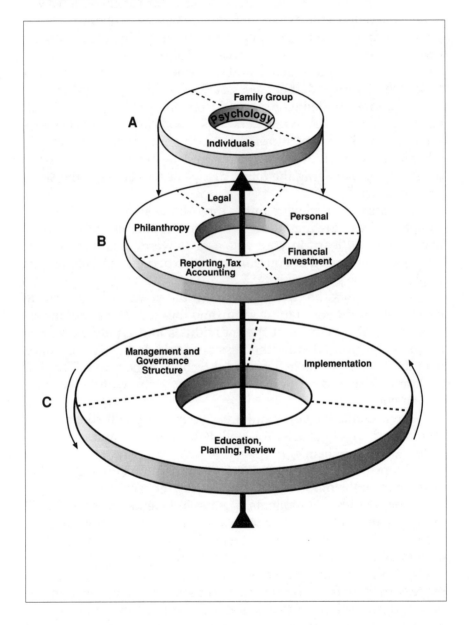

have as director or student. Over the years and generations, your family will move back and forth to different places at each level as circumstances dictate. But if you keep in mind that if *A*, the wealth holders and their psychologies, directs the establishing of *C*, the flexible foundation put in place (that is revised as needed to meet the changing times), then *B*, the key result areas, will operate smoothly and will accomplish the mission, goals, and objectives of *A*.

First, familiarize yourself with the wealth stewardship precepts in the following section. When wealth is newly available, most people feel they have to *do* something with it. They rarely think to just park it safely for awhile until they plan how to manage the new wealth and all of the activity it will inevitably spawn around them. These precepts are laid out in a sequence that is roughly parallel to the structure of the book and, most importantly, to the way your learning process should ideally unfold.

Second, a look at the most common types of wealth is a useful exercise for a new wealth manager. It is similar to a new mother who, when her toddler throws his or her first tantrum, asks other mothers with children this same age, "Is this normal or should I be worried that something is wrong here?" Part of your emotional and psychological profile is molded by how your wealth is created. Chapters 2 and 3 will address other factors in wealth psychology. You will see that by familiarizing yourself with your type, you can later make decisions about investment styles, management structures, and so on that are more relevant and useful to you. By understanding this, you won't think that you have to reinvent the wheel to do a passable job managing your affairs.

The more understanding you have, the better able you will be to fashion a good system by which to manage and direct your involvement in wealth stewardship. For instance, because our family business has tied family members together for six generations, we as individuals have decided we need independence in our personal financial management. Consequently, we do not operate our personal business out of company headquarters. However, a younger entrepreneurial business will operate both business and personal affairs out of the same location because all things tend to flow from the same source—family matters, business matters, and the wealth that the business and family generates and uses. Regardless of the source of wealth, the general precepts identified in the following section will apply.

WEALTH STEWARDSHIP PRECEPTS

The steps described here are presented in a sequence that is designed to maximize the book's value to you, regardless of what your profile is. Even if you choose to turn everything over to a bank or a brother to be managed for you, at least familiarize yourself with what is involved so that you can represent your interests effectively and with personal satisfaction when times for decisions arise.

1. *Be aware. Awareness is your greatest ally.* Without awareness and knowledge, you give your power away too easily. Unidentified emotions and secrets destroy great businesses. You read it in the paper and see it around you every day. No one is immune. Financial ignorance is no excuse. Wealth stewardship and financial literacy are achievable regardless of age, gender, background, or life interests.

2. *Define where your wealth comes from, its benefits and traps.* Don't ignore the fact that different types of wealth, personality, and psychology influence your personal decisions.

3. *Identify the family or individual culture in which decisions are being made.* Are you organized around single or common values? If not, do you want to be? How do you define them? What and who do you care about?

4. *Craft family and personal mission statements from which the process of planning and implementation can flow.* With them, conflict, information flow, control, and shared and diverse goals can be heard and addressed. These statements will serve as the foundation for the planning function that is so integral to satisfying wealth stewardship. A clear mission in times of extreme pressure becomes the sea anchor in the storms of great change.

5. *Embrace the art and necessity of planning.* Planning helps ensure peace of mind, personal control, and realization of goals.

6. *Get to know yourself and how you respond or act with professionals, peers, family, and across generational lines.* This will evolve as you do your planning. Gaining and maintaining personal confidence and control are your goals.

7. *Define key result areas—accounting/reporting, legal, personal, investment, and philanthropy.* Learn their particular qualities and determine your interest in and grasp of them. Decide what you don't know so you can set about learning what you need to learn. Identify important decisions within key personal and business result areas. Use this as a guide for building an agreed upon structure in which to manage the process. Employ a team approach in working with investment managers, professional advisors, and associates to address the disparate family and professional agendas.

8. *Within key result areas of your stewardship, treat investment categories in context.* Include core operating businesses, collections, and philanthropy as resources to steward, and give them value equal to the pure "investment areas." Asset allocation in the broadest sense includes *all assets* to which you devote time, talent, and treasure. Your model should be reflective of your personal interests and style.

9. *Identify your objectives.* Guided by your mission statement, construct personal and family investment and philanthropic objectives. Incorporate confidentiality (not secretiveness), honesty, and trust to ensure realistic goal-setting and action plans for the future.

10. *Define "risk" for yourself.* Every investment industry and asset class has an element of risk. Those you understand the least may appear to be higher risk, but in real monetary terms they may be less risky. Real estate developers are comfortable with debt; landowners are not. Which is the more risky position? It all depends on your perspective. Have a clear idea what you mean by "investment," whether it is for a targeted return, a gamble, for pleasure, or for a collection. Identify whether you are risking lunch money or extra capital. What is lunch money for you?

11. *Define a personal and/or family philanthropic ethic.* Make a specific effort to build philanthropic awareness as a useful and satisfying investment, planning, training, learning, employment, and enjoyment tool.

12. *Investigate avenues of investment and what they mean.* Where is additional training for the women? Integrate the next generation into the process early, by talking to and training the children.

13. *Define your own "investment (time) horizon."* Are you a market-timer or a long-term investor? This personal definition should be relevant to your age, and it will change with time.

14. *Be a patient investor.* Understand that cycles happen. Become comfortable with them as you learn more. Everything you invest in is cyclical to a certain degree. Try to stick with or learn from people who have ridden a few of those cycles in their industries—up, down, and back up again. As Julian Robertson and other investment wizards suggest, "Ask an old man."

15. *Collect tools of the trade.* These tools include continuing self-education; awareness; reliable professional advice; concepts of planning, creative asset allocation, and process; an open mind; prudent investment goals and actions; and hiring and firing the most appropriate advisors for the time, age, and place.

16. *Understand at the outset that the fact that a person is a friend or family member does not guarantee that she or he will make a good business partner or manager or have your best interests at heart.*

17. *Be a prudent and diligent investor.* Don't agree to invest in anything you don't understand just because someone else is doing it. Take your time, be flexible, expect and admit your mistakes, correct where you can, and move on. Spend 75 percent of your time on the revenue generation and 25 percent on cost containment.

18. *Get it in writing.* Ask questions before you sign anything, *especially* if it's between family or friends. To recoin a phrase from Robert Frost, "good legal documents make good partners." A family member or friend can disappoint you unexpectedly, especially when downturns in fortune occur for them.

19. *Understand the following verities.* You *will* lose money. Money *isn't* everything. "Riches don't alleviate, only change, one's troubles" (Epicurus). Once the word is out, you *will* be seen as a dollar sign; it goes with the territory. Seemingly trusted employees *will* steal, so take precautions. Money doesn't make you smarter than anybody else.

TYPES OF WEALTH

In 1984, 74 members of the Fortune 400 list of the wealthiest people in America derived their fortunes from energy (oil and gas); in 1994, the number was 21. There were 71 real estate tycoons on the list in 1984 but a mere 30 in 1994. In contrast, in 1984, there were 6 list members from financial institutions, and in 1994, there were 30.[2] Wealth sources are cyclical. A case for diversification can certainly be made from this, but more importantly, the types of wealth represented here are as diverse in their characteristics as the owners themselves. Having an idea of the characteristics that accompany general categories of wealth provides a way to identify for yourself what defines certain attitudes and values you want to pay attention to when discussing your family mission and values statements and designing your investment policy goals.

For instance, oil and gas operators are perceived as gamblers who are comfortable with leverage. Borrowing money to drill so that you can extract oil to sell to make money to pay back the money you borrowed and then some is the way the business works. But many oil and gas fortunes are actually held by landholders who just happened to have the stuff under their land. And everybody knows that ranchers and farmers are conservative and debt averse. This sets up a conflict within a single type. Where do you fit? What are your attitudes? Would you be able to operate with a conflict of this kind affecting your decisions?

The truth of the matter is, you are comfortable moving around in familiar territory where you understand what's going on. If you want to step outside that zone and try something new, be sure you learn at least the basics of the trade first. Don't just take someone else's word for it. Begin with knowing and understanding your own wealth source first—what its cycles are likely to be and what its strengths and weaknesses are—before you invest in other assets. Oil and gas prices go down just like they go up. Stock markets crash, and 80 percent or more of professional money managers underperform their benchmark indexes. If you don't actively manage your own portfolio, be careful who you entrust with your wealth. Know the area in which you want to invest.

Just as defining as the business itself is the type of wealth that describes your family. Wealth management types appear in several recognizable categories. Some will be in an organized management setting, either through the operating entity, such as a family wealth office, or through an operating company office. Other types are newly liquid and unsure of how to proceed. They will either go to a financial institution, investment advisor, or another established family office for management or guidance; start their own firm; or join together in a group of other wealth holders.

Entrepreneurial/Operating Business-Based Wealth

A family business is of two main types: simple (first generation) and complex (multiple generation). The largest segment of the private wealth economy is in the form of family-owned businesses or owner-managed companies. Owners begin as risk takers. If the company survives succession transitions, unless the majority of the family or other owners remain involved, the nature of the owners changes. They tend to become more risk averse, less committed to the whole group, and more individually motivated. Depending on the size of the company and the family, families usually grow exponentially faster than the ability of the founding principals and principles to sustain the demands of later generations. As a result, less than 10 percent of all closely held businesses in the United States survive to third-generation ownership.

Although first-generation entrepreneurs are risk takers by definition, they typically exhibit a risk-averse personal investment style and generally prove to be poor managers of personal wealth derived from that business unless they continue to roll it over into new entrepreneurial ventures, a world they understand. The risk in entrepreneurial wealth is business risk (a risk they understand), not investment risk (risking their hard-earned savings). Business owners understand and are comfortable investing in what they can control, and they can't control the stock market (unless the market is their business). For instance, if they become comfortable using derivative strategies in the business, they will be more likely to feel at home with them for their personal portfolios. At the same time, they might diversify only into bonds so as not to put the personal portfolios at risk in the stock market.

Another characteristic exhibited by most entrepreneurs is that they have the majority of their personal net worth tied up in the business until that business matures. First generations are planning averse, but experience teaches subsequent generations that succession, tax, and financial management planning must undergird many operating business decisions. This is because they might have been rocked by the impact of estate taxes on the company and the family after a transition. When a patriarch/matriarch retires or dies, the family may or may not continue in business as a group. Often, without a unifying central figure, the family will divide unless the group is highly mature and evolved. If there has been ineffective or no estate planning done, they might have to liquidate to settle the estate.

Common to this group is the public misperception of a family member's liquidity. Much of the wealth may be illiquid and dedicated to company growth capital, although there are visible exceptions to this characteristic. Within the family there are varying levels of education and financial expertise. This depends entirely on an individual's formal education and involvement in the family business.

Women in entrepreneurial families make decisions differently depending on their direct involvement in that business. Often, they are barred or sheltered from the business, and this affects their attitude toward managing all types of financial and other business decisions, whether they have an outside source of income or not. Most become involved in the company only if they are encouraged to do so from an early age. The women are more often involved in philanthropic efforts if those are a part of the family's profile.

Post-Equity Liquidity Wealth

This fastest-growing segment of the wealth economy is characterized by enormous early liquidity that becomes less liquid as the portfolio matures and diversifies. Management of new wealth very often becomes the new family business in various forms of family offices and family foundations. This new wealth management company is often technically unsophisticated at the outset and is besieged by service providers and salespersons, art dealers, and so on. But as it matures and the family expands, the characteristics gradually evolve to take on those exhibited by inherited-wealth families.

Unless philanthropy has been a part of the corporate or family culture, post-equity wealth holders tend to be philanthropically underschooled or unsophisticated. Because the capital has been directed solely through the business, they have not had the opportunity to practice philanthropy. There are exceptions to private personal philanthropy, such as the case in which a person is innately a giving person and is active in community affairs on his or her own, but the majority of this type has never had the opportunity to consider philanthropy. When the Stella D'Oro family sold out, most of the family members were newly emigrated Italians. The company had managed the money; it was all in the bank in trusts. As a result, the family members practiced no financial planning and had no idea that philanthropy was something they could do.

With massive liquidity comes a lowering of risk aversion unless old biases are still in control. Mistakes are made in a rush to get the wealth "under management", planning tends to come after the fact. Others can't wait to start a new business of liquidity management. But once an entrepreneur, always one, and entrepreneurs like having it their way. Traditional investment strategies are more palatable, and publicly traded or restricted insider stock often becomes the core investment asset that dominates investment strategy.

The educational level of this group is varied. Some have younger family members schooled in certain management strengths. Subsequent generations may have more technical education; they often hire aggressive managers from outside to manage the new business.

Performance by money managers might be the most important criteria for choosing a relationship, but as the portfolio matures and diversifies, performance loses its top billing, and service and confidentiality become the prerequisite for retaining the association. If the leader is older, the goal will more likely be capital preservation and the growth of buying power.

More women family members are involved in the business of this very interesting group. Where the women are actively involved in the family's office, they are often the managers; however, gender separation in the previous company generally perpetuates in the subsequent post-equity formation. Philanthropy is more frequently managed by the women.

Inherited Wealth/Established Office

Inherited-wealth families typically have mature, diverse, less-liquid portfolios. They might have a large segment of the portfolio in low-basis publicly traded stock or they might have a large portion in illiquid, closely held corporate stock. These families usually hold these assets in a large array of complex ownership entities. As a result, the estate- and tax-planning focus is singular and often drives many of the investment decisions.

Service, confidentiality, and performance are primary criteria for the professional relationships chosen by inherited-wealth families. But the historical goal of these families has been capital preservation, and that becomes strained by the liquidity needs of subsequent generations as they increase exponentially in numbers and demands. There is clear incidence of later generations living beyond their means but denying that they are doing so. This behavior can often be coupled with high incidence of substance abuse and other family dysfunction. Because of the distinct visibility of their wealth, this group tends to be the most private and secretive of all wealth-holder types.

Because of the availability of opportunity, these wealth holders tend to have high education levels, and the male family members have visible financial literacy, if not sophistication. Succeeding generations, particularly the women, may have little, if any, interest or guidance in active wealth management. However, the greatest level of philanthropic knowledge and sophistication appears in this group, and frequently, the family foundation is the largest segment of the business under management. As barriers break down, more and more young, female family members are asserting their rights to financial literacy and involvement.

Instant or Celebrity Wealth

This type of wealth holder is difficult to characterize because the sources of wealth are so varied. But generally, if the wealth holder has a career, she or he turns over wealth management to trained professionals. As a group, these wealth holders prefer one-stop shopping to eliminate distractions. Lottery winners and other new celebrities generally haven't a clue about wealth management and can be the most disadvantaged of any wealth group. Their lack of financial literacy and their inability to handle instant fame often leads them to make extremely poor choices about managers and investments. A current rock star earned $13 million in the last two years. He had an entourage of 20, and he spent $9 million for a home that is valued at no more than $4.5 million (if he can sell it). The *New Yorker* recently reported his bankruptcy filing.

As wealth managers, holders of celebrity and instant wealth tend to emphasize performance by managers rather than focusing on particular asset classes. Wealthy celebrities have little or no interest in, or knowledge of, investments and tend to be highly risk averse and conservative where financial markets are concerned. As for philanthropy, this group has rarely regular exposure or modeling for it. The commitments vary with personal inclinations.

These wealth holders most often turn management and decisions over to professional managers, some of whom are sadly opportunistic or incompetent. This wealth group is the one most likely to be "skinned" due to inexperience, lack of focus in this part of their life, and their personal, high visibility—everyone knows where they are and can get to them all of the time. Professional athletes, rock stars, and other creative artists make poor business people, often investing in bogus real estate and oil and gas deals, as well as other asset classes for which they have little training or literacy, such as art and venture capital. Of course, there are exceptions, such as Madonna and Claudia Schiffer. Hiring a good, honest gatekeeper should be the highest priority if this is your wealth type.

Professional Wealth

In some ways, professional managers who have amassed great wealth from salaries, stock options, and bonuses resemble the entrepreneur in wealth-management style. They have been busy managing a career or corporation, not their personal wealth. Individuals in this group possess a high level of education but less practical expertise, financial literacy, and desire to manage their individual portfolios. The exception to this, of course, is the professional money manager. But in general, certain characteristics are common across this type, which includes attorneys, physicians, upper-level corporate managers, and others like them.

Holders of professional wealth share a singular focus in common with all successful money makers, one that rarely includes involving their family members in investment planning and decisions. Instead, they prefer to turn management over to trained professionals, and they tend to prefer one-stop shopping to eliminate distractions.

For the corporate manager, the core asset is most often restricted stock or options in the managed company that will dictate the key asset management decisions. Peculiar risk profiles exist depending on the asset mix. Professional corporate managers may be conservative in their personal financial decisions. Sophisticated hedging and tax-planning techniques will require a financial sophistication that this professional might not possess. There is clear opportunity for folly and misguidance. Many physicians, believing they are wisely diversifying their interests, have invested in bogus oil and gas properties and start-up companies outside their area of expertise rather than concentrating on what they know—science, technology, and health care in their various forms.

The value of personal philanthropy is likely a new phenomenon to these individuals, although professionally, they might be corporate philanthropists for opportunistic or "good business practice" reasons. Likewise, the women and children in these families very seldom have the financial literacy necessary to comfortably pick up the reins of management of the personal portfolio when the inevitable succession or family changes occur.

The offspring of all of the wealth types discussed in this section will ultimately have the characteristics of each of the classifications, with an additional overlay of inherited wealth issues. Chief among these issues are trust and autonomy issues, exhibited by a lack of belief in oneself and one's ability to make it in the world; a garbled sense of values and mission, work ethic, and motivations; and a lack of practical training about money management. The chapters on the psychology of money and communications that follow will address these issues and the impact money can have on the deterioration of the family and its relationships.

In conclusion, regardless of your wealth type, assume that there are plenty of people in a similar situation who are all trying to understand and manage complex responsibilities for the first time. They are all just as afraid as you are of what they think they don't know. Fear is often the by-product of an innocent lack of information and of kept secrets. Secrets around money are endemic to our culture. It seems the longer a family has wealth, the more common are secrets and the more ingrained is the family dysfunction. The dysfunction, in turn, magnifies the secrets around wealth that families keep from each other and the outside world. Whether we like it or not, we play out our familial roles in our family business and family financial decisions. This extra weight of personal emotion in the mix creates the need to make a family transaction a business transaction. The more financially literate you are, the less emotional you will be when making decisions.

Thoughtful private wealth stewardship should be the preferred alternative to crisis management, where options are eliminated, decisions are made for you, control is weakened, families are divided, and fortunes are lost, taxed away, or otherwise dissipated. You and the world around you benefit the most when you use whatever power, wealth, and influence you care to have in a positive and satisfying way. Otherwise, your wealth will end up managing you and dictating your life and your relationships.

As William Cronin once said:

> Home, after all, is the place where we live. It is the place for which we take responsibility, the place we try to sustain so we can pass on what is best in it (and ourselves) to our children....It means looking at the part ... we intend to turn toward our own ends and asking whether we can use it again and again and again—sustainably— without diminishing it in the process."[3]

This is the goal of private wealth stewardship.

ENDNOTES

1. David Rockefeller, Sr. Letter to the editor, the *New York Times*, September 21, 1995.

2. Robert Williamson, Jr. "Food for Thought." Client letter, Donaldson, Lufkin, & Jenrette, May 4, 1995.
3. William Cronin. "The Trouble with Wilderness." *The New York Times Magazine*, August 13, 1995, p. 43. Reprinted by permission.

2

WEALTH IS MORE THAN MONEY

The Psychology of Wealth

Wealth is more than money. If not money, then what is it?

Wealth is a state of mind. Wealth is a personal psychology. Wealth is abundance in its many forms and how society, families, and individuals view the place that abundance holds in their lives. In this country, however, money is the predominant measure of wealth. Amassing wealth equates to the *sunum bonum* of success. Unfortunately, financial wealth can create heartache, broken relationships, and other problems when it is not put in perspective to the rest of our lives.

The psychology of wealth and money flows from several sources. It comes from the normal differences in male and female attitudes and psychologies. A personal psychology is also determined by a money personality that is innate, and another that derives from attitudes and beliefs born of family circumstance and upbringing as well as from the values shaped by societal, political, and religious structures and beliefs. In *The Silence of Money*, Lee Hausner defines the several psychological patterns we all live with but of which most of us are unaware. Bringing these various aspects to light provides a simple, basic knowledge to help you understand that making financial planning and action decisions often are not about the money or wealth itself. Personal financial decisions are emotionally based rather than being driven solely by quantitative or practical measures. Because of differences in money personalities, what appears practical to one person can appear frightening to another.

Trying to converse from different money perspectives adds to the diciness of communications on financial topics. For example, a successful Hollywood executive identifies her personal history as the driving force behind her conservative money management profile. She has invested everything in a bond portfolio. She was a child of the Holocaust whose family escaped Nazi Germany with nothing, and she was raised by a stepfather with a "depression era" mentality. Her learned money personality set her up for later conflict with her husband, a wealthy film director, whose free-wheeling artistic personality leads him to spend what he has just because it's there. Even though this woman has earned and accumulated much personal wealth by using other people's money to take considerable risks in the entertainment industry, her underlying conservative nature reigns when it comes to her personal financial decisions. She is so bound by her money personality that she convinced her husband to sell several homes he owned before their marriage. Now, they live in one home and stay in hotels when working in other locales. Understanding, accepting, and working openly with differences saves and strengthens relationships engaging in battles over money attitudes.

Research and experience tells us that on money and financial matters, women and men are by their very natures set at cross purposes, and we need to keep in mind that these underlying differences can create obstacles to personal goals when we work together. For instance, women are more "other centered," or relationship motivated, and men are more motivated by personal autonomy. Some common misconceptions about women, men, and finance include the one that argues that men know how to manage money and women do not. In reality, men often act as if they know even when they don't simply because they think they should. Even when women have a head for money, management, and finance, they will often defer in the presence of male advisors, siblings, and spouses out of some false belief that it isn't appropriate to do otherwise.

Two erroneous maxims are, "Men are allowed to ask questions" and "Women shouldn't have to worry about their finances." As a result, if a woman fails to speak up, she becomes a coconspirator in maintaining these faulty stereotypes. Other coconspirators are professionals who cannot or will not envision nontraditional roles for women as competent financial managers, despite the fact that many women are managing household budgets, teaching children to manage allowances, planning and saving for vacations, and managing their own salaries, personal finances, and investment portfolios.

In philanthropic decisions, a couple more often gives the greater support to the husband's philanthropy, and the woman tends to give smaller individual amounts to her personal causes. I experienced a lack of respect for my ability to make personal financial choices from my former spouse after making a philanthropic pledge to an institution we both supported. I was chastised for not discussing my intentions, even though the contribution was made from my separate account. Later, when I was asked to fill an unexpired term of another female trustee on the board of trustees of this same institution, my husband reneged on his capital pledge in protest against not being chosen to serve on the board, even though the board seat was reserved for a woman. I am relieved that attitudes are beginning to change as women act in their interests. Speaking up may not be easy, but it is sometimes very necessary.

I have explored how my own psychology influences how I relate to wealth because I was periodically in conflict with some family members and advisors when I made personal legal, philanthropic, tax planning, and financial decisions. Exploring some of the issues highlighted by Lee Hausner in the following sections helped me separate my responsibility and actions from those of others. I could have used her information a few decades ago. Instead, I learned very much by trial and error over many years of difficult personal and professional relationships involving investment and other financial decisions.

I have also wrestled with what unearned or inherited wealth means to me. I pay attention to how it impacts my attitudes and decisions. Much of what I experience stems from other people's false perceptions of women's roles as financial decisionmakers. I know that supporting myself and making my own decisions, regardless of the obstacles, helps me build self-confidence and self-esteem. I also know that I need and want to use wisely, manage carefully, and give away thoughtfully that which is my birthright (through no effort of my own). It is my responsibility, and if I want to sleep well at night, I can't abdicate it. Getting to this level of understanding has taken a long time, beginning with my first awareness of being part of a family business.

My family owns and operates an agribusiness company, a capital-intensive, low-margin business headquartered in drought-prone south Texas. My attitudes toward money were shaped by the unpredictable nature of stewarding the company's assets. My father was excessively frugal, and my mother was, and still is, a polar opposite—generous to a fault, with an eye for quality and largesse. My dad's attitude was partially due to backlash from his spendthrift father. My mom had her separate income, and was uneasy with the marked gulf between her attitudes and dad's. Dad wanted us to learn the value of hard work, commitment to a goal, and frugality. (You never knew when another drought or hurricane or a parent's debt would wipe you out.) Dad had spent his youth on an outpost division of the ranch in a small wood-frame house and, in his early years, he rode horseback to school across miles of rangeland each day. As an adult, he was a cattleman, unaffected by the oil and gas revenue stream the company enjoyed after he graduated from law school. My mother grew up in the city, the youngest daughter of a general surgeon and chief-of-staff of a large hospital there. She had lived in comfortable and spacious surroundings before marrying and moving to the ranch. She liked nice things and wanted us to have them, too. The tension between mom and dad over money was no secret, and the messages I received from my parents were mixed. There is no mystery about why I am conflicted about what money and wealth mean for me and why I have chosen an open, educative approach with my own children.

In my family, the five members of my grandfather's generation each had their own "money personalities" from carving out a living from the land before oil was discovered. Later generations seemingly should have similar "money histories." Instead, my fifth generation contemporaries respond to the management of personal finances and the role of the family company in our personal lives in myriad and often highly conflicting ways. Disparate family groups form opportunistic alliances to serve personal perspectives on control, power, and perceived unfairness in divisions of labor and management. If one cousin is in management, another family alliance wants its representative on the board of directors as a counterweight. Personal attitudes of the various factions and individuals toward money in their own lives further complicate the dynamic. Some of them are spendthrifts, others are frugal, depending on their innate money personalities. As the number of minority shareholders in the family company increases, struggles for power and control accelerate at a rate equal to the distance that a family member feels he or she is from effective management and control over the shrinking pot—the pot used to feed the growing number of hungry mouths. There are over 100 of us now; if we don't make an effort to understand the part this plays in our communications, our family business meetings can collapse over conflicts.

Lee Hausner understands these conflicts. She spent many years as a counselor in the Beverly Hills Unified School District, which is predominantly populated with families with great wealth. Her experience in working with family businesses and children and families of privilege gives powerful credence to the tenets that "wealth is more than money" and "the rich are different"—from each other. To paraphrase Epicurus, "Riches don't alleviate, but only change, one's difficulties." But wealthy or not, attitudes toward money dictate more of our external lives than we realize or want to admit.

Making decisions such as who to trust, who to work with, and who to choose as business partners can be greatly enhanced by becoming aware of how your psychology dominates your choices. Knowledge is power. This chapter is about you—the way you relate to yourself, your spouse, your parents, your children, your philanthropies, and your advisors based on what money and wealth mean to you. The chapter is also relevant when considering what messages young people incorporate into their attitudes and choices. Lee talks about substituting money for relationship in her "Hidden Meanings" section. In her section entitled "Money Personalities," Lee looks at predictable personality types that will help you define your risk profile and develop a means to accept why your profile and that of your spouse, parent, or sibling may be at odds and should be considered when making joint financial decisions.

Lee also defines how we turn money into something other than what it is and give it many different meanings in our lives. She provides us with an insight into what we need to look at under the surface that might be undermining our financial decisions and our willingness to have open communications about this last taboo. It is not her intention to resolve conflicts in such a small space. This information is meant to inform and define the issues for you. Whether you use it or not is your choice. Lee does provide some elementary exploratory questions for you. For most people, it takes years to comfortably incorporate their personal attitudes into all matters having to do with wealth and wealth stewardship.

THE SILENCE OF MONEY

Lee Hausner, Ph.D.

Taboo subjects are rapidly disappearing today. Books, magazines, TV talk shows, and dinner party conversations regularly address once prohibited subjects such as deviant sexual behaviors, drug addiction and recovery, and incest survival. But there still remains striking silence on an extremely important and emotionally charged subject, one that impacts everyone's lives whether rich or poor. Money and its meaning to a family collectively and to family members individually remains shrouded in a veil of silence. Although money is not a topic of general conversation, its impact is felt in every aspect of our daily life. Emotions regarding money issues can be observed in activities as diverse as

Discussing prenuptial arrangements.

Setting a fee for services provided.

Lending money to a friend and then collecting when the debt is due.

Arguing about an overcharge on your bill.

Dividing the financial assets following the death of a parent.

Acknowledging your financial assets to a friend.

Requesting a larger monthly allowance or asking for a raise at work.

Considering a purchase or making a donation that will result in disapproval from a significant other in our lives.

Career choices.

Arguments over money issues are responsible for the highest percentage of marital disputes and are often the root cause of divorce. And for individuals who have experienced the divorce process, it becomes immediately apparent that marriage is less about love than it is about the financial settlement. However, in the majority of these situations, only a small percentage of the problem lies with the actual lack of sufficient dollars to pay bills. Rather, these conflicts revolve around basic differences between individuals' attitudes toward money and how they actually choose to use it. The intensity, frequency, and emotional cruelty of battles over money are fueled by factors far more powerful than just dollars and cents. That is why attempts to resolve these types of problems by dealing only with the objective monetary facts (for instance, you have again overdrawn your monthly budget; let's set up a budget) without understanding underlying psychological and emotional issues related to money creates an impasse in resolving these tensions.

WHAT IS MONEY?

The dictionary definition of money is quite straightforward: something generally accepted as a medium of exchange, a measure of value, or a means of payment. However, how we earn and use money is one of the chief means for expressing who we are and what we value. Thus, it is no longer just currency about which we are talking. Money has become a metaphor for a wide range of positives such as security, education, travel, prestige, opportunities, desired material indulgences, love, hope, power, freedom, and happiness. However, it has also become closely identified with negatives such as shame, guilt, control, manipulation, intimidation, fear, envy, greed, anxiety, low self-esteem, and marital conflict. Money penetrates every aspect of our lives. It could more accurately be defined as the energy force of our contemporary society. It is important to know this when approaching any financial decision, not only when it is yours to make but especially when various attitudes and agendas in a larger family group are involved in how such decisions are viewed and implemented.

Negative Messages

Historical negative images associated with money have perpetuated the silence that surrounds this subject. We learn from the Bible that the love of money is the root of all evil. Sophocles felt that there is nothing in the world so demoralizing as money. We refer to the "filthy rich" or a "poor little rich kid." A financial windfall is categorized as "making a killing" (is profit being equated to murder?). Amateur athletics is considered a "purer" sport because money is not involved. Among the financially elite, it is considered poor taste and breeding to talk about what things cost. "If you have to ask, you can't afford it" appears to be the motto. Money causes everyone to worry. If you have it, you are concerned with managing it or the possibility of losing it somehow, and if you don't have it, you worry continually about getting it.

Various religions have developed norms to regulate or bring a balanced perspective to economic activity so that individuals will not strive to please only their material selves; rather, individuals are encouraged to always remain in tune at a deeper level with others and their own more spiritual selves, separate from material measures of worth. Buddhists speak of the middle way. Christianity admonishes one to love thy neighbor. Judaism speaks of the importance of mitzvah, and the Mormons maintain regular tithing. The medieval church permitted the exchange of money only for basic necessities, and considered business or trade morally dangerous. Material needs were not evil, but were to be considered secondary to the spiritual self. It was considered lustful when material acquisitions became the primary concern of the individual, thus creating negative images associated with the obviously materially successful individuals.

The Dual Nature of Human Beings

The search for spirituality in an increasingly complex, often hostile, world is a major movement in today's society. Does money demean our spiritual nature? If one holds this belief, money becomes even more taboo. But to deny the importance of the material drives of the individual creates additional problems. Avoiding or ignoring such a critical subject does not cause it to disappear. The effect of money on our behavior, whether positive or negative, continues to exist. If we remain unaware of the role money plays in our personal lives, we will not be able to make the necessary positive changes when its power creates problems for us. The challenge of modern society is to create a successful balance between the dual nature of human beings, that is, the material being as well as the spiritual one. Money should enable one to live a life of meaning rather than becoming the meaning of one's existence. An individual who becomes a slave to money is serving a fool of a master.

Hidden Meanings of Wealth

Below are some of the euphemisms for money common in our modern society. They develop from the range of emotions and attitudes intimately connected to the meaning of money in our lives.

Love

If a child grows up in a household where money is prevalent and things are readily purchased but affection and attention are minimal, money becomes a substitute for love. When frequently absent parents return laden with gifts; inappropriate abusive behavior is remedied with a "serious" present; and money is given to provide the child with opportunity to leave the home for amusement so that mom and dad do not have to bother to give their time and energy, then money becomes the love vehicle. With little experience in sustaining a loving, intimate relationship with parents, the child will grow up with the belief that love must be purchased, and the degree to which one is loved can be counted by the number of possessions one acquires. When this thinking is extended to the belief that friendships or other types of relationships are purchasable, the individual will generally end up bitterly disappointed and feeling used.

Happiness

The length of the lines of hopeful repeat purchasers of lottery tickets when the jackpot mounts might indicate that some people live their entire lives waiting for the magical windfall that they are certain will be the answer to all of their problems. If this is true, this fantasy gives hope that any day, all of their problems may magically disappear when they have access to excess money. Each day becomes bearable because of the continual hope of a brighter tomorrow, a day free from money concerns and full of the security that money can provide. If money is readily available, this illusion is gone. Those who come from an affluent background do not have the luxury of this fantasy. They are keenly aware of the fact that money will not suddenly cause all personal problems to disappear and, in fact, that money has often been the contributing cause of some of their personal distress.

Control

The Golden Rule is that those that control the gold make the rule. As the giving of money is frequently used to reward behavior that conforms to the expectation of the giver and the withholding of it is used as a punishment for behavior judged unacceptable by the giver, the controlling power of money is clearly felt and often bitterly resented. The struggle for the purse strings in family dynasties attests to the use of money to control others' actions and behaviors. There are incentive trusts created every day with built-in grantor-defined criteria that force beneficiaries to comply in order to "earn" their inheritance.

Self-Esteem

In a society that judges worth by the amount of money in the bank or possessions flashed about, money becomes closely tied to self-esteem. Watch heads turn on the street when an expensive, flashy car passes by. Viewers appear fascinated by the television show and accompanying magazine entitled *Lifestyles of the Rich and Famous*, and one of the popular city tours offered in Los Angeles is a visit to the mansions of Beverly Hills. In the celebrated play *Fiddler on the Roof*, one of the principals shares his longing for riches in the well-known song, "If I Were A Rich Man". One of the striking lines of that song—"if you're rich they think you really know"—again supports the popularly held notion that the rich are entitled to respect merely by virtue of their bank accounts. Additionally, sociological studies have demonstrated that people are, in fact, treated in a more favorable and respectful manner if they are perceived to have money.

Security

Money plays an obvious role in creating a sense of security, which comes from the knowledge that one has the financial resources to pay for desired goods and services and will not have to deal with threatening creditors. Additionally, money clearly provides the resources to create systems for physical security (such as alarm installations, bodyguards, gated and guarded communities). There is irony in the fact that the money itself creates the need for these elements of protection. If the only security comes from money, you will never feel at peace. The belief that money will create internal security is illusory. Real security is internal and comes from a feeling of being in control of situations through personal skills and ability.

Freedom

There is some danger of viewing money as the only vehicle for freedom. The "someday" syndrome sounds like this: Someday, when I win the lottery or strike it rich, I can start living. The danger in regarding money as the only vehicle to personal freedom is that it can become an excuse for not doing things (i.e., I have to wait until I can afford it) and serves as a cover-up for underlying lack of confidence and initiative.

Guilt

In families of inherited wealth, money can create a sense of guilt on the part of the heirs. What did I do to deserve it? Am I worthy? Can I handle the responsibility? Will people think less of me because I didn't earn it? Additionally, if a child is constantly told that he or she should be grateful for all his or her material advantages, when this child feels angry and unhappy, guilt accompanies these "ungrateful" feelings. If the original source of the family fortune was obtained illegally, this sense of shame can be passed down through many generations.

Power

When one experiences the power that affluent individuals appear to exercise, it is easy to make the connection between money and power. The danger in this thinking is when the individual becomes directed only toward activities in which it is possible to acquire large monetary sums in the misguided belief that they will then become all powerful. True power is internally based. If these inner resources are not developed, disappointment and frustration will ultimately result.

Action

The frenzied activity on Wall Street illustrates the connection between money and action. Certain individuals have acquired enough money to dispel any worries about personal finances. However, the obsession becomes the creation of more and more wealth, as the process of wheeling and dealing becomes the life energy force. When extended the common pleasantry of, "How have things been for you since we last talked?" a new business development officer for a large money-management house responded, "Not good, I'm afraid." When asked why that was, he said, "I've been on vacation." The inquirer asked, "And that's bad news? How so?" To which the officer replied, "I don't make any money when I'm on vacation."

Dependency

Most children begin their lives in a state of economic dependency on parents. As the individual matures, one milestone in life is the assumption of total personal financial responsibility. However, when money or, more precisely, the lack thereof is seen as a means of prolonging dependency needs, the individual will often exhibit behavior that prevents mature development. Examples of this include a female heiress giving total control of her personal assets to the man in her life, or young adults sabotaging any attempt to become successful, thereby creating situations where they are forced to remain economically dependent.

Resentment/Envy

If money is closely associated with the fantasy of happiness, resentment and envy are inevitable between those who have money and those who don't. For that reason, individuals of means will frequently report experiencing a greater sense of comfort when socializing with those of similar economic means so that they do not have to worry about jealousy and envy. Additionally, since siblings often perceive material items as a tangible way of showing favoritism for one child over the other, parents have to take care not to needlessly create destructive envy.

Tension

Money becomes the convenient focus of conflicts that often have deeper interpersonal meanings. One example of this might be a husband's monthly tantrums over the amount of the telephone bill when the real issue is that he has been feeling ignored while his mate passes the time chatting with friends on the phone. When children are continually exposed to these types of conflicts, it is easy to understand why the presenting focus of money appears to be the tension producer. The silent double message transmitted around money adds additional tensions and perpetuates into later relationships if not openly recognized.

Its a Guy Thing

In families where men assume major control of finances and financial decisions, it can be hard for their daughters to feel comfortable taking control of their finances. Even when these daughters are business, math, or economics majors at the university and are now professionally working in this area, they will often report a sense of discomfort bringing their monetary skills into their marital relationships unless the husband wants to voluntarily abdicate or share this responsibility.

Sexual Potency

As women have historically looked to the men in their lives to provide the financial resources, it often appears that men with money have an easier time attracting the women they desire. Men will also report feeling more sexually powerful as they achieve greater monetary success, or that they struggle with potency when married to a wealthier woman or one who earns more than they do.

Intimacy

Within relationships, feelings of intimacy can often be directly correlated to the manner in which the couple deals with money issues. One of the challenges of a healthy relationship is the ability to retain a sense of individuality while simultaneously creating a relationship of togetherness. How to still be "me" while committing to a partnership of "we" is one of the continual struggles within a relationship and is a common problem handled in the offices of marriage therapists.

In some relationships, any attempt on the part of one partner to maintain economic separateness creates a discomforting distance and lack of trust. If both parties share this viewpoint of economic independence, they can become happily connected and comfortably relinquish any individual power in financial matters. However, many individuals feel the need for some type of autonomy. Economic independence becomes one of the important areas in which to retain some control in order to avoid feeling that the sense of "me" is lost in a relationship of "we." If this position is interpreted by one's partner as a resistance to creating desired intimacy or a lack of trust, marital problems are inevitable.

With such a wide range of feelings and emotions attached to money, it is not surprising that these differences can cause stress, particularly in interpersonal relationships. Emotionally charged subjects are the ones that most people conveniently avoid dealing with in an open and nonconfrontational manner. Thus, the taboo around money is perpetuated.

DEFINING DIFFERENT MONEY TYPES

As a result of the varied roles money plays for people, several general money types can be identified. You will find yourself in one of these categories. When financial institutions understand these types and can apply that information in delivering better client service, more appropriate investment recommendations are likely to follow.

For yourself, if you know your type, you can more easily discern what investment activities and advisor types are more comfortable for you without wasting time considering those that aren't.

Deal Maker

For this type, the money high comes through the process of acquiring assets (money, properties, and companies). These individuals are often accused by their families and friends of being workaholics. In an attempt to convince them to modify their behavior, it is often pointed out that they have more financial resources than they could spend in a lifetime. This approach fails to recognize that these individuals never believe that one can have "too much." The excitement is in the hunt for acquisition, and that is what is continually driving the deal maker.

Investors

Security and stability play an important role in the life of the investor type. He or she likes to sleep at night with minimal worries. Like the deal maker, there is a drive to acquire a defined amount of assets. However, the satisfaction for the investors lies not in continual acquisition but in building security for the future and confidence in their money-management ability. Money means security more than power. Investors are more risk averse than the deal maker, and they are more disciplined in their spending habits. Maintaining a balance in their lives by spending quality time with loved ones will have a higher priority than acquiring an additional buck.

Spenders

A spender is the most self-indulgent personality type. You can look to the material possessions continually being acquired by this money type to recognize the pattern. Spending is the focus. "When the going gets tough, the tough go shopping," could be their motto. As fast as money comes in, the spender dispossesses it. Carried to its extreme, this compulsion to continually purchase quickly destroys many plans for financial security.

Relators

Insecure in their social skills, this type of individual views friendships as a commodity to be purchased. Money is used to win the approval, companionship, and loyalty of others. He or she is the one to always host a party, pick up the check in restaurants, buy extravagant gifts, and make generous loans with undefined repayment dates.

Hoarders

Spending creates panic for the hoarder type. He or she carefully saves as much as is possible. It is the process of guarding and preserving assets that creates a sense of comfort in the relationship with money.

Gamblers

Gambler types live on the edge and take great chances with their money. These actions create the emotional highs that the gamblers continually seek.

Dreamers

The dreamer believes in a more idealist state of existence in which money is only used to deal with basic needs, and philanthropic activities have greater meaning and purpose. Disillusioned children of wealth are often found in this group. Having had financial resources and blaming them for all the pain and unhappiness in their lives, they view money as the root of all evil. Thus, it must be given away.

The types of investments to which you are drawn, the partners with whom you do business, and the advisors you hire will need to be compatible with your money personality type. If that isn't possible, be aware how your type might play a role in negotiations and decisions. This understanding can enhance your perspective on the cause of any problems, and lead to acceptable compromises and solutions. You might even choose to change your type.

CONNECTING WITH YOUR MONEY HISTORY

Answer the questions that follow to the best of your ability. Through this type of self-analysis, you will begin to understand how the money messages in your family have determined what money now means to you. If this history has caused dysfunctional behaviors (money disorders such as compulsive spending, gambling, money hoarding, etc.) or conflicts in your present interpersonal relationships, increased awareness will enable you to take the appropriate steps to reduce the negative effects of your history. A discussion focusing on any one of these questions can structure the beginning of a more open dialogue about the subject of money.

What is your definition of "wealthy"?

Are you comfortable talking about your money?

How was money used in your family (i.e., for control, to buy love, as reward)?

What do you remember your father saying about money?

What do you remember your mother saying about money?

How did the attitudes of your parents differ?

Did your parents fight about money?

Were your parents ever in serious financial trouble?

Who controlled the money in your home?

How did you receive money when you were growing up?

At what age did you begin to have some money?

What lessons in money management did you receive at home?

Did you have to work for your money?

Is saving important to you?

Do you save on a regular basis?

What do you think is the greatest value of money?

What are the dangers associated with having money?

How much money do you need?

How much money do you have?

What are you willing and unwilling to do to get money?

What types of satisfaction have you received from money?

What types of satisfaction have you received without it?

Was your family philanthropic?

What is your current involvement in philanthropy?

Do you want greater or less philanthropic involvement?

Does spending cheer you up?

Are you anxious when spending for yourself?

Are you terrified about losing everything you have?

Do you feel that money makes you threatening in your interpersonal relationships?

Do you regularly insist on getting the bill, buying expensive gifts, or lending money because you want to be admired and included?

What role did (or would) money play in your choice of a
mate?

What are the attitudes about money that you would like to
teach your children?

What is your current money behavior teaching your children?

What are your priorities for the control and transfer of your
wealth?

Have these issues been discussed with the members of your
immediate family?

BEGINNING TO DEVELOP A HEALTHY APPROACH TO MONEY

1. As honestly as you can, trace the development of your
    money beliefs and try to identify what money means to
    you.

2. Identify dysfunctional beliefs and patterns in your life so
    that these problematic attitudes are not passed on to
    another generation.

3. Money is a good servant but a bad master. Don't exag-
    gerate or deny its importance. You must be in control,
    not be controlled.

4. Use money not as an end in itself but as a reward for
    achievement. Achievement is its own natural high. If
    you shift the focus of your energy into accomplishments,
    you will de-emotionalize the power of money.

5. Begin dealing openly and verbally with money by
    providing financial education to members of your
    family. This is often a more structured way to begin a
    dialogue about money.

6. Concentrate on your nonfinancial assets, which include
    the following:

    Health
    Education
    Family
    Community

Personal growth
Service to others
Talents (special skills and interests)
Creativity
Spiritual faith
Gratifying work
Nature

This is by no means all there is to know about how attitudes and circumstances impact the path you choose to secure a comfortable relationship with others concerning wealth and its place in your lives. These are tools to use along the way to inform your development into a confident wealth steward.

3

MAINTAINING PERSONAL CONTROL

Communicating About Wealth

The oldest generation is really a family bank. The Rothschilds are great examples. They lend money to their children. When the investment creates growth, the children pay back the seed money and keep the growth. Money is a tool for empowerment of people. The real assets are the people in the family. A balance sheet approach tells you that you see these human beings pursuing happiness. Aristotle says you don't know if your life was happy until you're dead. You only obtain happiness by pursuing a life of virtue, temperance, justice, moderation, responsibility. The wealth steward can see if a child is pursuing a life of happiness. If they see one derailing, they can say, "I'm not going to make you any more loans. You've used up your credit. Become credit worthy, I'll make you more loans." Discipline in families is part of the responsibility that goes with the rights of privilege and wealth preservation. Saying "no" is important, too.

James E. Hughes, Jr.[1]

Experience teaches that, in this society, perceptions more than reality shape attitudes toward wealth. Because of this, giving children knowledge and understanding to live in "the real world" is a greater gift than monetary largesse. Too often, just being related to wealth is construed as having it. But even without the incumbent wealth, people with "wealthy" names are judged by standards accorded to actual wealth, however unfair that might be. There are plenty of poor DuPonts in the world. As a result, children need to be educated about the impact of perceptions on them, regardless of whether they are going to have the wealth in the end or not.

Financial parenting is a tricky job. It makes sparks fly. Communicating openly, well, and wisely with children (young and adult alike) about wealth and money creates a firm framework for sound wealth management and stewardship practices in succeeding generations. Communication and education are important, whether they take place after the wealth is made or through the wealth-generating process.

Female children are more likely to be kept uninformed than male children. Assuming that a female child shouldn't be exposed to financial training or allowed responsibility for her decisions unnecessarily handicaps her. That has been the experience of many of the women in my family even though we are equal owners of our family company. In the past, male siblings, cousins, and uncles working in our business discouraged female family members from directly using their competencies for mathematics and business, even though we are expected to understand the dinner table and family meeting business discussions and to serve as executors and trustees for various family entities. Only a handful of women served in management positions (one in five generations) and on the board of directors. Much of the personal financial management remains the domain for the men in the family. A common outgrowth is the development of women with responsibility but no authority who later must ascend to authority roles by default. Lack of exposure to and training in financial matters result in unnecessary errors in judgment and little inclusion in the management process for these women.

Because I took responsibility for my own financial education and did so with little guidance from my family and by using allowances as tools, I began my own children's financial education when they were preschoolers. Lessons increased in complexity as they were better able to assimilate information. When they reached 13, to open their first accounts they called banks for information on checking account policies. They winnowed the selection of banks to three. After personal interviews, my elder son was turned down by his first choice, because bank policy didn't allow accounts for people under 18. His savings account had been there since his infancy (his trust fund was also there), and he was prepared to dedicate all of his savings to meet the required minimum for the new account. He went in with such confidence but came out angry for being denied. He moved his savings and trust accounts to a new bank. He learned the value of managing disappointment, negotiation, expectations, research, and account management. My second son learned from his brother's experience and went to a new bank that was hungry for business and that had no account minimums or service charges. (There might be a lesson in here somewhere for the banks.)

Teaching sound philanthropy to children is equally important in our family. The boys were encouraged to save from their allowances during the school year. They each had opened savings accounts into which went earnings and Christmas and birthday money. At the end of each school year, any allowance they had saved was matched. Fifty percent was donated to the charitable groups of their choice, while the other 50 percent went to their savings accounts. They have chosen volunteer interests on their own over the years. Today, as young adults, they continue ever more generous and thoughtful philanthropy. Occasionally we gift as a family unit.

Another mother of two, twenty-something offspring who manages her personal family office believes the following four key themes prepare children as wealth beneficiaries:

1. *Teach and be a role model for responsibility, stewardship, and philanthropy.* If children become responsible adults, they will be responsible in all aspects of their lives, including personal relationships, work, and financial management. The mechanics can be learned, but the underlying approach to life has to be instilled. Encourage involvement with financial, intellectual, human, and time resources; be a mentor and a model for them.

2. *Base their training in reality.* Involve them in the process early, gradually increasing their activities when they are in school.

3. *Let them know they have to work.* Managing assets is work, too. This is the real thing. Involve them in it.

4. *Teach young people how to identify and use mentors.* Inform young women that men can, and often do, serve as valuable mentors in the worlds of real estate, oil and gas, money management, and elsewhere, where men predominate. Be a mentor and encourage your children to

be mentors where their experience is of value to others, too. We often teach what we need to learn.

Lee Hausner has worked for many years with affluent families in counseling their children at school and as a consultant to family businesses. She has a great depth of experience and success in teaching the critical role of financial parenting. The suggestions she provides can help anyone become a better financial parent, the result of which is children who are better prepared to take realistic charge of their stewardship. The great benefit of this action can be stronger, more open family, business, and financial relationships.

CHILDREN OF PARADISE

Lee Hausner, Ph. D.

Successful parents generously provide their children with the best that money can buy: beautiful homes, designer clothing, prestigious private schools, exotic vacations, summer camps, a multitude of private lessons, and so on. Clearly, it could be expected that these lucky individuals would have a head start up the ladder of success. However, the accomplishments of these privileged youngsters are often very disappointing. Many find little purposeful direction; lack motivation; do poorly academically; appear passive, depressed, and/or angry; and become involved in various types of substance abuse and delinquency.

Does having money in and of itself sabotage families and corrupt children? Absolutely not. Parenting is a complex and demanding job. A majority of parents assume the responsibility for the task poorly prepared for dealing with these challenges, irrespective of the economic level of the family.

Just as poverty creates unique parenting challenges, so does affluence. Today, the effect of affluence on families is as much a concern to successful professionals, entrepreneurs, and achieving two-income families as it is to celebrities and heirs to the family fortune. Although the media appears to enjoy sensationalizing the problems of high-profile families, relatively little formalized research has been directed toward analyzing and evaluating factors that could produce problems for affluent families.

Over the years as psychologist for the Beverly Hills Unified School District, I have identified critical challenges for families of wealth on which I lecture internationally to an organization whose worldwide membership is composed of leading business leaders. These challenges include instilling realistic expectations, developing competency, increasing effective communication, avoiding overindulgence, taking responsibility for financial parenting, and providing financial competency training. Being aware of the negative effects and thoughtfully planning how to avoid them will ensure that your children grow up emotionally and intellectually prepared for successful, productive, and satisfied adult lives, using money to their decided advantage.

REALISTIC EXPECTATIONS

Children passionately desire the acceptance and approval of the two most important individuals in their lives: mom and dad. Each child is unique, with special strengths, weaknesses, and passions. However, as families become more successful and accomplished, parents often develop preconceived ideas of how their "perfect" child will behave and what life role he or she must play to support the image and tradition of the family.

When this parenting attitude is coupled with a larger-than-life image of the family patriarch or family history, is it any wonder that the young child might feel overwhelmed? Feeling that nothing he or she can do will ever live up to these unrealistic expectations, the child gives up or acts out the anger of this burden in a hostile, antisocial manner.

What can parents do? Give up your fantasies and look realistically at the child before you. What can you celebrate about this child? What are the child's special skills and talents? How does the child differ from the other family members, and how can that difference contribute to the family? Can you take out a piece of paper right now and list five special characteristics or interests of each child in your family? If parents can not identify unique talents, they generally will not notice, acknowledge, or encourage them.

Parents can foster the healthy development of their children's potential only if they are aware of and respect the ability and interests of each child. Then, the parents' role becomes that of actively encouraging all of the "baby steps" it takes to reach a final goal. The key word to note is *encourage*. If parents want to motivate children in a healthy manner, they must continually be aware of the following formula:

Activity + Good Feelings (from positive encouragement)

= Motivation

but

Activity + Stress and Pressure = Avoidance

Achievement is a continual process. Along the way, parents have the opportunity to make a child feel positive about important characteristics such as attitude, effort, ingenuity, and discipline even though the child might not always produce a spectacularly noteworthy end-product. There can only be a limited number of class presidents, straight-A students, star athletes, primary leads in the school productions, and beauty contest winners. But everyone can feel good about his or her efforts toward even the most lofty goals when parents are continually looking for positives in everything their children do. On the other hand, if positive acknowledgment is withheld until the child has reached a predetermined parental level of performance unrelated to the child's interests and abilities, then the child feels constantly pressured to reach this often unattainable goal; this type of unrealistic expectation can lead to disastrous consequences for the child.

Competence

Competence is the learned ability that children acquire when they are permitted to handle a variety of independent tasks, even if they do not succeed in all of them. Children who feel competent enjoy the thrill of their own accomplishments. They don't feel dependent on the all-knowing adults in their lives. They seek the challenges of new and difficult situations with eagerness and enthusiasm. "Let me try it myself" is their constant refrain. Children feel powerful and proud when they are able to do and think for themselves and to realistically put their unique skills and talents into action. When too much is done for a child, there is no opportunity to acquire this skill. Likewise, criticism of or lack of praise for a competence can cause children to smother their effectiveness and doubt their self-worth.

The wealthy family often provides too many adults (governess, nanny, housekeeper, tutor, driver, parents) to serve the needs of a child. Not only does this apply to physical needs, it also expands to include all areas of decision making: where the child will go to school, what course of study will be followed, with whom the child will socialize, what vacation time will look like, and so on. Driven, entrepreneurial parents who have created their own success are all too quick to continually direct all activities of their children so that their offspring can avoid any mistakes the parents might have made and proceed directly to their own success. However, it is often in the failures that the greatest learning takes place, and it is in the process of good and bad decision making that children develop confidence in their choices. When not permitted this independence, the end result is a passive, insecure individual who depends on others for directing his or her life, often with disastrous consequences.

Competency training begins at the earliest age with allowing a child to feed, dress, and handle personal grooming tasks independently, even if it may take a little longer than the adults may wish. As children grow older, thoughts, opinions, and the ability to make good decisions should be rewarded through verbal encouragement and enthusiasm for their contributions. Complimenting a child for his or her thoughtful work in choosing a bank when opening a checking account is a good way to reinforce competence.

Jobs can never be underestimated as a powerful means of developing competency. Many highly successful individuals began working at a very young age with the proverbial newspaper routes, after-school clerking jobs, or weekend car-washing and lawn-mowing enterprises in lieu of or to supplement allowances. While usually the result of financial necessity, these jobs pay considerably more than the obvious monetary rewards in the long run. The working child develops greater self-assurance by assuming responsibility and then accomplishing the task without the help or involvement of parents or substitute caretakers.

By contrast, most affluent children have little opportunity to make deposits into this "competency account." Household chores and other potential opportunities to develop competency through the initiation and completion of tasks are handled by others. Even the most basic tasks, such as cleaning their own rooms, are often done for them. This kind of "help" deprives a child of the chance to do it independently, and perhaps more importantly, to feel that he or she has personal power.

Parents can remain focused on the development of competency by practicing the following exercise on a daily basis. Whenever a child asks to be helped or asks "What should I do now, I'm bored?" ask yourself this critical question: Can my child handle this task or any part of it independently? If the answer is yes, then let him or her do so. Remove the helpers. Stop giving advice. Then, be sure to offer your positive verbal acknowledgment of the child's ability to handle things independently. In this manner, a competent child can develop.

Communication

Communication is the critical life skill—the combination of the ability to listen as well as to express ideas, opinions, and feelings. Effective communication is the most important method of creating positive relationships within the family, and it validates the personal worth of each family member. However, one of the most common breakdowns in families is in their communication process.

High-profile parents are often physically away from the family at critical times when children want to talk; this inaccessibility interferes with the communication process. Additionally, these types of parents are often much more accustomed to talking and directing others, as this is the role they often play in the world outside the family. Power is equated with the talkers. Bosses talk, workers listen; the chairman of the committee directs, the committee members follow their assignments. It becomes very difficult to shift to a listening mode around children. However, within the family, the roles have to be shared. Children need to do some of the talking, and parents have to be able to listen without interrupting, overreacting, criticizing, or shaming.

Listening is one of the most powerful methods of validating another person's worth. It gives the speaker an opportunity to verbally share his or her innermost thoughts, ideas, feelings, hopes, and fears. Through the listening process, the receiver can then validate the importance of the speaker. But listening takes time, patience, and the ability to focus totally on the speaker. Effective listening does not occur when a parent "listens" while cooking, reading the paper, or watching TV. When parents are truly listening to a child, they give the child complete attention, eye contact, and closed mouths. It has been said before that humans have been given two ears and one mouth to emphasize that listening is twice as important as talking.

Because the second part of the communication process must focus on *what* is said to children, if you are a parent concerned with the development of strong self-esteem, it is important to physically monitor your conversations with your child for several days. Keep a notepad handy. For every positive comment ("I love you," "Thanks so much for your help," "Come ride with me while I do my errand, I enjoy your company," "What a great idea!") give yourself a "+". For every negative, critical, sarcastic, or angry statement, be honest and give yourself a "–". At the end of three days, total your positive and your negative scores. If the positives don't significantly (at least three to one) outnumber the negatives, the balance must be immediately changed if the emotional health of the child is important to you.

Healthy families develop specific opportunities to practice their communication skills. One highly effective vehicle for facilitating healthy dialogue within the family is family meetings. Family meetings should be scheduled on a regular basis, for a specific length of time, and with a rotating chairmanship directing the activity. Any item can be brought up for discussion. The goal is to be able to listen in a nonemotional, nonconfrontational manner, developing a method of conflict resolution, consensus building, and support for the activities of family members. Annual family retreats are an excellent vehicle for expanding the communication skills developed within the primary family to include the extended family of grandparents, aunts, uncles, cousins and in-laws. Family meetings and family retreats provide an excellent forum for bringing in resources to educate family members in identified areas of need (financial expertise, foundations, specific conflict resolution techniques, asset allocation, etc.).

If the thought of an extended family meeting strikes terror in your heart, engage the services of a professional facilitator to begin the process. After several facilitated meetings, the family will learn how to manage this process independently so that successful family meetings can continue.

AVOIDING OVERINDULGENCE

The problem of overindulgence is not merely that it creates spoiled, bratty, demanding youngsters who feel that they are entitled, by virtue of their birthright, to indulge their every desire. When a child gets whatever he or she wants on demand, it fosters a youngster who will never learn how to delay gratification. It is the ability to delay immediate gratification that enables individuals to remain with a challenging or frustrating task until they eventually achieve success. And it is in this type of achievement that a child experiences the greatest natural high. How wonderful it feels to be successful through your own hard work and determination!

In a society that more often than not determines worth by dollars earned or generated, how does a child of affluence feel worthy if he or she played no part in the acquisition of the actual wealth? The answer lies in the ability to feel the power of personal achievement in the nonmaterial aspects of one's life. It is true that the child who learns the excitement of achievement brings this passion to bear in a variety of activities, which often results in the independent creation of additional wealth.

If they are to appreciate what they have, overindulged children need to be regularly exposed to people less fortunate than they are. Besides, they might not always have the wealth. Cosseting them away from the "real world" sets them up to be judged incompetent or to be victimized or despised in adulthood by that same real world. Another sensitive challenge is to walk the fine line between the truthful acknowledgment of privilege and encouragement of responsibility, and stress-filled urging and pressuring to perform outside one's competencies.

Financial Parenting

"I am afraid to talk with my children about our money because it might spoil them." A common dilemma for families of affluence is how much information to give to children regarding the financial resources of the family and when to give it to them. These concerns are often handled by complete avoidance. Many young heirs have told me that they knew very little about financial matters until, suddenly , they were informed that they would now have access to significant wealth through the distribution of their trust. Overnight, they were "money managers" with no skills. (See Chapter 4, page 54)

If your children will someday be in the position of having to manage money, it is important to begin their training as early as possible. This does not mean they have to receive audited financial statements of the family's assets. However, most children from prosperous families know there is money available simply by the lifestyle they are afforded and because outsiders focus on and remind them of their ties to wealth.

Today's youth is quite savvy regarding the cost of luxury items. They know that they are living in a substantial, often servant-staffed home in the upscale neighborhoods of the city. They may attend private school; vacation during winter, spring, and summer vacation; and have access to late model (or classic) cars. These facts are not a secret. In many cases, children may fantasize about having an even greater sum of money than the family actually has. Knowledge that there is family money will not in and of itself "spoil" your children. What will cause them to expect excessive indulgences is the behavior and attitudes of the parents.

Children should be told that the family has money and that one day, they will have the responsibility of being responsible stewards of these funds. Therefore, as a family, you are going to commit yourself to a proactive program of developing competency in money management. It is important to emphasize the notion of "stewardship." A steward is a person who manages property or other financial resources for the future use of others. If parents can create excitement about developing competencies in the skills of management, attention is directed toward those activities that result in the preservation and growth of capital rather than the self-indulgence of spending.

Financial Competency Education

Children become consumers as soon as they recognize an object of desire and request it. They are keen observers of how the world works, and most are eager students. What they need is guidance.

Allowances

The preschooler has little understanding of the difference between various denominations ($1.00 is the same as $100.00) or of long-range saving. At this level, their introduction to finance is simply learning that one must pay for items that are removed from the store and brought into the home. The grocery store is a wonderful learning laboratory. The child can begin to recognize numbers and can observe the parent giving money for the goods received. Parents can show how to tell how each item is priced and even demonstrate how to add the numbers together to form a total. By the time the child is in school and mastering arithmetic, a sense of greater or lesser values of money will begin to develop.

The actual dollar amount of an allowance will vary, depending on the purchases for which the child is required to assume responsibility. Most experts feel that under the age of 10, the allowance should be based more upon the frills the child might buy with it. The final figure for an older child will include more necessities (such as lunches, clothing, and transportation) than allowances for the younger ones. The general rule of thumb regarding the allowance is that it should never be so large that the child will not have to make some hard choices in spending, nor should it be so small that the youngster cannot have any meaningful experience with money. If your young child makes poor choices in spending, let the consequences of these decisions become a life teacher without parental comment, such as "I told you that cheap toy would break the minute you brought it home." It will not take too many disappointments to teach the skill of more thoughtful purchasing; you don't have to be the negative nag.

When children reach high school, ask them to submit a budget to you, over which you, as the parent and funds provider, have line-item veto power. This exercise will encourage adolescents to think realistically about known and anticipated expenses and will help them in mastering budgeting. Care should be taken not to demand too much control over any money independently earned by the early high schooler.

Should the allowance be connected to the completion of assigned chores? If the allowance is to be used in a punitive manner, it loses its effectiveness as a money-management tool. The failure to assume household responsibility might be handled in the following manner. Michael is to be responsible for cleaning his room. If his room is left in disarray, on allowance day, Michael will be given his full allowance with an accompanying bill from mother for the "cost" of hiring her to clean the room. Now, rather than a punishment, this situation becomes an important life lesson. If you do not wish to perform a task in life, you have to pay for someone to do that service for you. The child learns how to allocate a limited resource. In most instances the choice will not be to "pay" for housekeeping services.

Purchasing for Value

For the younger child, again, the grocery store is a wonderful laboratory. Teach your child how to read the pricing codes so that he or she can determine which product gives the best value. Give an older child the money to pay for the grocery bill and let the child learn how to count the change.

Saving Habits

Begin with baby steps. Save for a treat at McDonald's in three days or the movies on Saturday. Gradually stretch the savings payoff day. With each weekly allowance, allocate a percentage for savings. For the younger child, paste a picture of a desired object on the savings bank so the child will be reminded of the long-range goal. Establish a savings account at the bank. Teach children to understand the concept of interest earned on their savings.

Teach That Money is an Earned Commodity

If you as parents have not worked for your money, it is even more imperative that children understand and can experience some models for working. Determine what chores you would pay to have done and permit your young children to begin to work and receive payment for their efforts. Later, working only for family limits the range this exercise has as a teaching tool. Allow them to get their after-school and summer jobs on their own. Insist that they pay for half or all of a desired first automobile (or other coveted object) with money they earn themselves.

What is "Expensive"?

When a child requests an item that is too expensive, say so. Give a clear explanation as to why that would exceed their allocation of the family budget. (This also gives heirs the concept of using a budget.)

Teach Responsible Use of a Checking Account and Credit Card

Children must be responsible for any expenditures and should be taught how to understand the monthly financial statements and how to balance a check book. Don't hand them credit cards at too young an age, and set clear limits on how they can be used.

Educate Children in Investments

Give stocks in which the child might have a personal interest (such as McDonald's, Coca Cola, and Disney), and encourage them to follow the progress and understand what their dividend check represents. Give them opportunities to purchase stocks they have researched themselves.

Share Your Business and Financial Knowledge

Share your knowledge whenever appropriate and utilize the services of financial service professionals as additional teaching resources. Use them for the family at regular family meetings. Be sure the level of instruction meets the instructional level of the least sophisticated in the group so that everyone can feel financially empowered.

Financial Responsibility

Give your child the job of planning family activities (vacations, monthly outings, family entertainment) within a designated budget. Let them make the calls, research pricing, and present it to you for review and acceptance.

Identify Skills Necessary to Create and Manage Wealth

Develop a family action plan to facilitate the development of all these skills using the appropriate resources in the community as teachers or mentors. Make appointments with your banker, accountant, and other business professionals to introduce your children. Include the children in meetings where decisions will be made on their behalf, and let the professionals talk with the children about what they do and can't do to help the family.

Do Not Rescue Your Child Financially

Lend your support and encouragement by assisting them in developing a plan to solve their own problems. Teach them how to fish, rather than giving them a fish (i.e., a financial bailout.) If a child borrows money from you, hold that child to a payment schedule and charge a reasonable (to the amount borrowed) interest if the schedule is not met.

Create Working Business Partnerships

With older heirs, be sure that you deal with this family partner in a respectful, *collaborative* manner. Don't overpower your children and take control of all of the important decision making. For example, Sally's sons, now in their 20s, have worked with her in a shared office since they were quite young. The boys have a familiarity with balance sheets, income statements, trust structures, due diligence, and family meeting participation. The elder maintains his own household and professional practice budgets with ease, independent from the family office. Educating her daughter-in-law in these same particulars creates a new and interesting challenge, because exposure to family business and asset management was not a part of the daughter-in-law's personal experience. Early education of new family members is as important as the education of your own children.

Create a Family Venture Capital Fund

Use it to fund projects or business acquisitions of various family members, providing the projects meet a predetermined business criteria that has been established by the family itself. One family group set aside $3 million for the three siblings to invest in their own areas of interest. If that money grows, great. If they blow their third of it, that is all that is available. One is interested in investing in the movies (he's a writer), another is interested in a sports franchise, and the other one isn't sure yet.

Use Philanthropy as an Educational Tool

For example, permit your eight-year-old child to choose a charitable cause she or he would like to support. Ask the child to make a short presentation (either verbal or written) to either the "family gifting committee" or the foundation board (if the family supports a family foundation) justifying the need for the contribution. A donation will then be made, and the child will be responsible for presenting a report at the end of the funding cycle explaining how the money was used and whether funding should be continued. In this relatively simple activity, the child learns evaluation, due diligence, value return on money spent, personal satisfaction in helping a needy cause, and decision-making skills—the foundations for responsible stewardship

When parents take the time and expend the effort to develop a strategic family plan and fend off the problems of unrealistic expectations, lack of competency, poor communication, overindulgence, and the lack of adequate financial parenting, they can insure that growing up advantaged will not become a heartbreaking disadvantage to their loved ones. Spending time with children, introducing them to mentors, and leading them into situations where they can find a balance between material wealth and personal meaning in their lives is a noble endeavor that is well worth your efforts.

One Woman's Way

A Texas woman manages the ranching and oil and gas interests and investment companies she inherited from her father when she was in her late 20s. Her father exposed her to the businesses as a child when he took her into the oil fields, often forgetting she was around. She notes, "I knew if I was going to have any relationship with my father, I would have to learn to play gin rummy and know the oil business." But her father didn't involve her directly in the decision making. She had to learn that on her own. Now she has three college-aged children to educate about her business. She has been active in charitable pursuits and fund raising all of her adult life, but only recently has she created a charitable foundation. Although a beneficiary, her own mom has never been involved in management.

FIGURE 3.1

ONE WOMAN'S WAY

- ◆ "Don't feel guilty about having money."
- ◆ "Turn over assets to people who know, after comparison shopping. Each money manager has his own technique. I use eight of them. I visit with them at least once a year, face to face."
- ◆ "Never let *anyone* sign your name to a check. You cannot *afford* to give up your signature."
- ◆ "Attend *all* meetings about your "stuff." It's yours and no one else gives a _____. Ask questions. Read materials."
- ◆ "Hire smart, honest, caring people to help you invest, to learn from, to do the grit work, to manage day-to-day money. Inattention to detail can break you. If someone doesn't understand the difference between a Tax-free and a Repo—fire him!"

Continued

Concluded

- "Know that it's your money and it's almost harder to keep than to make. Enjoy managing it—it's a great privilege. People are willing to help, *but* find the good ones. You can't ask too many questions."
- "Take care of your health so you can do the best job possible."
- "Take care of your spiritual life. What goes around comes around."
- "Take care of your ego: God gave you this money for a reason. He can change his mind."
- "Teach your heirs early all of the above. Responsibility comes with the territory."
- "Take your time to think and learn. Decide on a strategy. Be cautious. Trust few."
- "Set up a foundation and have the time of your life giving some of it away."

ENDNOTES

1. James E. Hughes, Jr., Esq., interview with author, New York, NY, 18 August 1995 and 6 September 1995. James E. Hughes is a trust and estates attorney in New York.

4

THE IMPERATIVES OF PLANNING

Tax, Legal, Philanthropic, and Financial Considerations

> Multigenerational families who successfully wealth plan have a common view of their role as custodians or stewards because the older generation wakes up one morning understanding that they are conservators. "Is it painful for you to sell a piece of art?" "No, no, I'm only the custodian of these pieces." When we confuse ownership with conservation or stewardship, we fail ourselves. Most people go to bed thinking they own things. A few go to bed thinking they are custodians. When the latter rules the decisions, planning issues become simple.
>
> *James E. Hughes, Jr.*[1]

Family wealth planning is best thought of as a hundred-year process, not one of quantitative, short-term decisions. Every 10 years or so you can count on experiencing a defining event out of your control that has financial ramifications—death, divorce, financial reversal, business reorganization, a war, kidnap. This event has nothing to do with investment decisions, yet it forces a changed direction. Shortsightedness and reliance on quantitative measures to define the truth too often subvert the critical role of wisdom, patience, and planning.[2] Preparing for the challenges is daunting but possible. Good outcomes don't just happen, and good planning doesn't always create great outcomes when people and emotions and wealth meet. But without planning, unexpected and defining events cause people to slide into crisis management rather than move through smooth transitions. Calm management is supplanted, emotions rule, and foolish and irrevocable mistakes are inevitable.

Planning imperatives are concepts that families *should* understand and adopt. When they don't use them, they still seem to ask why their plans don't work. Some of these imperatives are generally applicable to wealth stewardship planning; others are specific to the legal, financial, or philanthropic planning processes. For instance, keeping good records is important for ongoing planning, monitoring, and implementation of any type of plan, but it is particularly important in the legal planning area. I will walk you through the most important planning imperatives so that you can get a feel for the value that planning has as a foundation for all wealth stewardship activities. There is benefit derived from using these imperatives in this loosely suggested order. They should be considered as building blocks that, at times, may seem illogical when you are experiencing a transition. You can be thrown into the middle of a process at a time when you would rather have the freedom to begin at the beginning and do it right. But the process is not a linear one; it is circular and random all at once. Therefore, you will need to use the appropriate planning imperatives for the relevant time, place, and event.

I learned the value of planning through an informal system that included osmosis and trial and error—my own version of crisis management—a more common process. I would have preferred a more formal education. From my earliest recollection, I heard grousing in the family about double taxation, corporate stock redemptions, and the terms *tax* and *estate planning*, which broadened my lexicon. Each time there was a death in the family or a dissident family member left the fold, the whole family was affected and the shared asset—the ranch—was at issue. The guiding family mission statement had been from earliest times, "buy land and never sell." Selling land or giving it away to settle an estate or an ownership or inheritance issue directly conflicted with that broad family mission. Planning was the only strategy we had to avoid that conflict from occurring with each transition.

GENERAL PLANNING IMPERATIVES

Planning Imperative #1

Wealth management and transfer planning issues are tightly bound.

Ongoing wealth management and the planning involved that insures successful transfer of that wealth to desired successors must be addressed concurrently and regularly. How property is owned and managed, while you are here and after you are gone; tax and legal implications beyond your control; market variables; personal and family differences; lifestyle requirements; personal risk tolerance; trust and management security demands; unexpected defining events; and location and residential variables all create unique planning requirements for each individual and family. Someone else's planning will not necessarily work for you. You must design and work through your own plans.

What makes planning so essential is also what makes it so complex and, at times, baffling and overwhelming to address and manage. Four topical themes run concurrently in planning for wealth stewardship—legal, tax, philanthropic, and financial planning. One area is just as likely as another to be a top priority at any given time, but this doesn't mean that the other three can be ignored. Just when you think you have your will in place exactly as you want it, a financial reversal or some other unforeseen event occurs, forcing reexamination of not only your financial planning but also your estate and tax planning.

To help you navigate multidisciplinary planning, this chapter is divided into three main areas. Most frequently seen tax and legal planning matters are dealt with as a unit because they are often intertwined when making planning and implementation decisions. The next two sections are supplied by two outside contributors. A discussion of philanthropic planning, which is often integral to tax and legal long-range planning, was written by Jane Gregory Rubin. Also, Louis Leeburg contributes the section on financial planning, which directly interacts with tax, legal, and philanthropic planning. At the end of the financial planning section, special attention is paid to the Prudent Investor Rule, which plays an increasingly important role in long- and short-term financial wealth planning, stewardship, and management, particularly for trustees in multigenerational management positions. Your planning works best when you can design a framework within which you can manage all of your resources.

Planning Imperative #2

Embrace the value of using a broad and encompassing mission statement as a springboard for learning, teaching, planning, and managing.

The planning decisions are clearly delineated if the individuals and family group first set out individual and collective statements of mission built on a review of the goals and values that are expressed in the way the group and individuals live their lives. The exercise helps clarify purpose and direction, but few family groups ever do this. (See Figure 4.1.)

As an example, over the 143 years as an operating family-owned company, the corporate and family missions have changed to reflect the family's principal goals. In 1853 the mission statement was simply buy land and never sell. In 1955, with five generations and five family branches involved, this statement had changed to, keep the family together to keep the company together. Today, we are six generations large with a mission that directs our enterprises to remain wholly family-owned while serving as responsible stewards of our resources. Historically, these evolving mission statements were broad parameters to lead us through complex, specific actions over the years. The benevolently despotic nature of the family's leadership did little to teach any of us the technical necessities of financial management or planning. Thus, in the family at large, corporate planning was required, but personal planning was not considered important and was neither modeled nor taught. My own father abhorred office work, preferring cattle work and training a good quarter horse over financial management and training.

Review the components of a typical mission statement to help you form a statement of your own.

FIGURE 4.1

THE MISSION STATEMENT

- Overarching commitment: A statement of philosophy, understanding, and inclusiveness of all affected owners (individual or group) in shared asset stewardship. Goals flow from a mission statement.
- Stated set of underlying values: A statement of what to do if these are violated or impinged, and determination of how to insure that these values will guide wealth management decisions.

Continued

Concluded

- A statement of rights and responsibilities of the family wealth holders and affected parties and how they are to be integrated into the chosen structure.
- A statement of how resources are allocated among family members—what their individual interests, needs, investments, and perquisites are.
- Answers the following question: What are our relationships with the community and our philanthropic priorities?
- Inclusive and built on consensus (not majority rule): All parties and dynamics are addressed and represented.
- Carries no legal authority.
- A statement of purpose that the group or individual can use to build specific policy.
- Framework for comprehensive financial plan for individuals and the group, and a point from which to begin when doing periodic reviews.
- Not an investment policy statement.

The following excerpt from the Steward family mission statement gives you an idea of how one family sets out to define its values and to design a framework and code of conduct for comprehensive planning:

> We seek to join together in a loose but committed federation of related individuals and family groups to guide and support each other on a mission to conserve, steward, thoughtfully use, direct, share, and enhance all resources for which we have responsibility and care.
>
> The interests and concerns of each of us are valued equally with those of all others, each reserving the right to *respectfully* disagree with others' individual priorities.
>
> Wherever possible, communications will be inclusive and open, with particular attempts to effect consensus leaving each member with the right to leave the group from time to time without being harshly judged for choosing to sit out a group decision.
>
> Each member acknowledges accountability for his or her actions affecting the group.
>
> All members will openly share ideas for joint investments and philanthropy projects as provided for in separate group financial

and philanthropic plans constructed by the group, realizing that in certain instances there is strength in joint commitment and action. Similarly, there are times when separate actions are equally fitting.

The family-at-large agrees that whenever possible, members of the group will actively serve as mentors to its younger members in personal and business matters.

Planning Imperative #3

When you aren't sure, appoint regents to manage for a *fixed* period of time.

Discussions to design your statement can take considerable time. You might have to appoint temporary caretakers or custodians of your resources while you are planning and getting your financial education. There is always someone familiar who could suffice in the short term.

The extent of my experience with any formal financial education or planning involved handling a checking account opened when I was 14 to manage a small allowance. I was married at age 20, and my real financial education began at age 21 with one of those defining events I mentioned earlier in this chapter. My new husband and I were graduate students in Austin, Texas. Life was simple. His father paid his law school tuition and our rent. A trust from my grandparents paid my tuition and certain school-related expenses. I had no clue of what planning meant, what my real income was or what bills I never saw were handled by my father's office while he was busy doing ranch work. His secretary served as informal manager for our family until this aforementioned abrupt change occurred.

Planning Imperative #4

Do not panic in a crisis or allow yourself to be pushed into making decisions that you aren't prepared to make.

You will be asked to operate up to or beyond the standard set by the prior managers of what you now control. This is difficult to do without extensive tutoring or mentoring.

Late one April 14th, a special delivery envelope arrived. Imagine my reaction when I learned that by midnight the next day, I had to pay the IRS 10 times our combined account balance of $300.00. I had never paid taxes before. (That all was done from my father's office.) I didn't know I even had enough money on which I could be taxed. Could we borrow from a bank on short notice? Should we borrow from the parents or grandparents already supporting us? I had never had more than $500.00 in savings. It didn't seem businesslike to borrow from my parents. In my family, debt was anathema. I had seen my brother lend money to friends and get stiffed so I didn't want to jeopardize any friendship by borrowing from a friend. In a panic, I called Dad.

Planning Imperative #5

Have the courage to be a student, but don't get drawn into the details too early or it will confuse you.

State clearly that "I intend to start a course of study for x years to educate and be educated. Over those years, I will decide what role I will play. I am making no decision now." You have the choice. It's not your advisor's choice to make. Don't be afraid to be an amateur.[1]

Determined to be more responsible for the future, my husband and I, with the help of a tax accounting specialist, designed a tax-reporting folder that grew in complexity over the years as the laws and our finances changed. My father tired of my increasingly uncomfortable questions, which he didn't want to address. His idea of planning was to buy life insurance and put the rest in a checking account. After my husband began practicing law and we started a family, I became household budget director and manager, assuming ever-greater responsibility. I found that the planning process required steady building and patient learning. Every new and more complex revelation generated fresh information to explore and then include or discard. Numerous related and unrelated decisions such as, "Do I want to pay someone to do the detail for our taxes or do I compile records myself to cut down on the expense?" had to be personally addressed. In the beginning, we spent a lot of time with accounting firms and attorneys until we developed a system. Fortunately, my husband was trained in tax and trusts and estate law.

Planning Imperative #6

Be sure you have a clear understanding that the interim job of custodian and caretaker is going to end.

Avoid conflict and the danger of using tutors as a crutch. Insure that their second job is to teach you what you need to know to take your rightful responsibility. Don't fall victim to inertia or fear of responsibility. Unfortunately, professionals don't like to lose clients nor have their work done by the client.

Cash flow planning, budgeting for taxes, and other contingencies became monthly exercises for me, first on a very small scale, and then on a much larger scale when there was a dramatic change in fortune in our family. Ten years later, when the changes did occur, this self-education served me well and proved its value in the face of another spate of unexpected challenges. (When these challenges come for you, expect to use advisors as needed.) Just then the distribution of substantial liquid capital to the shareholders of our company required me to move my personal planning and implementation from the dining room table to a staffed investment office shared with my brothers, mother, father, and grandmother. During the distribution process, the number of advisors ballooned to the same as the number of family members.

Planning Imperative #7

Planning is a team effort.

Planning covers all areas of life: investment, succession and wealth transfer, philanthropy, retirement, liquidity and tax, insurance, and medical assistance. One advisor cannot supply all the diverse expertise required, nor can planning be done in a vacuum. The affected person must be a part of the process and define its direction. The people involved will vary at different stages but might include your family (your spouse or companion, the generations on either side of you), investment advisor, attorney, accountant, financial planner, banker, trust company, trustees, broker, psychologist, custodian, insurance consultant, and family business consultant.

Defining event by defining event, I learned that families in business together rarely have the luxury of making independent decisions, regardless of the lifestyle and relationship distances. Especially in closely held businesses, a death, corporate reorganization, or other transition opens a window to such actions as a stock transfer or a recalculation of asset values, actions that expose all shared ownership to examination by taxing authorities. A whole team of advisors may be required to help you implement an action to take advantage of, or protect, your interest at these times. And more important than the team of professionals is the family teamwork it takes to maintain control of your planning education and goals, to keep peace in the group, and to get the job done.

Planning Imperative #8

Talk to your parents and talk to your children *at appropriate ages* about the important things.

Discussions on such topics as estate plans, wills, trusts, philanthropic goals, changing investment needs, medical directives, provision for aging, disability, burial wishes, and so forth need to be held at the appropriate times. Be wise enough to be uncomfortable in the short term in order to greatly diminish the likelihood of generations of anguish. Ignoring sensitive planning issues won't make them go away. Help your parents plan by educating them in the planning rules. Keep no secrets and encourage others not to keep secrets either. (Use the techniques and information found in Chapters 2 and 3 to help your personal communications.) The discussions of financial planning presented in Appendixes A and B are useful as discussion and planning aids.

Nobody should operate in a vacuum when shared assets are under management. Planning and communication are critical. Literacy in the areas of finance, legal issues, and tax issues allows you to wisely make complex decisions that no one else can make for you. Above all, remain flexible in your stewardship work.

Planning Imperative #9

Effective planning is a flexible and living process requiring living and flexible documents.

Commit yourself to shepherding such a process. Rigidity creates brittle, breakable, often useless plans. There is a difference between good planning and bad planning. Just because you have a will doesn't mean you have effectively planned your estate or management succession. Just because you have a tax plan for the year doesn't mean it is compatible with a money manager who doesn't invest "tax sensitively" for you. Just because you allot an amount to philanthropy doesn't mean it's compatible with your plan or the possibilities available. There is an interdisciplinary and intergenerational nature to stewardship planning. Surprises can appear generations later and from the least expected places—all the more reason to have a clear statement of mission as a springboard.

In the early 1980s my grandmother, already in her 90s, revised her estate planning as she routinely did, nudged by her astute and caring attorney to do so as she aged and as laws and circumstances changed. In the review process, the attorney found that an unclear

will signed by her father in the 1920s muddied ownership and con-
veyance of her assets in the next expected asset transfer. This discovery threatened to turn several estate plans upside down, including
those of my grandmother and those of many more individuals in
three subsequent generations in our family.

Planning Imperative #10

Use a businesslike planning process.

Keep an eye on cost effectiveness but don't ignore the "people
issues." Meet at least annually with your advisors to talk about wealth
planning. What's new in Congress with the tax laws? What changes
are there in the family—a new child, impending marriage, illness,
death, pending death, a divorce—and how does this impact the
group, specific individuals, and planning changes? What are the issues that affect those to whom I wish to leave my assets? If Papa, my
great-grandfather, had followed this rule as his daughter subsequently did, she and the family would have been saved countless
legal and court expenses and the considerable personal stress that
ensued over the clarification of the intent of his will.

Although wills are not estate plans, Papa believed his will suf-
ficed as an adequate plan at the time it was written. Four generations later, my grandmother's attorney suggested that the adopted
great-grandchildren, my first cousins, might or might not inherit the
commonly held ranch property in the Texas Panhandle after my
grandmother's death, depending on Papa's *intent*. In his own hand
Papa struck and initialed the words *pro rata* in his will, penciling in
per stirpes. Because of this, my grandmother could not clearly transfer her property without a clarification. A "friendly lawsuit" ensued
in which all parties were separately represented (including attorneys *ad litum* for minors and unborn children) to insure fairness to
the future beneficiaries. The court was asked to determine Papa's
intent to avoid pitting one branch of the family against another and
to allow fair partition of the undivided property at a future date.
The family at large thus retained friendly relations between cousins
while effectively unclouding the estate planning options for my
grandmother.

By understanding the benefit of taking the time to do her own
planning, my grandmother limited the time, expense, and emotional

stress inherent in waiting for an adversarial situation to endanger future family harmony. As your planning process unfolds, you will address specific issues of legal, tax, philanthropic, and financial planning concurrently and separately. The following planning imperatives are applicable to the remainder of that ongoing circular process.

Planning Imperative #11

Decide what priority wealth holds within your family and the position you or others hold in the family.

Are family members managers or are they leaders? Are they followers? Are they weak or strong? Understanding your individual position in the family tells you what kind of help you need. In Chapters 6 and 7 and Appendix C, the structuring, governance, and management of resources and the hiring of advisors and staff will be covered more fully. But philosophically, when wealth "happens" to you, this planning imperative must occur first, before you design structures and engage a staff.

Planning Imperative #12

Know what your assets are and how they can be used to effect a plan for you.

Expect your plan to be creative but viable and in keeping with your overall interests and goals. Begin by familiarizing yourself with the Third Restatement (the Prudent Investor Rule), which will serve as a guide for investment and financial planning (see Figure 4.3 at the end of this chapter). The section entitled, "Financial Planning Imperatives" by Lou Leeburg in this chapter and material in Chapter 5, "Apportioning Investment Resources," continue discussion of the planning process you can follow. Naturally, as you implement, monitor, and review these actions, your asset and goals assessments become the basis for reviewing the plan as you go. This was a particularly difficult exercise for me when I first approached it because of the fluctuating nature of the manageable cash (oil and gas royalty payments) and the uncertainty of the impact of my father's health and his estate planning (in progress) that coincided with this new asset base for my family. Another complicating factor was the undivided nature of the ownership in several assets that muddied valuation on which to base the assessment.

Planning Imperative #13

Expand your goals as you expand horizons, communicating them before assuming or planning for ownership or investment.

These goals serve as guides to your advisor, someone who knows how to refine and expand those goals *with* you, rather than dictating what they should be from his or her perspective. You can drive the process rather than be driven by another person whose goals might be quite different from yours. As you read this book, pay particular attention to the key result areas for investments you might consider as you do your planning and implementation strategies. Involve your teenage and older children in the process, too.

Planning Imperative #14

Keep good records.

Keep records to track investments and care for your long-range planning. Keep duplicates out of the house, either in a safe deposit box accessible to another trusted party in the event of your death, or in counsel's office—preferably both. Be sure your family knows what and where they are. Computer-generated record keeping should be backed up daily in the office. All computer files maintained by persons or firms retained should be backed up at least monthly. What to include in these records is addressed in the legal planning section of this chapter and in Appendix B. Monitoring investments and achieving short- and long-term planning objectives rely heavily on reporting and record keeping.

Planning Imperative #15

Implement, monitor, review, revisit, and replan.

Stay current at every level. Stay abreast of changes that might affect you, and keep your advisors informed of them. Likewise, request that they do the same for you, such as letting you know about tax law changes. If charity is your goal, investigate and stay current. Has the charity changed? Have your interests changed? Do the bylaws need changing? Is the charity still in good standing? Do the directors know that your ideas have changed? (Build in regular reporting requirements from the philanthropy as a prerequisite of continued support.) In short, maintain ongoing, regular communication.

Once you have a firm grasp of these basic planning imperatives, you are prepared to deal with any issue that arises as your life as a steward unfolds. Events and issues will not come to you as neatly wrapped and orderly as this process has been set out for you, but you can have skills to address the particular conditions and challenges described in the following sections. Ultimately, what follows can be used as ready reference glossaries when you encounter the hurdles along the way.

COMMON TAX AND LEGAL PLANNING ISSUES

Tax is voluntary. You only pay if you don't plan.[3]

A basic knowledge of the tax issues that are relevant to your situation and how and why they affect you leads to better decisions. Many jurisdictions have designs on your assets, from local authorities to those of foreign countries where you might be invested or where some of your family has citizenship. Although the axiom, "Don't let the tax tail wag the investment or planning dog" is sage advice, you can't ignore the tax impact of your choices. Knowing the types of taxes (ordinary, capital gains, transfer and business) and their impact bolsters confidence and leads to knowledgeable discussion with professional advisors. Terminology such as *cost basis* and *tax basis* is required lexicon for anyone affected by either one. Personal planning will be impossible without the vocabulary.

The short-term financial planning you implement can result in long-range tax and legal consequences. You must think both ways. Fifteen years ago, as a Texas resident, I invested in oil and gas in Oklahoma. Today, I still must file Oklahoma state tax returns. Fees to prepare the return now exceed the current declining revenues from that asset. I didn't ask about that then, and I'm paying the price now.

Another investment I made in a basic, long–short, U.S. equities hedge fund in 1981 grew and gradually metamorphosed into a "macro" strategy. The short-term results have been nothing less than spectacular, but the ongoing, unforeseen impact has been the generation of tax consequences in several foreign countries. Also, ordinary income taxes from bond positions rather than more preferential capital gains have become the commonplace tax treatment for the portfolio. This changes my tax planning. Understanding the difference provides me with a clearer understanding of after-tax performance and the impact on my cash flow of severe undulations in the taxes I report and pay. This understanding minimizes my discomfort and allows me to stay in the context of overall portfolio results, in which losses might have occurred to offset gains, thus helping me keep my situation in perspective.

The most important variables that impact tax planning are what, where, and how your assets are owned. A general knowledge of common ownership structures, types of taxes, and currently available tax strategies are all useful tools to strengthen your future planning. Knowledge of the actions that advisors take on your behalf that impact or lessen your tax burdens helps you to converse effectively, ask the right questions, and read reporting information with tax-wise eyes.

Common Taxing Conditions and Challenges

Familiarize yourself with what the taxes actually are, as defined in Appendix E. Taxes include personal investment taxes (capital gains), income taxes (FIT), business taxes (income and excise), real property taxes (ad valorem), transfer taxes (estate, gift, and generation-skipping), and alternative minimum taxes (AMT). The most common situations wealthy families must address begin with ownership in the family company that creates the wealth.

Low-Cost Basis Publicly Traded Common Stock

This type of stock often occurs in inherited or recently merged or traded company ownership, as well as in compensation packages for upper management. This category of stock creates several challenges: how to diversify a portfolio without paying enormous tax or depressing the market by trying to move a large block of stock. For larger blocks of this type, very few options are available to minimize the tax effects of transferring stock except for a private equity swap and a transaction called "short-against-the-box" and other arcane strategies that are under fire as benefiting the very wealthy. Pressure mounts to eliminate these strategies altogether.

Gifting low-cost basis stock in trust to a philanthropy while retaining income protects the market value but shelters the taxpayer from gift and capital gain tax when the charity sells the stock to realize the cash value of the gift. (See the discussion of charitable remainder trusts in this chapter, Appendix E, and Chapter 8.)

If you are passing your stock to the next generation via a will, a "step up in basis" occurs, increasing the value to the beneficiary at no tax cost to them should they decide to liquidate all or a part of it soon after the transfer. This action doesn't protect the estate from death taxes, it only protects the beneficiary from capital gain tax. The main danger is the individual's lack of appreciation of the concentration risk. The factoring in of the tax cost against the risk reduction of diversification should be analyzed by a qualified professional to be sure that the tax tail isn't wagging the investment dog.

Closely Held Corporate Stock

Closely held corporate stock often proves to be a highly illiquid property with devastating transfer tax implications. Next to raising expansion capital, the single largest reason for companies going public or selling out is to solve this lack of liquidity/estate tax dilemma. Family limited partnerships are becoming increasingly common to better address this problem while keeping the company in family hands. Transfer of closely held stock to a family foundation partially addresses the problem. If family corporations don't normally throw off adequate income to accommodate the 5 percent distribution rule, the family foundation is not a viable option. Also, foundations may only hold a small percentage of the company's stock. If the company is a C corporation, it is subject to corporate *and* individual tax liabilities. If it is a Subchapter S corporation, the corporate tax liabilities flow through to the individual shareholder. If the corporation doesn't supply sufficient income to the shareholders to cover the liabilities, the shareholder is at risk personally and the company is at risk from shareholder revolt. Buy–sell agreements and other exit strategies have to be instituted when addressing closely held stock ownership. Understanding your options for tax, investment, philanthropic, and estate planning will increase your sense of security and satisfaction when planning for closely held stock transfers.

Portfolio Turnover

Portfolio turnover is probably the most overlooked tax consequence generator. High turnover, depending on the timing, can generate hefty short-term (treated as ordinary income) and long-term capital gains in any given year. Lack of control over a manager's timing of sales or a mutual fund annual distribution and turnover rate, or failure to plan adequately to compensate for these implications erodes investment performance by an average of 3.5 percentage points, not including state and local taxes.[4] (This calculation assumes a 28 percent tax and that only capital gain taxes are paid, not the higher ordinary tax rate of a short-term gain. If the tax rate were 20 percent, performance would have to be 2 percent greater than the benchmark measurement to overcome the capital gain tax impact.) Over a period of years, the amount to reinvest is eroded exponentially due to built-in tax effects of portfolio turnover. The higher the turnover, the more taxes you pay and the less there is to reinvest for growth. In the case of a mutual fund, even if you invest near year-end, you are liable for your pro rata tax on the fund's *annual* tax calculation.

Tax Implications of Business Ownership Structures

How you hold your assets affects the level of your tax liability. More detailed definitions of structure types may be found in Appendix E.

Multijurisdictional Ownership

Multijurisdictional ownership creates interesting problems. Anglo-Saxon law allows U.S. citizens to choose where, to whom, and how much they give away to heirs. Other countries such as France (under Napoleonic law), Germany, and Japan dictate these terms. Trusts are not available under the Napoleonic Code and thus can't be used as a planning tool in France. Equities in nearly all foreign countries are taxed at the estate rate of that country, unless they are held in corporate form. A partnership does not protect them. There are annual tax implications that must be adhered to and returns that must be filed. Limited-liability corporations won't exempt you from estate tax in any foreign country. There is no marital deduction for the spouse of a U.S. citizen spouse if the surviving spouse is not a U.S. citizen.

Limited-Liability Corporations

Limited-liability corporations are not permissible in all states. These hybrid ownership vehicles have the characteristics of both a limited partnership and a corporation. See the Glossary for a detailed definition.

C Corporations

C corporations (C corps) are the structure of choice for many larger family companies because they allow for orderly succession planning and management and provide liability protection with the corporate shell. Since 1993, the top C-corp tax rate has been lower than the individual rate. From 1986 through 1993, this wasn't the case.

Many companies elected to become Subchapter S corporations during that time. Corporate profits are taxed to the corporation, and dividend distributions to the owners are taxed at ordinary tax rates—near 50 percent for the wealthiest owners.

Subchapter S Corporations

Subchapter S corporations (S corps) pay no corporate income tax. Instead, the income and expenses pass through to the individual owners, who are taxed at individual rates according to their income, thus eliminating double taxation.

Proprietorships

Proprietorships are less costly to form than a corporation because they have only one owner. Like partnerships, they suffer no business income tax, but their *net* income is taxable to the owner. However, proprietorships don't escape excise and sales taxes on their goods and services.

Limited Partnerships

Limited partnerships are similar in characteristics to proprietorships, but they have multiple owners. The general partner is responsible for management decisions, although the limited partners must agree to changes in the partnership agreement. Like the S corp, the partners are taxed on the type of income received annually (whether long- or short-term capital gain or ordinary income) according to their ownership interest in the partnership and the type of income the partnership generates. Beyond the annual tax implications, particularly for a business partnership between family members or unrelated business associates, estate taxes on a partnership are calculated at a discount to the survivors and to the estate due to the binding nature of the structure and minority status of ownership. If the partnership forcibly binds disparate personal interests merely to spare tax dollars, potential discord among these undivided but incompatible interests might outweigh the planning and tax benefits of this type of structure.

Personal Holding Company

A personal holding company holds the entities under which ownership is managed—partnerships, C corps, and S corps (under certain rules). Both corporate and individual tax implications arise from this hybrid structure, but it is used by many larger family companies in which the family members are quite diverse in their interests and involvement in the company. The tax implications for this type of entity are complicated. The company can't hold more than 79.9 percent of an asset as an S corp to avoid a double taxation burden to the owners. As a C corp, owners pay both corporate and individual taxes, and under personal holding company rules, the holding company may be subject to tax penalties unless it pays minimum dividends to shareholders, thus *insuring* the owners of double taxes. And, of course, the ownership interest is subject to estate taxes at death. However, like the closely held company and family limited partnership, the illiquid and minority nature of the holding company provides a deep discount for gift and estate tax valuation purposes.

Retirement and Pension Plans

Retirement and pension plans sound like a great idea, but IRA, Keogh, 401(K), and profit- and pension-sharing plans are not tax protected, they are only *tax deferred*. The astounding fact is that if anyone of these is in an estate at the time of death, it is subject to an 85 percent tax depending on the state in which you live (when imputing estate, income, capital gain, federal, state, and local taxes). If the plan is given to a private foundation, there is only a 15 percent excise tax burden and the children can be designated as the managers. In the case of an IRA, a beneficiary spouse can postpone the tax liability by using the spousal rollover. This might not be advisable with sizable sums because of the 15 percent excise tax imposed on larger accounts. This particularly impacts the families of highly paid managers.

Pooled Portfolios (LPs and Mutual Funds) versus Individually Managed Accounts

Pooled portfolios (LPs and mutual funds) and individually managed accounts have different controls for tax planning. The latter allow some control over timing of investment loss to offset gains, whereas the former do not. Only very recently have portfolio managers begun to work with clients to address their tax planning concerns without diminishing the power of their overall management style and philosophy. Looking only at year-end unrealized losses limits tax planning flexibility and portfolio management efficiency.

Annuities and Life Insurance Contracts

Annuities and life insurance contracts are among the last investment vehicles that permit tax-deferred growth on virtually unlimited levels of assets. The annuity may be partially or totally taxable. Careful analysis must weigh the costs of administration against any overall tax savings. On average, an annuity must be held for longer than seven years to zero out the cost. Only then can you begin to calculate the gains and benefits.[5]

Other "Taxing" Considerations

Ownership structures that are useful for tax planning often appear more beneficial, but with investigation, you will see certain downsides. This further highlights the need to be familiar with the muddy nature of the alternatives.

Philanthropic Gift Structures

Philanthropic gift structures are touted as the answer to your tax problem. The charitable remainder annuity (CRAT) and charitable remainder unitrust (CRUT) provide tax deductions or tax deferral of capital gains in perpetuity, although the income received by the donor is taxable as income in the year received. However, the Internal Revenue Service closely reviews charitable transactions to test for lack of charitable purpose. Avoidance of capital gain as a purpose for the trust is not alone sufficient to qualify a gift as a charitable act. The most important variable is the terminology of the trust. Only a professional trained to write a trust should be trusted to design one for you—not an investment professional using charitable planning as a "hook" to sell investment product.

Age as Tax Planning Factor

Age is a too-often ignored variable for beneficial planning efforts for the whole family. The different ages and stages of the family members determines the tax planning and investment focus. Because there are four or five taxes to pay (federal, state, local, ad valorem, capital gain, estate, gift, and Malthusian—more mouths to feed as generations expand[4]), you must get the growth (capital gain) down to the youngest member of the family and have the older members in low-risk, low-tax-cost assets. What is good for mama isn't necessarily good for junior.

Maximizing Tax Code Provisions

Tax code provisions such as the marital deduction, lifetime giving and the generation-skipping trust are three ways to transfer assets in order to minimize the erosive character of multiple tax burdens. Giving real property in your lifetime rather than through your estate eliminates a tax on a tax. Future appreciation of property is transferred free of tax to the recipient, and only individual gift tax on the amount above your lifetime exemption (as of this printing, $600,000 for an individual, twice that for a couple) is assessed. If transferred after death, both the value of the property and the amount the beneficiary received to pay the tax with are taxable at 55 percent. To transfer $1.00 in assets at death will cost $1.22 of liquid assets in estate tax as opposed to 55¢ in cash as gift tax paid during a lifetime transfer.

THE LEGAL IMPERATIVES

Several generalizations must be highlighted as guidelines for legal planning. These imperatives hark back in part to the general planning imperatives but are specific to the legal issues that every family and individual faces when stewarding assets and families.

The Decisions You Make Today Have a Very Long Reach

If you don't communicate your intentions and motives clearly, how they are perceived is out of your control. You must be the keeper of the values and goals you wish to see passed on. My grandfather's estate planning is a case in point. In his will, he bequeathed one-quarter of his estate to my father in a life-tenancy that flowed through to my brothers and me upon my father's death. Dad was also designated trustee for the other three-quarters of the estate on behalf of my three aunts. Because of this structure, there was no estate tax payable by dad or the estate at the time of my grandfather's death. But, should dad later predecease his sisters, steep estate taxes would inure to the sisters and their children because, unlike my father's portion, there was no generation-skipping feature to their inheritance. This perceived injustice later compelled the aunts to pressure my grandmother to rewrite her will, to disinherit my father's offspring and to name the aunts and their children as her joint heirs ostensibly to compensate them for the "unfair tax bite" they anticipated and for the lack of control they had over their own affairs. I don't think my grandfather or his attorney (who was also that family's corporate counsel) had any idea what ill feelings would arise from what they saw as a wise estate plan.

Know What Your Goals Are Before Making Irrevocable Legal Decisions

Your ideas and priorities will change. Regularly revisiting decisions and reviewing goals especially with each major event such as a birth or marriage, supplies flexibility that creates comfort. Too often we make our decisions based on our expectations of what we want our children to be, when we should see them as they really are. Jay Hughes suggests that estate planning flows from only one question: How wealthy do you want X to be?[1] I suggest that it is more complex than that, but that the question is a good place to start.

Surround Yourself with the Best and Right Legal and Tax Advisors for You

What *you* want to have happen actually pays the bill and insures personal comfort. You need competent general counsel with a thorough understanding of tax and property law (beware the attorney who professes to have all of the answers) and an accounting professional not dominated by income taxes. Look for general counsel who understands family dynamics, who encourages no secrets, and who clearly cares about you. These key advisors should have superior access to technical specialists. Insist on continuity, not a constant stream of technicians-in-training at your expense. (See Chapter 7 and Appendix C for more on this topic.)

Don't Allow Taxes to Drive the Process

This cannot be stated too frequently. Tax planning is how lawyers and accountants get paid. Planning is an art. It applies judgment and personal mission to conflicting information and to the motives of those you pay to help you. Too often the accountant is measured by tax savings performance, not by good team planning skills.

Without a Will, Government Makes Your Choices for You

A thoughtless or careless will causes generations of distress. Many wills don't have trust provisions, but many model ones do. The disposition of assets and care of the grantor and beneficiaries should be clearly addressed in a coordinated fashion. Study Figure 4.2 and review the Wills and Trusts Toolbox that follow in this chapter to prepare an effective plan for your family. At the very least have a will that you have signed and keep it current.

Keep All Legal and Recordkeeping Documentation Current

Besides your wills and estate plans, additional documentation should include irrevocable insurance trusts (the value is not includable in an estate), other insurance documentation for protection of assets of exceptional value, personal property inventory (on computer disk and video as well as hard copy), advanced medical directive (living will), medical power of attorney (in the event that you can't speak for yourself), durable power of attorney for investment management (in the eventuality of your incapacity to manage business affairs), letters of instruction for next of kin spelling out what your wishes are for burial, a separate letter articulating special bequests, and particular trust documents. By being this specific about where you want things to go and what you want to have happen, your heirs and assigns will receive what you want them to have. (See Appendix B for a complete listing of important documents.)

Keep Documentation Safe but Not Secret

In the event that anything unanticipated happens to you or your family, these items, or copies of them, should be kept in several places and made accessible to trusted others besides yourself. Repositories such as a safety deposit box in a responsible other's name and your attorney's office prevent inaccessibility in a time of great emotional stress. Ask your loved ones to do the same with their affairs, and then let each other know where the papers reside. Too often, the family has no idea "where she or he kept those things or what she or he wanted done." (See Chapter 14 and Appendix B for more information on this topic.)

Key Family Members Are Entitled to the Same Protection as Nonfamily Members

Indemnity agreements for responsible family members are a prudent business and legal planning imperative. For all fiduciaries to have the broadest possible investment options, any agreement should stipulate the "lowest standard of care"; that is, only gross negligence is indemnified (a fiduciary can be negligent but not grossly negligent). Negotiated agreement is preferable to merely implicit understanding that "Uncle John" will do a good job for you just because he is "Uncle John." Uncle John should be held to the same standard as any outside fiduciary, and he should be given the same protection because you expect him to act exactly the same. In fact, you expect him to act better *because* he is Uncle John. (See Chapter 14, "Insurance on Liability" and "Director's and Officer's Insurance.")

Educate New Family Members

In-laws and others may have dissimilar backgrounds. When they are just entering a family accustomed to doing business together around financial issues, certain suspicions and misunderstandings might arise in a person unfamiliar with wealth as a business. She or he might see the requirement to sign a legal document as an act of mistrust or aggression. The new family member needs to understand his or her rights and to be clear about what the release covers. He or she also needs to learn the value of working with the family plan by not remaining fearful or ignorant of it as it evolves.

A Trust Is an Effective Estate Planning Tool

Whether revocable or irrevocable, the basis for which type of trust instrument to use is a matter for the individual family and the advisors to work out over time. A trust serves as a shield, with the assets in the trust's name. But it cannot insure wise business decisions, happy and productive family relations, work ethic, or moral values. Study the following section, "Wills and Trusts Toolbox."

FIGURE 4.2

ELEMENTS OF EFFECTIVE ESTATE PLANNING

- Provide flexible current language for future contingencies.
- Retain clear control.
- Protect and enhance assets.
- Establish investment and administration guidelines.
- Define payment schedules.
- Minimize tax impact for beneficiaries.
- Minimize probate costs and delays with dispositive trust language.
- Establish system for the safekeeping of records.
- Meet the needs while curbing the desires of future generations with flexible, creative incentive provisions.
- Provide for unexpected incapacity.
- Design privacy-shielding mechanisms.

WILLS AND TRUSTS TOOLBOX

The components of the planning documents that will withstand the tests of time and family and business changes are available and are useful as well as necessary. There are more bad wills, estate plans, and trusts than there are good ones. Lawyers and accountants make more money undoing inadequate instruments than writing and executing good ones. It is much more cost effective to invest the time and money up front to do it right than to end up in court to clear up muddy or debilitating terms and conditions for later generations. With the previous planning imperatives clear in your mind, you can now access the tools available for your own wealth stewardship planning.

An Effective Trust Has Clear, Flexible, Current Language for Future Contingencies[3]

There are 10 elements that contribute to the creation of an effective trust. Including these in any instrument of this type that you design places you in an advantaged position to know that your plans will actually unfold the way you hope.

1. The power to change the trust in the event of any law change (11 major tax law revisions occurred in the span of one professional career).

2. The power to administratively change trust (trust protector's role).

3. The power to change the trust substantively (modifying ages of distribution, etc., as a result of unexpected changed lifestyles of beneficiaries and dashed expectations, and altering future beneficiaries in trust language).

4. Provision for care for special assets such as art collections and operating companies.

5. The capacity to lend and borrow money with repayment provisions.

6. Investment responsibility.

7. Administrative and distribution responsibility.

8. Incentive provisos to meet needs while curbing desires.

9. Dispositive language built directly into the trust rather than the will to shield the estate from costly legal and

court proceedings (a trust remains out of probate if it is written properly).

10.   The power to change the citus of the trust.[1]

Choosing Appropriate Trustees

Designing a trust is a challenge for an estate plan. Most trusts are control instruments and irrevocable; thus, they are difficult to change. Trustees are chosen for many reasons. A bad or inappropriate one can undo all of your careful planning and compromise your family's future. To choose well, be sure to match abilities with the responsibilities and your family's needs, ensure that accountability provisions are in place, and hold the trustee separately responsible from fiduciaries involved in other aspects of the family and the business.

Potential corporate trustees should be scrutinized from a checklist that includes examination of experience and stability, rate of staff turnover and dependability, and attention to your account (how many accounts can one officer manage effectively?). Also important to the selection are reviews of administrative and distribution efficiencies and excellence, investment management focus, performance, and the track record in the management of like assets. References from other clients about their experiences with the trustee reveal much about trustee appropriateness. Is there an affirmative policy of resignation? (Many trust companies have them.) The fees, though sometimes negotiable, normally run 1 percent of asset value under management, regardless of the quality of management provided. Consideration should be given as to how equally liable cotrustees would interact.

Wholesale Institutions

As trustees, institutions wrestle with whether they are conservators of assets with an investment department or whether they are investment advisors with an administrative department. Retail money management institutions have decided they are investment advisors with an administrative role to play. You must be clear about what you want in a trustee for the long term. From the client perspective, if the trust company decides to preserve 50 percent of the talent reserved for the administrative function, services will be excellent. If only 25 percent of the talent is allocated to service, the services will suffer. Conflicts of interest arise over time when policy changes with management objectives. Ask the institution up front, "Where is your

emphasis— administration or investment advisory?" If it is important to you, ask, "What are your capabilities and track record in philanthropic administration?" What the family needs most from a
trustee is excellent administration and distribution decisions. There
is a clear conflict of interest when the trustee only looks to itself as
the best investment advisor for every trust asset they manage. Fortunately, some institutional trustees are becoming wise to this and
are making long-overdue changes to diversify asset management.

Private Trustees

Multigenerational, complex families must have handmade trusts.
Families who have sufficient assets to make a "make or buy" decision to hire any person to provide any service ask "Since I can make
anything a commercial service provider has to offer, what is the benefit of using an outside provider? Why not choose to make my own
or use a customized private trust company with a proven record
that is already representing and managing similar families?" The
advantages of outside trust management are (1) not having to manage it, (2) not having to deal with disgruntled family members, and
(3) more experienced service. If you decide as a family that you are
in the long-term preservation business, you are already prepared to
put forth more effort on your own behalf than an institution that
serves a client base that is not necessarily compatible with you.

Family as Trustee

The family is the most often used trusteeship method for wealthy
families for many reasons, the most important being that family will
better care for family than will nonfamily, regardless of the level of
appropriateness to the task. However, having family as a trustee can
create tragic and unforeseen tensions and outcomes if it is done without serious thought and discussion.

   When my aunt wished to redeem her shares in the family company, my father, because of his conflicting business and familial roles
as chairman of the board of the family company and trustee for his
sister, was forced to ask the court's protection against a possible liability claim by requesting a declaratory judgment. To have the court
decide fairness in the redemption value for her shares was his best
protection against future claims. He was legally bound as a fiduciary to sell at the highest price for his sister, yet he was bound by his
corporate position as chairman to negotiate the lowest possible price

in order to protect the company's cash flow for the other family shareholders. Be realistic about the ramifications of family trusteeship. There is merit in an independent perspective. The William A. M. Burden family chooses to use individual family members, not banks, as trustees. Succession of the trustee, flexibility, and education of individual trustees are benefits of this choice.[6]

Choice of Executor

Like a trustee, executor choice is very personal, if not as important. The executor, the first person to deal with the bereaved family after the will is read, must have authority to carry out your wishes. Being compatible and fair is of extreme importance. The executor is responsible for carrying out all of the details until the estate is settled, which can take several years in the case of a complicated and substantial estate. If the executor is a younger family member, a coexecutor is prudent, depending on the maturity and training of the family member. Compensation for the executor should be decided in advance with the help of tax and legal advisors.

Removal Clause for Trustees

Including a trustee removal clause lessens the burden on your family in the future should they want to move the trust. Removing a trustee for "cause" can include assigning trust officers with less than five years experience, for changing corporate trustees more frequently than every five years, for relocation from trust origination, for demanding unreasonable compensation, and for failure to comply with written agreement on the operation of the trust. No matter who you choose, lengthy discussion is necessary to disclose your goals and the willingness of the trustee to serve, especially if the trustee is an individual.

Trust Protector

Providing for a trust protector is a useful tool for contingency conflict resolution because it supplies an independent voice of the protector who can say yes or no to the removal of the trustee to avoid frivolous or mean-spirited actions. One cannot assume that the beneficiary is always right . Because of the expanded liability issues and the Third Restatement (Prudent Investor Rule), there should be oversight. Paying a private trustee to oversee a trustee responsible for administering the trust creates unnecessary expense. The protector is paid no fee, has no investment role and therefore no liability. The protector's only responsibility is for overseeing the trustee's prudent handling of the terms of the trust. The only liability in the protector position is the arbitrary and capricious use of the removal power. Initiating removal of an incompetent trustee is not his or her responsibility. The protector has to be asked to act, but once activated, he or she is all-powerful. For example, where great wealth is at issue and a marital property agreement is advisable but one-half of the couple balks, an independent facilitator might be necessary to ease the path to agreement. However, when agreement is not an option, a revocable management trust with a trust protector is a viable alternative.

Advisor and Trustee Succession Provision

This provision must be established when the trust is initially formed. Because inertia exists in all matters to do with planning and management, inappropriate or ineffective service providers can linger long after their effectiveness has ended. Trustee competence and performance need regular review, as do all working relationships with staff and outside advisors and trustees. Always ask, "Is that person appropriate to the situation?" Just because you have always used that bank or that law firm means that perhaps it is easier, but not necessarily best, for you to choose or keep them as advisors and trustees. A long-time relationship is harder to sever even when the advisor has not acted in your best interest. The relationship then becomes acrimonious and financially costly. Forced removal of bank trust departments as managers is not peculiar to my experience. Where active oversight of bank trustees by families is the norm, this action is commonplace.

Special Assets Provision

This provision requires careful evaluation and choice. Private trust companies are particularly appropriate where there are special assets to manage, such as operating businesses, extensive real estate holdings, substantial special collections (if they constitute more than 5 percent of the estate), and so forth. Most public or individual trustees aren't equipped to make the underlying investment decisions appropriate to these assets. For instance, familiarity with environmental risks in managing real estate, hiring employees, and being engaged in businesses that are not in their normal activity range require special management expertise. If a private trust company is not appropriate or affordable, for whatever reason, then an individual or group of special trustees whose authority is limited to that particular asset should be appointed. Trust language defines parameters. This frees other trustees from responsibility for managing that asset. This system benefits the family's long-term goals and the capacities of the various trustees. Family business consultants often advise against appointing the child who will manage the business as trustee for that asset if he or she is to be effective in leading the business. She or he must be the advocate of management and retention of wealth in the business. She or he may be conflicted over meeting other family members' goals and needs when they are at cross purposes with those of the business. Family companies go out of business over this very conflict. The natural instinct is to keep trusteeship in the family, but it is risky to consider business separately from human relationships, especially when it is all in the family.[1] The earlier example given of my father and his sister's trust is a case in point.

An Outside Board of Directors

Having an independent board of directors is a special requirement for the operating company managed in trust. This is applicable as a tool for the beneficiary just taking on complex or large holdings who needs a working board of experts that can teach and shepherd him or her. Trust language can provide for an advisory board for succeeding ownership. Too often, the advice for the new owner comes with a buy/sell approach before he or she has time to decide the direction he or she wants to take the assets. Ulterior motives may exist for the "expert" to buy the business himself or herself at a distressed value or to give the opportunity to a partner to the exclusion of the best interest of the owner. For instance, a real estate broker asked to give advice on a potential development property would not have an unbiased opinion. Independence and lack of bias, along with needed familiarity with the particular asset class, are key qualifications for a board of this kind.

Second Family Trusts and Adopted Kin

Remarriages and adoptions present unusually sensitive challenges. In planning a trust for a second spouse who is not the parent of the future beneficiaries, that spouse's assets should be segregated from those of the children in the first family. The fiduciaries for the second marriage beneficiary should be different from the fiduciaries for the first marriage beneficiaries. Putting income or trust control in the hands of a second spouse while passing it to the children of a first marriage can create irreconcilable conflict. The beneficiaries and their remaindermen will second guess the unrelated party as long as they live. The Averill Harriman Family trust is illustrative. Also, how an individual feels about nonblood (adopted) and blood issue can complicate matters unless the wording and intentions are clear.

Provision for Incapacity

Special legal provision should be made in the case of a beneficiary who needs his or her affairs managed due to handicap or other incapacity. A revocable trust with a pourover will provides protective management in later years. The beneficiaries are the grantors *and* the beneficiaries at a time when most personal faculties abound. The beneficiaries choose their own trustees when they are capable. An institutional trustee is *not* a good candidate for a situation when guardianship is a possible outcome.

Active Beneficiary

Encouraging a beneficiary to be active may appear unreasonable because he or she is often a minor when many trusts and wills are drafted. But if regular review is a part of an active planning and management process, beneficiaries grow up during that continuing process. A trust is a formalization of a three-way conversation between the grantor who funds the trust, a trustee with distribution, investment and administration responsibilities; and the beneficiaries. The trust agreement assumes that the beneficiary is the major actor. The trust assets are there for the benefit of the beneficiary, not the trustee. If the beneficiary doesn't meet with the trustee once a year, or even more frequently, if he or she does not make the trustee aware of who he or she is as a human being, not just his or her balance sheets, the beneficiary loses. Trust is built as the relationship is built. If the beneficiary writes once a year and says "These are my needs, thank you," and gets a check once a quarter, he or she will get good service but will not get that to which he or she is entitled. If this occurs, the fault lies with the beneficiary.

Having designed the plans, learned the vocabulary, and kept the managing process in mind puts you far down the road to satisfaction in what wealth stewardship can provide for you and your family. All that is left is the enjoyment of the journey—understanding that where you go from here is going to be much smoother than what you believed it could be when you first took on the challenge of directing your own business.

PHILANTHROPIC PLANNING IMPERATIVES

Jane Gregory Rubin

Individuals with names associated with wealth are regularly approached to part with their available assets for the benefit of a charity. This has become a fundamental fact of existence in the United States and abroad, as other nations experiment with the "American model" of private philanthropy. How to appropriately respond to such requests has become a life skill. The philosophy of this book is that stewardship of private wealth includes philanthropy, and it is important that you gain control of the process of giving. This is done by learning about issues about which you care and focusing on where your assets can make the most difference.

The high level of private giving in the U.S. as compared to other nations that we consider our peers (the U.S. is second to Canada) exists primarily because fundamental services such as hospitals, schools, and major cultural institutions have, in large part, been historically dependent on private largesse. This has resulted in uneven distribution of such services and has provided donors with enormous opportunity to effect social development.

To some extent, government funding at all levels has attempted to even out the distribution of public benefits associated with charitable institutions. These attempts, at least at the moment, are being discredited and increasingly eliminated, with a renewed call for "private" philanthropy and volunteerism to replace government involvement, again creating more opportunities for the private donor. Religious philanthropy, which accounts for over one-half of the generosity of Americans and accounts in part for the statistically high level of giving in the United States, is not appropriate for government subsidy for constitutional reasons.

The government provides indirect public support, in the form of a tax policy that allows generous deductions for most lifetime philanthropic gifts. The general working rule is that the least amount of tax benefit is available where the donor is seen to exercise the most control. Within the spectrum of tax benefits, the least benefit is available for lifetime gifts of appreciated or self-created property to private foundations. The most tax benefits are available at death, where a charitable deduction is allowed for the full market value up to 100 percent of the estate. Income and estate or inheritance tax regimes in some states and in other countries can be more limited. A donor with dual citizenship or residence in more than one jurisdiction for tax purposes must be especially careful when planning for charitable giving.

In Chapter 8, there is broad discussion of implementation issues related to philanthropy, with in-depth discussions of various techniques of giving. The philanthropic planning discussed in this section will focus on special cases in which the imperative for lifetime gift planning is clear—the case of the person of wealth who has no heirs or who has stewardship of certain kinds of assets that are not seen to be appropriate as family bequests. Absent special circumstances, most donors should begin a philanthropic program during their lifetimes to insure that their intent is carried out after death.

In the first instance, the individual with no immediate heir must provide adequately for him or herself, given that there is no one to provide the family function. This is especially true when there are relatives who are considered "next of kin" under the law applicable to the donor's estate but who are not persons the donor wants to control or inherit his or her wealth. In such cases, the choice of advisors (covered in Chapters 7 and 8 of this book) is critical. To be effective, the philanthropic disposition of what is not needed to support the donor's lifestyle must be an ongoing process.

Planning Stages

If an incremental strategy is used (as described below), the group that is assembled is generally the following: the investment advisor, with knowledge not only of investment strategy but also with a working knowledge of income tax issues; the donor's personal accountant, who has a sense of the complex tax issues confronting the donor and can advise the donor, based on the tax situation in any given year, of how much should be given away; lawyers experienced in the interplay of estate and income tax, family dynamics, and charitable organizations; and the donor. If a private foundation is set up by the donor during his or her lifetime, it is increasingly advisable to have separate counsel for the foundation.

Step One

Examine the areas of the donor's personal and professional lives about which he or she cares most and then explore the broad issues affecting such interests. There also need to be candid discussions about how important it is for the donor's name to be associated with his or her giving. This can be an imperative, for many donors regard the projects they fund as a way to keep the donor's name alive, particularly in the case where no certain heir exists.

Step Two

If there is no family gift-giving mechanism in place, such as a foundation or philanthropic component of a family office, either segregate a block of assets, the income and/or principal of which is to be given routinely to charity, or create a trust to hold the assets that go to charities at the death of the donor. A trust is especially useful if there are relatives in whom the donor has no interest. At this point it is not advisable to do anything irrevocable. If a trust mechanism is used, it is generally a "grantor" trust, the terms of which can be easily changed. Charitable remainder trusts, defined in the Appendix E and discussed in Chapter 8, can be used effectively if there is low-basis property or closely held stock and the trustee has broad powers to choose the donees.

Directing the Gift

Directing the gift is an action by the giver that has many variables.

A Case for Anonymity

A research process is begun into what institutions are involved with the issues in which the donor is interested, including donor groups or policy institutes working in the area. Because the most effective grants are made after careful personal inquiry, "philanthropy support groups" may not be a good idea until the donor has some experience in actual giving. One of the most effective ways to proceed, particularly when the individual is a professional working within the environment he or she hopes to benefit, is by anonymous giving. Anonymity gives the donor the ability to identify needs, to carefully articulate the terms of the gift, and to gather knowledge of how effectively the money has been used without altering colleagues' behavior toward the donor. The contact with the donee can be one of the advisors (usually the lawyer) or a community foundation with "donor-advised" grant-making programs. The techniques of isolation of a block of assets and anonymous giving are equally effective as a starting point with younger-generation donors of inherited wealth.

If several institutions have been identified as doing responsible work in the area of interest, small gifts to a number of institutions for the first several years is informative, giving the donor the chance to meet the administrators of the organizations to generally see how responsible they are in dealing with donors. Once confidence is established, larger grants to fewer organizations or specific promised gifts can be put in place. Confidence and information are especially important if the donor is interested in becoming a member of the board of directors of a donee institution.

A Case for Private Foundations

With the individual who plans to leave the bulk of his estate to charity, philanthropy can become a life's work. More formal steps, such as the creation of a grant making or "operating" private foundation are appropriate. An operating foundation is a foundation that does not make grants to third-party organizations but spends its income on the furtherance of its own charitable purpose; for example, a medical doctor or scholar creates his or her own research foundation, or a teacher creates his or her own school.

This structure is likewise effective in family philanthropy to allow younger-generation professionals a career while acting as a steward for family assets devoted to philanthropy. The goal is to create a structure that will provide for continuity. By far, the most fragile time in any philanthropic continuum is during the administration of an estate. Control passes to a new set of individuals or institutions. With a charitable trust and/or a private foundation, the donor has created the institutional history.

Protecting Donor Intent

The lack of heirs can also be at other than the donor level. It is quite common to provide for close relations and then make a conditional gift to a charity or give directions as to charitable intent, for example, "to help homeless women," and allow the fiduciaries to make the arrangements. Generally, it is not advisable to word the provisions so that a charitable deduction is allowed or the charitable interest is vested. The interest of the charity should be contingent enough and the donor's preference to benefit the family stated clearly enough that the charity does not acquire sufficient interest to interfere with family matters.

Sometimes in such cases, a charitable deduction is desired for estate tax-planning purpose. For example, a widow has two children, one childless, but she does not want family assets to pass outside the bloodline, nor does she want to disfavor the child without children. Her estate plan divides the assets of her estate into two equal parts, one for the benefit of one child and his or her descendants. The second half is structured to give a charitable deduction while providing a lifetime income for the child without children. This can be done in various ways. The most intergenerational involvement with the process is usually created by the child establishing a foundation during the mother's lifetime for the purposes in which the child is interested. Moneys, either from the child's own funds or from parental annual giving, are passed through the foundation, giving the child grant-making experience.

Charitable Planning with Objects as Assets

Liquidity creates flexibility in charitable giving, but what of the case of wealth that is inherent in objects? In the United States, there are at present no national patrimony issues (other than those associated with native American objects). An individual is free to dispose of valuable collections. Again, this may not be the case if the donor resides abroad and holds cultural property such as art and antiques of historical importance in the country of residence.

This freedom does not mean that there are no moral imperatives associated with the possession of certain objects, particularly when there are no family members to care for the work in the same manner as the donor. For most major collections, either of work created by third parties or a successful artist owning a substantial body of his or her own work, the placement of such work in appropriate institutions is of major concern. Holders of such objects are generally known and are constantly approached for donations; they also tend to be very sophisticated and understand how their property will fit into the context of institutional or other private collections.

The usual target assets for charitable donations are those to be donated in-kind, in which the donor has a low basis and which are not part of the long-term investment plan. If a tax benefit for the donation is important, the most significant decision is to what extent the donor is willing to part with the object(s) during his or her lifetime. In some cases, formal deeds of gift are executed transferring title, but the transfer does not take place until death, resulting in estate tax benefits but no income tax deductions during the donor's lifetime.

In the case of the collector and/or artist who knows where he or she wants the work(s) to be placed, the institution should be approached by the donor. Sometimes there is interest, but an institution cannot afford to take the piece without an endowment for conservation funding. Unless there are particular circumstances (such as the donor not having other assets—which does occur with some frequency), it is generally a good idea to make such an offer as part of the original approach. This insures that the inquiry will be responded to quickly and that the piece(s) will be cared for when the donor is not around to ask questions. It is also responsible stewardship of the assets.

With very large collections, with difficult-to-place objects, or if the negotiations will, for various reasons, be protracted, it is advisable to transfer title to the collection to a trust, with the donor as trustee and a named successor trustee who is fully familiar with the contemplated transaction and in whom the donee institution has confidence. Even with research, care, and thoughtful structural planning, many such negotiations break down quite far into the process, when it becomes apparent how much the expectations of the parties differ. Those differences can be small, such as how the collections are to be treated within the institution's catalogue system, or they can manifest in larger institutional issues of display and de-accession.

Discussions concerning any tailored gift to a large institution may be dramatically dependent on the personality and interest of an individual within the organization, for example, a particular curator might want to build the collection in a specific direction. If that person leaves the position, the attractiveness of the institution as donee may diminish. Particularly if transfers over a long time period are contemplated, great care must be taken to create agreements that are not dependent on individual preferences and do not carve out exceptions to institutional procedures. Unless the gift is of extraordinary value, these conditions will probably not be followed. A recent gift of $20 million from a wealthy donor was later withdrawn when the donor's intent proved to be in conflict with the use of the grant by the recipient educational institution. The institution lost the $20 million gift and the donor walked away frustrated in his intent to aid the institution.

Many collectors and artists contemplate creating their own museums, and some have been successful. Because they are very expensive, a business plan is essential. Unless the donor plans to endow the operation to cover the costs, either alone or with additional family funds, a realistic projection of possible third-party funding sources must be made.

There are also archival collections and objects that have little monetary value and/or intrinsic worth but are absolutely irreplaceable and present moral imperatives of a special kind. These collections, such as a scholar's work documenting other cultures, are very difficult to place, particularly if the scholar is not well known or the results are unpublished. The classical repository of such work would be in the library at the university with which the scholar was affiliated. However, this is not realistic given budgetary constraints and the fact that most scholars who have worked internationally may have been associated with, or have materials located in, many different places.

In such cases, it is critical that the scholar, or others who have knowledge of the work, make sure that arrangements have been made to deposit the work with an archive in the United States and at least have a catalog of the material made available in the country that formed the basis for the research. The only general rule in all such situations is that the desired result can be obtained provided the donor starts early enough and is focused.

Because private philanthropy occupies such a special place in our social fabric, individual donors should treat such activity as an important part of his or her civic obligations. To the extent possible, a holistic approach should be taken, recognizing the importance of such planning within the parameters of business and family life.

FINANCIAL PLANNING IMPERATIVES

Louis Leeburg

Financial planning is a term that has had more than its share of use and misuse in the past 10 or 20 years. When someone speaks today of financial planning, the wise investor will ask, "Tell me, what do you mean, financial planning?" You will hear definitions ranging all the way from "anything and everything to do with money" to "what you do in order to help insure a comfortable retirement."

The precursors to financial planning are (1) a statement of the mission you have defined for the wealth for which you are responsible (Figure 4.1), and (2) a statement of the financial objectives that must be met in order to accomplish your mission. I define financial planning as the combination of strategy and tactics you will employ in order to achieve that set of financial objectives.

The mission statement should be clear and concise. Certainly, it should be committed to paper, preferably no longer than a page or two. Wherever possible, the mission statement should be the product of consensus among the beneficiaries of the wealth. The Steward family statement presented earlier in this chapter is an example. Your financial objectives in support of the mission should leave no room for a variety of interpretations, and they should be measurable.

With your mission and financial objectives in hand, you will be ready to begin the work of financial planning, keeping in mind that all financial planning is based on the fundamental principles outlined in Chapter 1, below, and in the section entitled "The Prudent Investor" that appears later in this chapter.

1. *Look to the past.* How have assets been allocated in the past? What has the annual yield of the portfolio been? What has the cash yield of the portfolio been? What have the spending requirements been?

2. *List your priorities and put them into two categories: short term and long term.* Long-term goals might include wealth preservation that keeps up with or is surpassing the cost of living. Examples of short-term goals are providing liquidity to fund a personal philanthropy and supplementing a child's earnings as he or she gets started in a profession.

3. *Describe your situation as it stands today.* Create a snapshot of assets, liabilities, and net worth. Once you know your financial position, you will be able to assess the amount and timing of cash receipts from assets and cash needs to meet liabilities.

4. *A family budget is the next order of business.* This can range all the way from a simple schedule of family maintenance costs to a complex array of disbursements in support of a program of philanthropy. Review this again and again to be sure that you have not left anything out and to be certain that you have not underestimated cash requirements.

5. *Compare historical cash flow to your budget.* If cash flow exceeds anticipated cash requirements, is there a policy and a plan for reinvestment of excess cash on a timely basis? If cash flow will be insufficient, can the shortfall be made up by liquidating assets that will not fit your plan of investment?

Throughout, rely heavily on common sense. Once you have decided what you want to do and have a plan for doing it, your instincts, your logic, and your common sense should have a major role in working your plan. Force your advisors to explain the "why" of their recommendations; have no hesitation in asking "how." Last and most important, refuse to submit to the enchantments of the willing suspension of belief. Sally's summary of what comprises a prudent investor will assist you toward that end.

THE PRUDENT INVESTOR

Familiarity with the principles of prudent investment is a valuable foundation tool for the wealth stewardship process. Anyone reading this book is a fiduciary (being in a position of trust and responsibility). How much better a legacy can you leave to your heirs than one that provides skills, memory, a sense of family, and creative and purposeful philanthropy, all of which can generate immeasurable fun in the doing? Begin by thinking of yourself as a fiduciary for yourself, and then apply it to those who will follow you.

Under prior rules adopted by most state governments, when defining the rights of beneficiaries and the responsibilities of fiduciaries, a person could not invest in speculative investments. Simply preserving capital in a prudent fashion was an acceptable level of care. But inflation, technology, economic forces, and modern theories have changed all that.

The investment principles upon which the Prudent Investor Rule rests derive from modern economic and portfolio theory and are required for formally appointed trustees in many states. Because they are being employed by large institutional investors, the entire investment community is incorporating them as a general standard. Informal management relationships in family asset management groups under legal pressure from an affected party could be held accountable if these principles are not observed.

The price of an asset is affected by two factors: the anticipated total return of the asset and the risk that the total return will fall short of expectations. Total return is the sum of income received (dividends) and appreciation/depreciation (capital gain/loss) over a specific investment period.

Risk comes in two forms: market/systemic risk (the risk attributable to any investment in the same market area; for example, all commercial rental real estate, all oil service companies, all stocks, and all bonds) and specific/unique risk (an isolated risk factor such as the weather affecting prices of corn but not other commodities, such as orange juice grown in another part of the country).

The free market will compensate for the systemic risk by price adjustment, but specific risk will not be protected by price adjustments in the free market. Diversification is employed to offset specific risk.

Risk management implies acquiring assets with responses to specific influences that will cancel or offset each other in order to diminish the volatility created by inherent risk. Since market risk varies from one market to another, the prudent investor must determine which markets to include in the investments. Selecting several markets with varying risks to approach overall tolerance may be most appropriate. But the beneficiary's tolerance, distribution requirements of the trust or individual, the likelihood of cash needs, term of the trust or age of the individual, and general goals and objectives are all factors in determining prudence. Once determined, risk must be monitored and adjusted when necessary.

Capital markets are efficient and are rapidly reflected in the prices an investor pays, theoretically dictating that passive investing (buying the market indexes) is the most prudent exercise. But because cost control is an issue of prudence, actively managing (hiring investment consultants in addition to money managers or your own staff person to actively oversee the portfolio) may be more cost effective if portfolio gains above the indexes justify the cost of paying for active management.

The Prudent Investor Rule (f.k.a. the Prudent Man Rule), as recently revised, is frequently referred to as the Third Restatement of the Prudent Man Rule. Under the Third Restatement, what were once considered speculative investments (oil and gas drilling, hedge funds, and venture capital) are commonplace in accounts of trust today. Depending on where the trust resides, different state trust laws are binding, but the definition of what is prudent according to the American Law Institute prevails in many of them. Many states have already adopted the Prudent Investor Rule, and fiduciaries of all types are adopting it as their guide.

Below are the four tenets of the General Standard of Prudent Investment:[7]

1. The exercise of reasonable care, skill, and caution must be applied, not in isolation but in the context of the trust portfolio and overall investment strategy, incorporating risk and return objectives reasonable to the investing party.

2. In making the investment decision, the duty is to diversify the investments unless under the circumstances of the trust, it is prudent not to do so, such as in the case of an operating company managed in trust.

3. The trustee must conform to loyalty and impartiality standards, prudently deciding delegation of authority and selection and supervision of agents, incurring only those costs that are reasonable and appropriate to the investment responsibilities of the trusteeship.

4. Trustee duties must conform to any applicable statutes governing investments by trustees in the location of the activity, and to the specific investment language in the trust instrument itself.

Use the ready reference guide provided in Figure 4.3 as you work through the financial planning and investment policy decisions (discussed in the next chapter). You will find the summary information for the Prudent Investor Rule very helpful at other times, such as when you are cast in the role of fiduciary for family members and others or when serving on not-for-profit or corporate boards.

FIGURE 4.3

> ## TENETS FOR THE PRUDENT INVESTOR
>
> - Prices reflect market risk but not unique risk.
> - Neutralizing unique risk requires diversification.
> - Markets are highly efficient; thus, attempting to outperform the market is a questionable exercise.
> - Total return objectives must include protection from inflation erosion of purchasing power.
> - View an asset not in isolation but in the overall context of investment strategy.
> - Have an articulated investment strategy.
> - Exercise care—reasonable effort and diligence in making and monitoring investments.
> - Remain within the guidelines of the stated objectives.
> - Delegation of strategy implementation may be the most prudent action, providing the choice is made with reasonable care .
> - Bear in mind the objectives of safety and reasonable total return.

Author's note: I especially credit James E. Hughes, Jr., Esquire for his forthcoming and expert counsel in helping prepare the tax and legal sections of this chapter. He shared his professional experience of working with families and enlisted the help of his colleague, Don Kozusko, who contributed to the glossary appendix on legal and tax planning terms. His critique of the finished chapter and a significant portion of the body of knowledge concerning general, legal, and tax planning subjects was invaluable.

FIGURE 4.4

The Process of Managing Wealth: An Overview

Planning	Implementation	Montioring
	Investment Oriented	
Set investment goals Determine implementation strategy Provide benchmarks to measure performance Produce "real time" investment reports	Allocate assets Select managers/brokers Design investment reporting system	Review performance Consider changes in · personal needs · economic climate
	Financial Management	
Consider asset/liability oriented issues Assess cash flow considerations Review hedging options	Design financial reporting system Produce "real time" financial reports Establish banking/credit relationships	Analyze results vs. projections Continuously update · budgets · projections
	Tax Related	
Identify tax saving opportunities · controlled company oriented · employer company oriented · investment related · interfamily driven · residence driven · transaction driven	Prepare periodic tax projections Prepare tax returns Manage IRS and state tax audits Periodically review estate plan	Consider changes in · tax laws · investment products · business relationships · employee benefit plans · family relationships
	Administrative/Controllership	
Consider assets/liability management techniques · insurance alternatives · custodial alternatives · cash management systems Determine optimum information flow	Select advisors/systems Pay bills/collect receipts Handle domestic staff Negotiate house closings, mortgages Coordinate "the process"	Consider changes in · new products/services · personal circumstances · professional relationships Revisit "the process"

Source: TAG Associates, Ltd.

ENDNOTES

1. James E. Hughes Jr., Esq. Interview, *Legal and Taxation Considerations*, New York: 18 August 1995.

2. James E. Hughes Jr., Esq. *Tax Intelligent Asset Allocation*, Speech delivered at the *Tax Issues Affecting Private Clients Seminar*, New York: The New York Society of Security Analysts, Inc., October 25, 1995.

3. Roy M. Adams. *Do Children Manage Money or Does Money Manage Children?* Speech delivered at *The Second Annual Wealth Management Forum*, Institute for International Research, New York: Plaza Hotel, September 1995.

4. James P. Garland, The Jeffrey Company, Columbus, OH, WYSAWYG *or Why the Meek Shall Inherit the Earth*, Speech delivered at *Tax Issues Affecting Private Clients Seminar*, New York: The New York Society of Security Analysts, Inc., October 25, 1995.

5. Alvin A. Clay, III, President, Pitcairn Trust Company, *Its What You Keep That Counts*, Speech delivered at the annual conference of the Family Firm Institute, Scottsdale, Ariz., October 1994.

6. Jeffrey A. Weber, Managing Director and Chief Investment Officer, William A. M. Burden & Co., LP, *What Families Want From the Financial Institutions That Serve Them*, Speech delivered at the *Second Annual Wealth Management Forum*, New York: Institute for International Research, September 1995.

7. John E. Martin, "*A Preface to the Prudent Investor Rule*," In *Trust & Estates*, Atlanta, Ga.: Argus, Inc., November 1993.

8. TAG Associates, Ltd. "The Process of Managing Wealth: An Overview," Distributed Professional Materials, New York, N.Y., 1994.

5

APPORTIONING INVESTMENT RESOURCES

The Fundamentals of Allocating Assets

Perhaps the most technical area newcomers encounter is money management. In reality, there are similar intricacies to all investments. Allocating resources is the most useful and effective way to keep the technicalities under control. Armed with these asset allocation fundamentals, a good understanding of the Prudent Investor Rule, and a basic due diligence process (see Chapter 13), any investment policy decision is manageable.

Because it is known that 90 percent of the returns in an investment portfolio are attributable to asset allocation, dividing the total pie of your assets into the correct size pieces to fulfill your mission and reach your goals requires considerable attention. Using the tools suggested throughout this book, but particularly in this chapter, will help you decide how you want to divide and shape that pie.

You can't really use someone else's asset allocation plan. Each family or individual needs to have a customized plan to fit the particular investment goals, risk tolerances of the group, the short- and long-term expectations, and varying cash flow needs. A personal investment policy grows from evaluating and expressing these variables. Because of the technical nature of this exercise, special advisor assistance is required. Because investment policy is the key to a successful financial investment management plan for any family group,

I have asked Louis Leeburg to elaborate on the steps to successful asset allocation and investment policy planning. He provides definitions of the common terms within his chapter, but these and others are also found in Appendix E.

Lou, as a long-time investment counselor and financial advisor to private clients and families, has an easy, clear style especially useful to a beginning student. After you have read his straightforward description of what asset allocation is, how it is accomplished, and how it relates to investment policy, take a few minutes to study Figure 5.1 shown on page 107. This flow chart will help you envision the place these features have in an investment process typically used by wealthy families.

TAG Associates, Ltd., a multifamily office in New York, uses this flow chart to educate family members in a simplified way about the basic components of managing the details of investment decisions. This model describes the same process in slightly different terminology from that used by Lou. The important thing to gain from reviewing this figure is that asset allocation, investment policy, and personnel decisions are fluid. You won't just make one set of decisions and forget about it. In addition to the initial goal setting, investment policy making, and investment manager selections, Lou addresses the monitoring of investment results, reviewing and changing of objectives, strategy, and managers, and the ongoing rebalancing of your allocation plan. These keep your evolutionary financial life relevant, current, and expressive of your needs.

ASSET ALLOCATION AND INVESTMENT POLICY

Louis Leeburg

Asset allocation is the diversification of one's investments into different forms of assets (technically called classes of assets), such as stocks, bonds, real estate, and cash, in a manner designed to enhance return on investment while minimizing risk. The investor cannot do much to influence the performance of an individual stock or bond, but there is a broad range of strategic positions open to the investor who seeks to influence the overall performance of his or her portfolio of assets.

History is the primary guide to asset allocation—not the history of a particular stock or bond or real property, but the performance history of *all* stocks, *all* bonds, *all* real estate through as long a period of time as you may wish to measure. History serves up detailed data in great abundance, and an army of analysts in the securities industry sift the data on past performance to produce powerful indicators of the future risk and reward characteristics of each class of assets. First, they calculate historical averages for each class, and then they analyze the degree to which each varies up or down from its historical average. When you hear the word *volatility* applied to a class of assets, it refers to the size of deviations from the historical average of performance.

With these historical perspectives as your guide, you can distribute your funds into various classes of assets with a fair idea of the returns to your portfolio as a whole, provided that each class continues to perform through time as it has in the past. Because the various classes of assets do not act in unison in response to events, diversification of investment usually reduces the volatility of the portfolio as a whole.

Beginning with your family's investment spending requirements, you can use these tools to adjust asset allocation to best meet your objectives, whether to maximize cash income, increase total return, or provide for an orderly liquidation over a fixed period of time.

REVIEWING YOUR ASSETS

The shaping of an asset allocation policy for an individual or family begins with a review of the existing assets of one's portfolio and then a frank review of your needs and your expectations. It is far from unusual for the portfolio with which one begins to contain assets that are the product of unique circumstances and cannot be readily converted to other classes of assets. In some instances, the conversion would have adverse tax consequences; in others, the lack of a ready-made market for the assets makes their conversion impossible or unwise; or perhaps it is the case that the assets constitute a large block in a family-controlled corporation and their disposition is controlled by a shareholders' agreement that prevents ready sale.

Whatever the circumstances, begin by listing the portfolio's assets by class—that is, stocks, bonds, real estate, and cash—with their fair market value, if it can be determined. Next, list the cash distributions to be realized from the portfolio in the year ahead under the assumption that none of the assets will be sold or converted. Now you will be in position to assess the impact of any changes you may consider making in the portfolio.

The next step should be an assessment of the issues specific to your portfolio that would influence a decision of whether to dispose of or convert any of the assets. Many articles and books on asset allocation begin with the assumption that all assets are liquid and that cost to convert from one asset class to another will not be excessive. Only rarely is this the case. Only rarely does one come into responsibility for a portfolio that is clear of concern for the consequences of a low tax basis or unreasonably high disposition costs for some of its components. In many family situations, certain assets are locked in by past commitments that prohibit their sale except under carefully prescribed circumstances. In making your portfolio listing, assets that will not be converted, for whatever reason, should be segregated from the other assets or highlighted within the portfolio.

At this point, you will be ready to estimate annual returns on the portfolio as a whole by using historical returns for each asset class as your guide.

Domestic stocks are typically measured against the Standard & Poor's 500 Index. The index is designed to be representative of the performance of the public market for stocks at any given time or in any given period. Historical analysis will suggest what you can expect the stock market to earn or average and what you can expect in terms of variances from those averages. Fortunately, all asset classes can be indexed (some with greater accuracy than others) so as to provide you with tools for creating different scenarios.

You can try your hand at this without changing a thing in your portfolio: You can shift assets from one class to another on paper and then pretend that you invested accordingly 2 years ago or 10 years ago. By playing these "what if" games, you can become familiar and knowledgeable without leaving your desk and without putting a single dollar at risk. All the while, it is vital to remind yourself that the next year or the next few years will not necessarily duplicate exactly the ups and downs of the immediate past. But this exercise will soon begin to show you which characteristics you will want your portfolio to have. It will also enable you to compare your expectations with reality. It will allow you to realistically assess whether it will be possible for the portfolio to earn what you expect it to, given the level of risk you deem acceptable.

As much as 90 percent of a portfolio's performance is attributable to the asset mix decision. That is why the steps recommended here focus on classes of assets and your becoming familiar with various mixes of asset classes. Once you have decided that you are comfortable with a particular mix of asset classes, you can then choose investment professionals on the basis of the expertise and track record in the management of specific classes of assets.

With your portfolio neatly segregated into various asset classes and with a clear picture of restrictions on certain assets, you will be ready to evaluate your spending and investment policy.

SPENDING AND INVESTMENT POLICY

I use the term *spending policy* to represent your estimate of the funds you will need to withdraw from the portfolio and the timing of those withdrawals. The policy can be expressed either in dollars per year or as a percent of the value of the portfolio. This policy will powerfully influence the range and character of investment policies you will be free to consider.

If you decide that you wish to spend 10 percent of the total value of your portfolio each year, for example, you will know that it is likely that the portfolio's real value will shrink over time if the historical long-term returns from the various asset classes is less than 10 percent. As I will illustrate later, that figure will be further reduced when inflation is factored in.

Historical returns for domestic equities have averaged near 10 percent for the time period from 1926 through 1994, while domestic high-grade bonds for the same period have yielded over 5 percent. The returns generated each year vary significantly and are also impacted by inflation, which has averaged 3 percent in the same period of nearly 70 years.

If withdrawals from the fund equal the increase in value created each year, the fund would deflate by the inflation rate to reflect the decrease in purchasing power. Therefore, if your goal is to preserve the asset base that you currently have, you should evaluate your portfolio on the basis of real return, whereby the gross return is adjusted for inflation.

Thus, in our example above, the real return of domestic stocks from 1926 to 1994 has not been 10 percent, it has been 6.9 percent, while in the same period, the real return from high grade bonds has not been 5 percent plus, but rather 2.1 percent. The yield of cash in those years was a mere .6 percent.

EVALUATING ASSET CLASS RETURNS

The swings of the past 20 years, then, illustrate how important it is to use averages calculated for long periods, such as in the following table, where I have shown the real return (gross return less inflation) and the standard deviation for each class of assets, using the longest available periods for which good data is available.

	Actual Annualized Real Return	Standard Deviation	Return Period
U.S. equities	6.9%	15.6%	1926–1994
Non-U.S. equities	6.3	18.1	1960–1994
Emerging markets	5.7	25.8	1976–1994
Real estate	1.8	9.9	1960–1994
U.S. high-grade, fixed income	2.1	8.6	1926–1994
Non-U.S. fixed income, hedged	2.1	7.0	1960–1994
Cash	0.6	1.8	1926–1994

By carefully manipulating the proportion of each invested dollar that goes into various classes of assets, with special attention to the volatility of each, it is possible to produce returns with a minimum of variance from historical averages. The importance of doing so is underscored by the huge difference in standard deviation shown in the historical record—that is, from a low of 1.8 percent to a high of 25.8 percent. There are many computer-based programs designed to find the "right" mix—optimum return with lowest volatility—based on the historical data. It is important to recognize, however, that the best of these models do not eliminate volatility altogether. Their function is to take into account all the known variables (historical price movements, deviations from average, the degree to which one class of assets performs independent of another, etc.) and then to suggest the best mix to achieve a given set of objectives.

But while the computer can magnificently model the past, the human mind remains—for a while at least—the best observer of the present. What is happening today can be just as important as anything that has taken place in the past, and sometimes more so. Analysis of today's events and trends should be a vital factor in deployment of your resources. Take for example the two 10-year periods, back to back, of the 1970s and 1980s:

◆ The 1970s produced large cap stock returns of only 5.9 percent for the decade; long-term government bonds earned 5.5 percent, and the consumer price index averaged 7.4 percent. The 1970s produced negative real returns because neither major asset class could produce gains greater than inflation.

◆ By contrast, the decade of the 1980s saw large cap stocks grow at a rate of 17.6 percent, while long-term government bonds grew at 12.4 percent. Inflation as measured by the change in the consumer price index rose 5.1 percent annually during the decade. Therefore, during this decade both asset classes generated real returns far in excess of their historical norms.

To take the appraisal of performance a vital step further, if we combine the two decades, 1970–1990, we find that real returns are 5.5 percent and 2.7 percent for equities and fixed-income instruments, respectively. The average for the 20 years, then, is below the historical long-term returns for stocks, while the returns on fixed-income securities for the period are greater than the historical average.

REBALANCING AND INVESTMENT POLICY

Most investors cannot afford to deal in 20- and 30-year time frames, and many will not adjust their portfolios unless a major market correction occurs. Changes made at those times typically result in lost opportunities, while a consistently disciplined approach to balancing has historically added value. If you are working to preserve or enhance an established spending policy, the chances are that you will want to "rebalance" your portfolio once a year in order to meet your objectives.

For example, if you began in 1970 by putting 60 percent of your assets in equities and 40 percent in fixed-income securities and did not rebalance the portfolio or withdraw funds, the effect of the 20-year differences in growth and returns of the two classes of assets would be that the portfolio would have been 72 percent in equities and 28 percent in fixed-income instruments in 1990. Thus, without rebalancing, you would have a distortion of your asset allocation and a portfolio with risk factors and other characteristics quite different from those you had established at the outset.

The advantage to combining asset classes is that it becomes

possible to lower the standard deviation of the overall portfolio (that is, its variance from the historical average) yet still maintain a relatively high rate of return.

The wise investor will commit policies and objectives to writing—spending policy, cash flow objectives, and portfolio investment policy—so as to be able to keep them fully in view when making asset allocation decisions. (See Chapter 4.)

If you seek to maintain your existing purchasing power, a key objective will be to maintain or increase the real purchasing power of your portfolio after adjusting for investment returns, spending, and inflation.

BASIC ASSET ALLOCATION MODEL

Let's say you begin with a portfolio of assets worth $2 million and you want to spend a minimum of $100,000 per year, or 5 percent of the portfolio's value. Let's assume that in the first year the portfolio gains 8 percent in value. It is all too easy to think that the gain will permit an increase in spending, which would appear to be the case except for the unpleasant business called inflation. If inflation has been 3 percent or more, the purchasing power of the portfolio has achieved no real gain, so spending should remain at the $100,000 level if you still wish to gear spending to 5 percent of the portfolio's purchasing power.

Investors who seek to maximize their total return normally will make a significant commitment to equities of 50–80 percent, but they will also maintain a 20–30 percent commitment to fixed-income investments as a source of high current income and a deflation hedge, and a commitment to real estate of 5–15 percent to maintain an inflation hedge.

Alternative assets such as venture capital, emerging markets, oil and gas investments, private placements, and derivatives are typically considered separately with an eye to the individual investor's knowledge of and experience with these alternative forms of investment. Many of the alternative investments have the potential to increase the overall return of the portfolio, but there is no guarantee that the potential will be realized. Here, one's own knowledge and expertise must have greater weight in decision making than any other factor. However, if these investments are limited in size, 5–10 percent of the portfolio, they can provide the possibility of strong gains without seriously impacting the volatility of the portfolio.

With the assistance of your financial or investment advisor, you should be prepared to evaluate your portfolio and determine how it meets or does not meet your objectives. If it does not meet your objectives, you can evaluate what changes can be made to achieve your objectives or whether you need to revisit your spending policy.

MANAGER SELECTION PRIMER

Within the asset groups there are different manager styles to consider. For equities, there are large, mid-size, and small capitalization managers who distinguish their style by the size of the companies in which they invest. In addition, some managers select growth characteristics or value traits, while others may take a modified index position. The styles of the managers should be carefully considered by your advisors, because the various styles will generate performance histories that will vary.

You should evaluate managers as you do asset classes, by looking at performance statistics versus the index of the asset class you are considering, so that you can determine how their historical performance compares both with the index and with their professional competitors of similar style. (See Chapters 7 and 9.)

Hired managers should be given written guidelines to insure that they do not surprise you by their investment choices. Guidelines for equities managers and fixed-income managers could be structured as follows:

A manager to whom you assign your *equity* investments should not be permitted to do the following unless specifically approved by you:

1. Engage in short sales.
2. Lend securities.
3. Purchase on margin.
4. Engage in option purchases or sales.
5. Make any private placements.
6. Purchase any securities of foreign companies (unless this is a non-U.S. equity manager).
7. Invest in real estate or commodities.
8. Purchase any fixed-income instruments rated lower than those outlined in point 2 that follows.
9. Purchase convertible securities.

A manager to whom you assign the *fixed income* portion of the portfolio should be limited to the following investments unless specifically approved by you to include other assets:

1. Direct obligations of the U.S. government and, if an international manager, direct obligations of major governments that have credit ratings comparable to the U.S. government.
2. U.S. government agency debt.
3. Corporate bonds rated A or better unless you are hiring a high-yield manager or someone with a specific discipline that you have evaluated and agree works for your asset mix.
4. Commercial paper rated A-1 or P-1 or better.

Once you have assigned responsibility for components of your portfolio to professional managers, it is important to evaluate and monitor their performance and to evaluate your portfolio against your original objectives on a regular basis.

If your expectations are not met, you will need to review your allocation to determine differences resulting from asset allocation or manager selection. Over reasonable periods of time, adjustments may be necessary in either your asset allocation or your choice of managers—or both.

FIGURE 5.1

The Investment Management Process

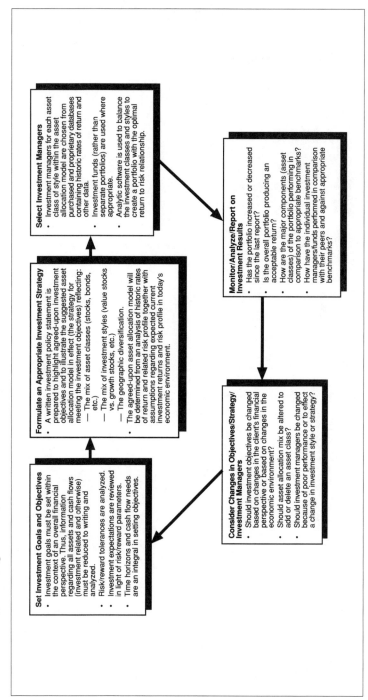

Source: TAG Associates, Ltd., New York, N.Y., 1994. © 1994 TAG Associates, Ltd.

This figure is illustrative of an investment policy management process followed by a multifamily office in New York City. Study this figure to understand the process Lou outlines in the foregoing chapter. Notice how the process is circular and ongoing.

ENDNOTES

1. TAG Associates, Ltd. "The Investment Management Process." Distributed professional materials, New York, N.Y.,1994.

6

FOUNDATION CONSTRUCTS FOR MANAGEMENT

Private Wealth Governance and Control

Besides a clear grasp and understanding of the initial actions of planning and education and their critical value to the management of resources, a wealth steward must place equal importance on governance structure and the governance procedures that flow from that structure. Precisely because stewardship is a process, not a series of unrelated transactions, nowhere else is clarity of mission, place in the family, and purpose more important than in governance and management. Perhaps the most critical decision a person makes about managing his or her wealth is the determination of the structure and governance criteria from which to work and with whom the work will be done. These fundamentals usually evolve over time, if wealth is grown gradually, or they erupt out of a defining event that brings wealth management responsibilities to the fore in a rush rather than from a clear plan.

Once set in place, a structure is difficult to alter. It is worth waiting, learning, and *temporarily* putting your affairs under management before committing to a structure chosen merely by default. It is not as simple as "Oh, I'll just hire a secretary to pay the bills and keep my books for me." Wealth management, in effect, is a business for you or the family, whether you go it alone or as a group, and only you can decide which way is most suitable for you. The processes and structures are as varied and unique as the individuals and families themselves.

Family wealth stewardship is a family business. The most common weakness of family wealth management arrangements is their failure to operate at a level of professionalism required to negotiate the family relationship minefield inherent in the business. The several situations, or "mines," that create hazards for most families include family intrigue and emotional attachments that hamper and infect practical business decisions. These include family members with unresolved familial issues performing management and trustee functions for family members and entities; trusting unrelated employees without fail-safe procedures in place; expecting other family members and advisors to automatically "know" what you are thinking without openly communicating with them; and expecting long-standing business professional relationships to remain static and reliable without regular review regardless of any historical association (not all trust officers or accountants are equal even if it was grandfather's firm or bank). Other hazards include assuming that friends and family are more trustworthy business partners because they are friends and family, and that you don't need to check their credentials or their deals as closely as anyone else's; assuming the family agrees with your values and priorities just because you're family; assuming that, in business, family members will always treat you as an intelligent adult because you are one; and assuming that the family business and family wealth management are mutually exclusive when they are inextricably related.

This minefield offers compelling reasons for thoughtfully choosing and implementing the structure and process for effective wealth stewardship. The least effective way to control your process is to simply accept things the way they are or the way they have evolved.

Through four generations, my family's management process was simple as long as the number of family members participating in ownership of the family asset remained controllable and all family members accepted the hidebound family culture and personal lack of liquidity. The company office managed everything for everyone through the business itself, diversifying and growing the company, and using the corporate liquidity to do so. In the late 1970s, when the fourth generation began fraying at the edges and the large, diverse and vocal members of the fifth generation reached their early 30s, internal pressures mounted to force the company and senior family members to provide flexibility for the disparate needs and lifestyles of the expanding family. The corporate office was not the place to manage those personal style differences.

The consequent corporate reorganization resulted in a distribution of certain corporate assets out to the shareholders. This event spawned the establishment of no less than 20 individual or group family offices to manage this new liquidity. In most instances, these offices sprang up randomly, like toadstools after a storm, out of perceived need but with little research or planning. They were formed and remain in varying random configurations to manage interests among siblings, two- and three-generation family groups, and cousin groups. Within one branch of the family there are four different business office locations representing three generations. Management is informal and fluid but not necessarily efficient or wise.

MANAGEMENT STRUCTURES

Most families have, if nothing else, a place where their personal business is conducted, whether at home, with a part-time secretary/bookkeeper, or off-site with larger staffs, depending on the complexities of the affairs under management and the desires and abilities of the cooperating family members. A combination of family members and hired assistants and advisors often form the management team. How involved you are or want to be is up to you and others who share the facilities. What you begin with won't necessarily stay the same as your business evolves and grows. In Chapter 7, in-depth techniques for hiring appropriate people to do the job at any specific juncture are discussed.

But rather than staying with a structure and people with which you begin, you may, in time, need to change structures and hire different personnel as your business evolves. For instance, a good administrative assistant or personal bookkeeper might not be qualified to manage and track complex financial assets, philanthropic entities, and legal details for a busy CEO, entrepreneur or recently liquefied pool of capital for a larger, extended operation or family group.

The array of management structures available to manage family office needs in this country, which are as varied as the types of families who use them, are of two primary types, private and institutional. The most common are defined below. In Chapter 9, "Money Management," brief descriptions can be found for types of family offices that serve as pure money management structures.

Choosing structure alone is not enough. Family stewardship requires realism, creativity, and flexibility to accommodate and manage the idiosyncrasies inherent in the ownership and governing group (at times in conflict) and in the type of structure itself.

Private Family Offices

Elements common to most private offices include individual services support; family group services such as family meetings, communications, and education; ancillary support for family owned businesses; individual and family financial planning, management and coordination; philanthropic management, and execution; trust, estate, and succession planning and/or administration; and back-office technical support and execution. As they are private, personal attention, customization, and flexibility are their leading strengths, but their insularity can be a weakness that results in loss of objectivity. (See Chapter 9, "Money Management.")

Private, Full-Service Family Office

A fully staffed office might cost $1,000,000 per year; $50 million of assets has been cited as the critical mass required to justify this level of expense. There are as many configurations and complexities as there are family types; these offices can either be dedicated to serving one family or to serving several families that all require similar services. Many of them have begun to expand their dedicated positions to open their doors to families *not* requiring full service, as long as a stated minimum in assets is committed to management. Pioneers of this type are Rockefeller & Company and Pitcairn Trust Company. Wealth Management Associates, Inc. (the Cox Family Office in Texas) and others are opening to outside families. An example of the dedicated, single-family office that remains single, internally managing all operations including investment management, is the Bass Brothers Office in Fort Worth. Their brother Robert maintains a separate dedicated family office of his own. Some of the above have evolved to institutional proportions through expansion. A full-service, major family office would provide services similar to those in Figure 6.1.[1]

FIGURE 6.1

Professional Family Office Services

I. Family Planning			
Family decision making process	Family member education	Periodic family meetings	Charitable giving and family foundation

II. Financial Planning			
Monthly financial reporting	Succession and wealth transfer	Personal financial plan	Tax planning strategies

III. Investment Planning			
Philosophy for investing	Investment policy guidelines	Asset diversification	Selection of investment managers
Short-term cash management	Custodial services	Performance measurement and reporting	Asset allocation rebalancing

IV. Personal Services			
Recordkeeping and bill paying	Cash flow budget and projections	Investment partnerships	Tax compliance
Property management	Insurance assessment and consolidation	Security and protective services	Secretarial and travel services

V. Family Office Services			
Family office structure and administration	Employee selection, compensation, and benefits	Management of information systems	Policy, controls, and procedures

Source: Family Office Exchange, Inc. Reprinted by permission. © 1993 Family Office Exchange, Inc., Oak Park, IL.

Family Investment Management Office

This type of office is limited to liquidity management as an unadulterated service. It exists when a family group dedicates their work to a devised investment philosophy. Liquid capital is pooled among the family members, and family members and/or dedicated professional money managers actively manage the portfolio or group of outside managers for the group. The philosophy of the founding family defines the investment approach. These offices are either for a single family or are open to other families. Ashbridge Capital Management (a branch of the Grace family), Milbank Winthrop Co. (Milbank and Winthrop families), and LJH Global Investors (the

Hedges family) are examples. Rockefeller & Company accepts outside clients for investment management only but provides other extended services to Rockefeller family members. The Bessemer Trust Company (the Phipps family) is also open to outside clients for investment management and trust services.

Family Office Service Companies

These are often referred to in the trade as multifamily offices. They are not dominated by the culture of one lead family or philosophy, but instead, they serve as a consortium of several families using investment management, estate and tax planning, and other operations to manage wealth and personal needs. Asset Management Advisors (the Perry family) began as a multifamily, full-service office. Associated Family Services and TAG Associates in New York are also examples of this type of office.

Family Office Cooperatives

In these cooperatives, several families join around issue-specific interests to effect economies and management simplification for individually managed insurance products, fee-favorable custody and trading arrangements, and other services. The economies of scale are valuable. The legal hassle of setting up binding partnerships to manage assets is bypassed by a system of this kind. There is freedom and flexibility to pursue other unlike interests and needs individually. Examples include the Boston-based Triple C Alliance (Pitcairn and Corning families) and the Witan Company in St. Louis.

Private Trust Companies

Private trust companies are formed within a family group for more direct and effective personal trust management for family trusts (often trusteed by related family members) without arcane and restrictive philosophical and bureaucratic institutional management by relative strangers. Their value is the centralizing (and personalizing) of management, custody, trading, trust accounting, record keeping and reporting, compliance, and trust administration when the assets are large, complex, binding and multigenerational. Consider that the Pitcairn family group had the daunting task of managing over 1,000 family trusts when they decided to form their family office. Weigh costs against the multiple fees of paying other institutions for management, custody, trading, and administration. Most trust departments charge a fee of 100 basis points (1 percent) of funds under management in the trust itself. All other costs will be in addition to the management fee.

Back-Office Specialty Management

Back-office management companies provide coordinated, customized services that often include record keeping, tax compliance and reporting, personal and domestic services management, family communications, financial gathering and reporting, and cash management. With efficient technology, long-distance personal service is available. Dellwood Financial Services, begun as a back office for the Archer and Daniels families in Minneapolis, has expanded its services to other families across the country. They offer all of the stated services in addition to educational and monitoring services for family members, historical tracking of personal and technical information for continuity purposes, philanthropic administration, and outside advisor coordination and management. They also serve as an objective balance to these other resources.[2] There are other providers of fee-based, technical, back-office management services.

Institutional Wealth Management Structures: Banks, Trust Companies, and Investment Management Firms

Despite their large size and restricting regulatory parameters, there are still several institutional management structures that are beginning to address the diversified needs of wealthy family groups more effectively. Of course, personal attention and product customization are difficult to provide due to the institution's very large client base and its lack of flexibility. Each type of management structure has its strengths and weaknesses and should be thoroughly reviewed by the decision maker before recommending it for the family group.

Concentrating their focus on the private wealth client, banks, trust companies, and investment management firms are the alternatives to private trust companies and offices. Because they are institutional, the customized service is compromised, but the efficiencies of size, product formation, and availability (depending on your requirements) might offset these concerns. Money managers are also opening private trust companies to capitalize on the growth and the annuity of the fees generated by a service of this kind, but they are not directed to serve only one family or carefully selected clients. Their activities are inflexible for many reasons, not the least of which are the regulations under which they operate, the impersonal nature created by staff turnover, and the often long-distance decision making inherent in large companies. A Fidelity Trust office in Houston, Texas, doesn't manage trusts in Houston, but in Boston, where policy is made. Several large providers have made names for themselves as being particularly knowledgeable in private client wealth management. Some of them are J.P. Morgan, originally the family bank for the Morgan family; Brown Brothers Harriman, originally a family office but long since institutionalized; U.S. Trust Company, in New York; and Northern Trust and Harris Trust Company, both in Chicago. Very few provide philanthropic management services and expertise although the Morgan bank has knowledge and some ability in this area. None can insure continuity of personnel, nor personal ancillary services such as hiring domestic help and other like services. These institutions often gain their clientele from families who feel they don't know where else to turn for multigenerational management and trust administration. Once a large institution is made trustee it is exceedingly difficult to remove regardless of its inappropriateness for the client.

Responding to institutional inadequacies, Fiduciary Trust Company International in New York designed a family resource management service incorporating the goals analysis, strategy, and policy tenets of the Prudent Investor Rule, recently adopted in New York State. This service uses a team approach to strategic planning, global asset allocation, trust and estate planning and administration, investment management, tax advice, custody, banking, and multicurrency reporting in a coordinated and customized manner for client families and institutions. They stress their individualized focus per client and their sensitivity to staff turnover. Inflexibility in most institutional trustees is candidly addressed by encouraging and recommending that trustee and executor removal powers be included in any legal documents. Direct access to investment managers is structured into the process. This enlightened approach is rare and indicates that officers are responsible for relatively small numbers of clients to insure personalized and responsive service. Turnover in personnel is not addressed, but the fact that institutions are waking up to the dissatisfaction that exists among institutional clients bodes well for increased choices for families and individuals.

Further hindrances to effective institutional management are their limited abilities to actively diversify into real estate, oil and gas, and venture capital investments. Some institutional firms are now buying outside specialty companies to satisfy the diversification needs for clients. The danger of this is the loss of independence in choosing your partners in your investments when you have the capital to choose your own, and the narrow risk profile the bank or trust company will serve due to regulatory constraints.

TAKING MANAGEMENT CONTROL

Before you make any permanent decisions about structures, how much control you want, how you want to be involved, and at what level you want to be involved, talk to other people. Visit the different kinds of offices described in the previous section to get a feel for your own style. The following example describes an unstudied approach to how a style of management control evolved for one three-generation family.

A Living Example

Without any real study, I joined in an office share with my children, father, mother, a grandmother's management trust, and three brothers and their families (15 people and 16 entities). It seemed like a good idea at the time, and we needed to work closely together to fashion a complex estate plan for my father, who was very ill. Originally, the office consisted of an office manager with general abilities and a small, back-office staff. We held meetings as needed until it was clear that we had to formalize our meeting plans. Outside professionals—advisors in money management, oil and gas geology, real estate, legal matters, and tax reporting—were used only as needed. We shared ownership in several assets, including the family corporate stock, but investable assets were held individually or in trusts. We reviewed deals and opportunities as a group, learning as we went but without a formal structure such as a partnership or corporation to organize us.

Within six months of officing together, factors clearly suggested that our investment and philanthropic philosophies and styles were very different—as different as the lifestyles and children's financial educational priorities we embraced. I severed my informal arrangement with the rest of the group. We continued to serve as trustees for one anothers' childrens' trusts and stayed loosely affiliated when legal matters and other events concerning shared assets periodically linked us. Fifteen years later, the arrangement continues, with my children and me in one office (four individuals and seven entities) and my siblings, their families, my father's estate, and mother in another (16 people with 18 entities.)

The family culture that was in place before the office existed determines the way business gets done. Doing business with the family is a challenge. Even when communication is timely, direct, and in writing, there are misunderstandings. For me, business is business and family is family. Setting aside nonfamily time to review what I am signing is important to me. Too often a document is handed out for decision or signature as a fait accompli rather than through a business process. Thus, I once exclaimed in frustration, "I won't sign one more surprise legal document on the trunk of a rental car at one more family graduation."

Removing personal blinders and biases enables you to be more professional, to separate the emotional baggage from the business at hand even if it means severing the business relationship to maintain the personal one. At a recent investor's conference, one young woman commented that she "got [her] brothers back" when she severed her business relationship with them. An arrangement such as hers or mine is often complicated by the actions of personal planning professionals who don't have an understanding of the family as a whole or who have limited professional experience with families in business together. These appointees often make recommendations for one family member that can subvert the delicate family balance that is so difficult to maintain. For example, a family limited partnership designed by the attorney for the matriarch in a family presents a partnership interest as a "gift" to a member of the family (which requires a signature). This new partnership will reconnect them to a family group with which they had severed business relationships many years before. Although the mother's estate plan was well served by the action, the offspring's estate planning, tax planning, and management goals were turned upside down. Their objectives were in conflict from the beginning, but the lawyer was unaware of the prior agreement to sever the business ties. No conference with all affected parties to discuss the pros and cons was ever held. The family member did not sign the agreement, and the lawyers are redesigning the agreement to consider all the issues, not just one. Ideally, the family members would talk with one another to settle the differences, but that was not the case in this instance. Thankfully, professionals are beginning to get the message about the importance of intergenerational considerations and open communications.

After you have seen how others do it, you will need to do some basic research about fundamentals that help define your own management objectives. The final result can be a governance structure that includes the general and customized elements (in the third section of this chapter) that are best suited for your situation.

First Things First

1. In the beginning, formulate your personal and family mission statements to serve as a foundation for the management process. (See the discussion of mission statements in Chapter 4, "The Imperatives of Planning.") From this and a clear understanding that your needs are unique, you can build a framework for managing your affairs.

2. Be clear about whom the office serves and what its purpose is. Is the purpose business only, or is it both business and personal? Is it managing for outside entities and individuals doing your business, or is it a business in its own right that is prepared to take on outside clients while serving your unique profile?

3. Be realistic in your expectations of operations, costs, and desired results and know how to evaluate them. Some of these measurements are qualitative and hard to evaluate, but strive to define realistic comfort needs and security levels.

4. Decide what role you will play—now and as you evolve in the future—who you want to work with, and how much you want to learn (especially if you don't want to work in the office regularly). Much of what you do will be decided as you learn and grow.

5. Determine the role philanthropy and its administration will play in your affairs. Is there a foundation? Will it be managed by the office or managed separately by choice or necessity? Some see the responsibilities and opportunities as complex and daunting; others approach it with a willingness to learn, to make mistakes, to seek guidance, and to trust others' experiences and their own abilities, and they find in it a satisfying vocation. If philanthropy doesn't hold a central place in your administration, being familiar with the forms it can take and roles it can play in your life increases your ability to practice meaningful ad hoc philanthropy. (See Chapter 8, "Philanthropy.")

6. Build financial education into the process. Use the family management office as a school for teaching the family the investment process, the responsibilities and opportunities of wealth, and philanthropic and personal values. Hold regular family meetings with interesting, educational, and personal topics using your staff as instructors. All family members need to be involved in the education and communication functions. They need guidance regarding philanthropy, accountability, and the value of saving, working within a budget, family culture and history, and personal competency. The need for this is essential in families of great resources. Even if the resources are not directly available to the individuals, the lifestyle they are exposed to and the perceptions of their peers and the outside world will force them into a role they will not be prepared to handle without guidance and information. If you ultimately choose an institution as primary manager for your affairs, remember that a bank or trust company rarely has the expertise to prepare younger generations and surviving spouses for assuming responsibility and dealing appropriately with wealth.

Forming the Structure

Once these key decisions are made and steps are taken, the forming of a governance structure to reflect the group requirements begins. This needs to include representation for all parties, including the family business. If available, the board of directors of the business can be a valuable resource for the owners' wealth management business, although it can't serve two masters. Consider forming a board of advisors for wealth stewardship. But with celebrated cases such as the Doris Duke Estate and Harriman Trust as beacons, and the Third Restatement of fiduciary investment policy standards, carefully consider whom you choose for fiduciary roles. Be sure they are competent to meet the governance requirements. Purchasing liability insurance is often a costly requirement before even family members will agree to serve on a board of advisors or as a trustee.

Great care must be used when beginning to choose the professionals you hire. They are there to educate and work with the family, not to disempower the wealth holders from becoming responsible managers and decision makers. Because a caretaker role is often expected by a family, carefully investigate the psychological profiles of persons seeking employment as family office manager. Family members should not become dependent, and employees should not become caretakers and enablers. The professionalism of the trust relationship is paramount in this setting. Executive search firms proliferate in this marketplace, some of which are more knowledgeable than others about the intricacies and needs of a family office. One such specialty search firm is the Rankin Group in Lake Geneva, Wisconsin. Larger executive search firms more often specialize in hiring technical specialties such as chief financial officer (CFO) and chief executive officer (CEO) positions for family offices.

Besides fair salaries, the employees for family offices must be given adequate incentives to strive for the goals that the family must clearly state in advance. When the Bass family established their office in Forth Worth in the late 1970s, they hired unproved Richard Rainwater, a Stanford Business School associate of Sid Bass, to work with them to design policy and manage their investments. He was compensated primarily by agreed-upon percentage participation in the successes he brought to the Bass investments. He has since gone on to form his own office, managing the great fortune amassed by doing so well for the Basses. Although not all hires are of the economic value of a Richard Rainwater, incentives must be realistic and competitive if a family expects good service and high-quality advice and help.

Additional staffing for personal requirements takes a different set of agencies and compensation standards and is addressed separately than for daily business office staff. Agencies, personal recommendations, due diligence into background, and the experience of other families are all required when looking for those who will live closely with the family. Wage requirements vary by region and scope of job descriptions. Mahler Enterprises, Inc. in Milwaukee, Wisconsin, specializes in customized, nationwide searches for high-level domestic staff. Other interesting resources are military installations. Decamping military aides have provided excellent "Fridays" and security personnel for several privileged individuals.

Security requirements and systems must be formalized and have clear structure. High profiles, and even low profiles with great wealth, have realistic concerns. The inclusion of confidentiality agreements, with the clear understanding of what confidentiality is, should be a requirement for all staff members and outside providers and board members. Some agreement as to what is included should be reached, and an understanding should be held as to what information is confidential and why, and what the consequences are for any violation of that understanding. Dismissal for misuse or abuse of that agreement should be swift. Some service providers can't help dropping names to impress potential clients. No matter how good they may be, breach of confidentiality is inexcusable. Be vigilant about lending your name to outside advisors. There should be no time limit on the agreement, even beyond termination of the employee or advisory relationship.

Give serious consideration to purchasing kidnap, fidelity bond, and liability insurance. Consider making prevenient arrangements with a bank and security firm for threatening eventualities. Embezzlement-proofing your personal transactions against even seemingly trustworthy staff is sensible and not to be taken lightly. (See Chapter 14, "Security and Insurance.") All systems of wealth management need two levels of checks and balances for protection. The simplest safeguards include putting a limit on the amount for which an employee can write a check and requiring two signatures on checks over a certain amount. Do not permit the same person who makes disbursements to reconcile bank statements. Embezzlement is a common crime in wealth management. Long-time, trusted employees can become common thieves. Remove temptation.

Decide on your communications goals and reporting requirements. Strive for standards that keep all affected parties "in the loop." This loop should include educated, responsive, and responsible family members and advisors alike. Reports should be regular, accessible, timely, businesslike, and understandable. Regular reports should include those for financial, trust, investment, and personal affairs such as family meetings. All families regularly fail themselves by not acting businesslike when working regularly with their advisors. As circumstances require, but at least once a year, review financial, legal and tax issues, and ask the group and outside advisors, "Where are we? What do we need to be considering? Are our plans up to date?" You will need good reports to be able to accomplish this review. When staffing is done, you can work on the particular ways to meet these specific goals. If you aren't sure what it is you will need to know, work with advisors to help you determine your reporting requirements. They will change as you learn more.

Deciding what back-office (behind-the-scenes, technical) support you need flows from previous decisions. Record keeping, investment monitoring, and tax compliance and reporting are the minimum back-office functions required for a family of means. Accessible specialty services uniquely capable of managing these functions for large, complex, wealthy families are available and can be contracted on a fee basis. They need not be brought in-house.

Contracted back-office services generally include personal and tax bill paying, tax return preparation, record retention, domestic employment hiring, personal and small business accounting and financial statements, family information gathering and dissemination, cash management, simple investment security transactions and tracking, estate and tax planning assistance, and insurance maintenance custody for certain nonmanaged assets. The personalized, educative, and confidential nature of these specialty providers makes them the answer for families, many of whom have complex and far-flung relationships to manage but who do not have a centralized, cost-effective way to manage them. Because the back-office provider is not in-house and charges a fee based on service type rather than on the size of the assets or sale of a financial product, they remain objective and essentially service directed.[3] Some of these services are available from larger institutional providers, but many are not. A combination of personal and outside facilitators is often necessary.

Technology requirements that flow from wealth stewardship can seem daunting. Whether brought in-house or linked electronically to outside suppliers, much depends on personal decisions in staffing and in monitoring of the individual investments and entities managed by your office. Whether a choice is made to directly control technological information and investment management or to link up with outside, fee-based providers (often bundled with monitoring and investment services), the existence of the Internet makes personal control readily available. Decide how to use the opportunities to suit your needs. Consider hiring a systems analyst to evaluate your needs and recommend the combination of in-house systems and outside technology providers. Much that used to be only available by sophisticated providers is now available in personal software packages, including accounting and reporting, tax planning and research, direct stock analysis, interfamily E-mail links, electronic and provider banking that limits transaction costs, standardized legal documents, and general pre-tax portfolio performance measurement. Oil and gas accounting and real estate investment evaluation, historically only attainable from accounting firms, are more readily accessed by private investors today. Proprietary software has been developed by technology specialists for these and other specific industries.

Delicate and realistic consideration is required for decisions addressing office cost and cost allocations to the individuals and groups served. Costs should be monitored and structures reviewed periodically. Do you pay fees to outside managers and banking institutions or manage internally, paying only necessary fees to specific providers? How do you allocate the costs among those using the services? The family members might not use the office equally. Some will be more demanding than others. Does the head of the family pay all the costs or just the basic costs, charging out allocable services to other family members? Do you set up a fee structure internally and charge accordingly? Do you charge according to time and use a billing software system to track individual accounts? What works best for you within the tax reporting scheme (who needs the deductions and has the cash flow) or largest time demands will be determined by your specific family. Outside management fees might or might not be negotiable, depending on the services required and the size of the asset pool under management. Because transaction services are farmed out, excepting the largest family offices, choosing your global custodian and prime brokers and traders primarily requires a cost-measurement investigation and banking and investment relationship management analysis. (See Chapter 9, "Money Management," and Chapter 7, "Picking People and Choosing Professional Resources.")

Stay regularly informed about what's new—in Congress, and in the tax and business codes—that might affect your family business plans. Ask staff and advisors to help you, and keep your advisors regularly informed about any changes in your family. As part of the communications plan, regular reviews and revisions of planning, investments, office structures, and personnel should be included for updating all affected parties. Is there a new child, illness, pending death, actual death, or divorce? How will this impact the group, individuals, planning, and changes? What are the issues that affect those to whom you wish to leave your wealth? If your beneficiary is to be a charity, has the charity changed? Has your interest changed? Do foundation bylaws need changing? Are the charities still in good standing? Do the directors know your ideas have changed? Businesses do that. Families don't. Then they wonder why things don't work.[3]

Control your own process. Be involved. Be educated. Be professional.

ENDNOTES

1. Family Office Exchange, Inc. *Professional Family Office Services*. Oak Brook, Ill.: Family Office Exchange, Inc., 1993

2. Darla. L. Keller. Distributed professional materials, Dellwood Financial Services Company, Minneapolis, Minn., 1996.

3. James E. Hughes Jr., Esq. Interview, Legal and Taxation Considerations, 18 August 1995, and 6 September 1995, New York, NY.

7

PICKING PEOPLE AND CHOOSING PROFESSIONAL RESOURCES

Getting Good Advice

Hiring good people is an art. It can be generalized to a point, especially when hiring permanent staff, but in the end, as much as competency and job fit are important, personal chemistry and style sometimes have more to do with what makes a satisfactory working relationship. The ones you "feel most comfortable with," whether it's with their style or investment ethic, are the ones with whom you will want to work.

Decisions, decisions—is there a simple way to make so many decisions? With over 17,000 registered investment advisors in the United States, all technically qualified to meet your money management needs and many more who aren't registered (at last count there were more than 4,700 hedge fund managers), the task of finding a money manager, or two, or ten, is daunting. Statistics show that 80 percent of investment advisors underperform the marketplace in any given year. This means that there is only a one in five chance that you will make a correct decision based on performance measurements alone. Even the best managers have bad years, and their numbers don't tell you the really important stuff you need to know in order to be secure about the manager with whom you are working. A lot of what will help you make a good match is understanding how star managers became stars: with focus, discipline, obsession with performance and their jobs—they live and breathe them—and an instinct and deep knowledge for the business. As people, these successful managers are seen by some as idiosyncratic and hard to understand. Try Bryant's following system and refer to Appendix C for ways to make the choices easier.

Figure 7.1 illustrates the array of advisors a family group regularly uses for wealth stewardship and displays how interconnected everyone is. Philanthropic advice and management, though not shown here, is also necessary. You can see that the personnel introduced here need to be able to work together. As a management consultant, Bryant Cushing makes a living showing people how to define their needs to find the personnel to fill positions like these. His formula has worked for many companies. Wealth stewardship, being a family business, is no different from other businesses when it comes to needing the right people for the right job for the right reasons at the right times.

FIGURE 7.1

Family Investment Office

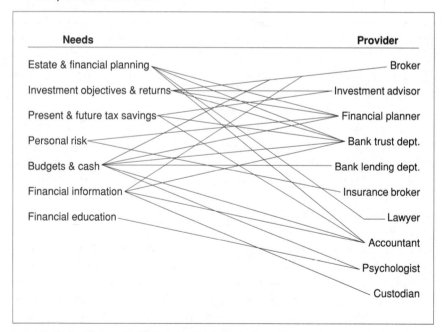

Source: Pitcairn Trust Company. © 1995 Pitcairn Trust Company, Jenkintown, Penn.

Bryant shows you how to develop X-ray vision to look through initial impressions to see what long-term relationships might be like for you as a client or employer. I must have talked to several hundred people over the years to get other perspectives on the handful of advisors and service providers with whom I have worked. Just like the relationships, my family's needs change again and again, and knowing when to say goodbye is a part of working with people. Some who stay too long can hurt you far more than the short-term underperformers. It can be difficult to fire money managers, accountants, or lawyers who become personal friends and still keep them as friends. Others appear to be your friends until your needs and theirs diverge. Bryant will show you how to compensate for this. Listed below are personal principles I use to guide me through professional relationship choices and changes.

Four Principles

These four principles guide me when I talk to people with whom I work—long- or short-term—when seeking advice, buying services, and reviewing existing relationships. They are especially useful during times of great change.

1. Be clear about who is in charge of the relationship, who keeps the many parts together, and who represents your view. In the end, it must be you. Naturally, you need to know what you want and you must be able to articulate that to anyone with whom you wish to work. The buck starts and stops with you.

2. Understand someone else's motivation and beware when it is in direct conflict with your priorities and best interests. A compensation structure can be a simple clue into discerning another's motivation. A bank marketer paid according to new funds brought under management is apt to be less attentive to your account after you have bought into the system. A stock broker is paid by transactions generated, not by the return he generates for you.

3. Keep your business relationships professional at all times. Because of the sensitive and confidential nature of the business, a long-term trust relationship breeds familiarity and closeness but also a lack of perspective and freshness to the working relationship. Also be aware that the wealth management marketplace feeds dependency. Keep the boundaries clear.

4. Don't let inertia keep an inappropriate relationship in place. Knowledgeable individuals and family groups change advisors because needs change as ages and life stages evolve. Families don't change banking relationships often, but banks can be affected by management changes. Staying with long relationships just because they are too much trouble to change is dangerous for your financial health. The same holds true of lawyers and law firms that become outdated. Heirs to the practice aren't necessarily as gifted as the founder was when the relationship began. Accounting firm changes and bank personnel turnovers can be especially irksome when managing an ongoing, complex business.

Following my divorce, I renegotiated *all* of the working relationships I had when I was part of a couple. It was at that time that these principles helped me the most. Several primary advisors did not survive the review. In one instance, asserting my preferences was misconstrued as distrust. Women who are dealing with service providers, financial advisors, and managers on a regular basis will find that some are comfortable with you as a client and some are not. Generally, women prefer more information more frequently if they are the primary decision maker. Male communication styles and lexicons predominate in accounting, law, banking, and money management, where men have historically been the providers and decision makers. When women step into that world in an active way, it causes ripples and misinterpretations. It is not uncommon for women and younger people to experience thinly (or thickly) veiled condescension in these arenas.

In this chapter Bryant can show you the system he has found to be so successful when looking for the best people. In Appendix C, I have also supplied some job specific considerations for your use with this chapter and at hiring time.

PICKING PEOPLE AND
CHOOSING PROFESSIONAL RESOURCES

Bryant Cushing

The instant you have wealth, the moment you hold wealth on behalf of others, your need for skill and wisdom in picking people and professional resources moves to the very top of your list of priorities.

This chapter has two purposes: to teach you the principles of picking people and to show you how to apply those principles. The goal is to equip you to do six things well: (1) identify what you should look for in candidates for any position; (2) prepare and set the stage for interviewing candidates; (3) structure and control the interview; (4) ask questions that will lead the candidate to reveal whether she or he fits the job or role; (5) evaluate what the candidate tells you; and (6) check references.

The principles and methods put forward here will apply whether you are picking a manager for the family office, a new law firm, or a housekeeper for your home. You will quickly get to the point where you will be able to weed out those who are not right for you. With practice, you will dramatically improve your ability to select individuals and professional firms wisely and well. When you find that your appraisal of a person was "in the right church but the wrong pew"—that is, close but not right on—you will know what you missed and why. You will be better armed, so as not to make the same mistake again.

You will also be light years ahead of the typical corporate director or professional manager in business. It is sad but true that less than 1 percent of America's executives and managers have had training in the art of picking people. A recent survey revealed that not a single graduate school of business offers instruction in picking people. So you will continue to see the same headlines repeated year after year in the business section of your newspaper signaling the departure of yet another top executive from yet another leading company. The news of the separation will be cosseted in those immortal words: for personal reasons. Nine times out of ten, the real reasons are that someone failed to read that person for what he really was when he was hired or promoted, or that the executive himself failed to read the company situation well enough to understand that he and the company would not make a good fit.

Failure in picking people can be traced to one simple fact: The decision makers did not have the tools for the job. Worse, they thought that the selection process began when the first candidate came walking through the door. Most employers learned from their predecessors that they would need only two documents to be ready to interview a candidate: a job description and an application or resume. That is a fatal error, one that is repeated day after day in hundreds of offices throughout the United States.

Picking people doesn't begin with candidates and job descriptions and resumes. It begins with homework. Homework is of three kinds, and only you can do it. When you complete these three home-work assignments fully and accurately, half the work of interview-ing is done—and that's *before* you've seen a single candidate.

HOMEWORK
Part I: The Context

For this segment of your homework, we will practice taking the measure of your family, and then we will size up the entity, such as a family office or the business that continues to generate the family's wealth. We will assume that family members have an important stake in your stewardship. We will assume also that you, as steward, con-trol the entity that produces or manages the wealth—or that you share control with others.

Your tools are pencil and paper—and a lifetime of interaction with and observation of your family. Your task is to list the family's characteristics. Ask yourself the following questions about the fam-ily. If the most important ways of describing the family are not present, you will know what to cross out and what to add.

Is this an essentially peaceful family or one that is internally contentious?

Is the family large or small in number of stakeholders? Are they geographically concentrated or at great distances from each other?

Is there a natural leader? Are there "wannabe" leaders?

Are there family members who are emotionally needy?

Is there a prominent fault-finder in the family?

What is the approximate level of financial sophistication among stakeholders?

How are decisions made in the family?

How long does it take, typically, to reach a consensus? What does it take?

Is the family accustomed to being run by a single authority figure? Or, as a polar opposite, is anarchy a better descriptor?

Is a sense of humor present? If so, what kind of humor? What form does it take?

What are the family's attitudes toward people outside of the family's close circle?

Are individual differences among family members respected or criticized?

What holds the family together or, conversely, acts to drive it apart?

When your list of family descriptors is complete, select the three statements that, above all others, must be included in any realistic family description. Number them one through three in order of their importance in family affairs.

Now repeat the same process in describing the family office, if you have one, or in characterizing the family's wealth-producing entity. Listed below are characteristics of organizations large and small that often determine whether one person will succeed in working with that organization and another person will fail miserably. Add and subtract from this list just as you did in capturing the prime descriptions of your family.

What is the level of professionalism? Is this an entity that young aspirants want to join because it is an outstanding place to learn?

What are the required standards? Is this an entity that sets and enforces high standards of performance—or something less?

How are decisions made? Do those who do the work of the entity have to wait excessively long for decisions, or are they made promptly?

What is the communication style? Is it informal and easy, restricted or open, regular or in the breach?

What is the direction of energy? Is it focused on internal struggles or on dealing successfully with the outside world?

What are the available resources? Are the resources adequate to support the work of the entity?

What is the exhibited level of self worth? Is the entity populated by people who are proud of themselves and what they are doing—or, at the other end of the scale, do you find people who have little value in themselves?

What are the internal politics? Are they present or absent? Occasional or continuous? At an acceptable or unacceptable level?

What are the thinking and planning ranges? Have the people of this entity been taught to think in short- (weeks or months), intermediate- (one to two years), or longer-range time frames?

What is the fire-fighting level? All organizations must fight fires from time to time due to periodic stressful circumstances. Some, however, know no other way of conducting their affairs, resulting in a continually stressful environment.

Part II. The Reporting Relationship

This should be a searching, honest appraisal of your own personality, working style, preferences, taboos, and yes, your idiosyncrasies. Many executives who have made a self-appraisal in the ways outlined here have later commented, "I thought I knew myself pretty well. Now I realize I should have recognized some of these things about myself long ago."

Are you a project-oriented or process-oriented person? The answer is vital to recognizing how you function best. People who are more at home with projects prefer work that has a clear beginning, middle, and end. When they have finished one project, they like to go immediately to another. The process-oriented person, on the other hand, likes long-term efforts that have no beginning, no middle, and no end. He or she likes working for the long pull. Where the project-oriented person would soon find a way to divert from a process to embark on a project, the process-inclined person can't wait to get back to the process if it becomes necessary to tackle a short-term project. This is not to say that everyone is one or the other; many people are comfortable in both situations, but most of us have a natural inclination for one or the other that will strongly influence relationships with subordinates.

What does it take to make you angry? The list may be short or long, but it is important that you identify the triggers. Perhaps it is sloppy work by a subordinate, people who are habitually late, individuals who procrastinate, people who tell half-truths, or those who won't tell you when something is going wrong until it has reached disaster proportions. The only unacceptable answer to this question is, "But I never get angry," because everyone does.

What do you do with your anger? Do you immediately confront the source of your anger; do you count to ten and then let go; do you muffle it down inside and keep it there? If you communicate your feelings, how do you do it—angrily, quietly, sarcastically, firmly, or in some other manner?

How do you like to send and receive information? Some of us much prefer to hear what another person has to say. Others want it in writing. People who send information in one form usually prefer to receive it in the same form. The manager who likes to hear things face-to-face usually has little time or patience for long reports. But then there are executives who are basically readers; they make their decisions based on what they see on paper, not on what they hear. Mismatches between superiors and subordinates in this dimension of preference can create subtle but very real friction. (This disparity between chief executive and subordinates was so pronounced in Jimmy Carter's first year in the presidency that it became the subject of a front-page story in *The Wall Street Journal*.)

How often do you need to see or talk with subordinates? Opposites do not work well together here. If you put together a superior who likes his subordinates to make contact only when there is a decision to be made or a major problem to be solved with a subordinate who has a deep-down need to be in frequent contact with an authority figure, both will be continually distressed. And there are, indeed, people who have a need for repeated contact, whether or not the work requires it.

Do you see yourself as a conceptualizer or as an implementer? Architects design structures; contractors build them. A small percentage of the world's people can do both. Most of us tend to be one way or the other. Why is this an important ingredient in your self-appraisal? Because two architects will have a hard time actually making a building!

Part III: Position Requirements

Concern yourself less with the surface requirements of the position to be filled than with the attributes and characteristics the candidate must bring to the situation, to the position, and to you in order to succeed. Certainly you will need an inventory of the basic requirements of knowledge, experience, and specific skills that the job requires. That information should be coupled with a separate inventory of personality descriptors designed to tell you when you've found the right match. Decide what the "make or break" qualities are for performance in the job or role.

Does the position require short- or long-range thinking? Not all jobs require the long-term view, but when they do, the short-range thinker will be not only a misfit but also a problem.

Is this a staff or line position? Line jobs are the "doing" jobs, the ones that involve the core work. Staff people support and complement the line's doers. Know which description applies to the position you seek to fill.

Is there a need for negotiatory ability? Excellent negotiators are few and far between. If the position requires it, you will want to be absolutely certain that your candidate has it.

What is the ability and willingness to delegate? Many have the ability, but they are simply not willing. Equally undesirable is the person who delegates and then believes he has no further responsibility.

What are the available relationship skills with authority figures, peers, and subordinates? Most positions require constructive relationships up, down, or across—or all three. Some will perform admirably in one direction and poorly in others, such as the person who does handsprings to have a positive relationship with authority figures but tramples all over subordinates.

Is there a required ability to judge situations for what they are? This can be the most important single ingredient in one position and of little importance in another. Staff accountants must only concern themselves with factual data, the letter of the law, that someone else gives them. There is no situation to judge or personnel to direct. On the other hand, a managerial-level accounting position will require the ability to judge the nuances of the circumstance or within the gray areas of the tax code, recommend treatment, direct the inquiry, and make sure it gets done.

What level of social skills is present or required? Which fork to use, how to keep a conversation going among people who are strangers to each other, and a dozen other social skills may or may not be important to the job. Failure to recognize the importance of matching the social skills to the work environment can lead to disappointment, frustration, and embarrassment.

What is the balance of rigidity versus flexibility? Is flexibility actually a requirement in the position, or would the more rigid personality be a better fit?

What is the need for initiation versus reaction? We can't all be initiators, and in many situations, more than one initiator is too many. But you may need someone in the position who reacts quickly and appropriately to changing circumstances.

Is the ability to set standards or adhere to them present? Standards and their enforcement usually make the difference between a truly professional organization and one that is not. If the job requires setting high standards, the candidate should be a person who does so naturally and out of strong conviction. If the context is one in which standards have long been set, you will not want a person who is oblivious to standards.

Is being a resource to others important? Does the job require teaching others or serving as their resource? Some people revel in that role; others are just not cut out for it.

Is the ability to persuade important to the position? In many positions, one's talents of persuasion are vital. In others, you may want the job to be done in comparative isolation.

Homework Review

Part I: Size up the context in which the candidate will work. Size up the family home (a private setting; informal, small office), or the company responsible for generating wealth (a formal operating company office), or the separate office (dedicated to the personal family or individual's business) in which the candidate will work to give you a basis for judging what kind of person will fit in the work environment and who will not.

Part II. Apply a pair of calipers to the person to whom the candidate will report. Assuming that person is you, identify what it will take to create a good fit between you and someone who will assist and serve you.

Part III: Put a measuring tape around the position so that you will know what the candidate will need to bring to the job in order to do it well. This will give you a basis for judging what it will take to perform well or what kind of person won't work out in this role.

THE INTERVIEW

When your homework is done, you are ready to interview candidates. You will need to take only one piece of paper into the interview. Divide the sheet into three sections and list the three important characteristics of context, self-appraisal, and position requirements.

Résumés are limited documents at best, and in today's world, we never know whether a résumé has been prepared by the candidate or by a professional résumé service. The sole task of the résumé is to help you decide whether you want to meet the candidate. It is then up to you to probe behind the résumé's assertions to learn more about the candidate than he knows about himself. That is the goal of the candidate interview.

Set the stage for the interview by holding all of your telephone calls and other interruptions. Plan to seat yourself in parity with the candidate, not behind a big desk. This is not the time to play "boss."

After you have introduced yourself to the candidate, explain how you are going to proceed. First, tell the candidate that you have a responsibility to him or her as well as to yourself and your family or company. You are responsible for making sure that the candidate and you are not a mismatch. A company usually can survive a parting of the ways easily; for the individual, a mismatch can result in losing a year or two of a career.

Second, say that you want to devote the first part of the interview to learning as much about the candidate as possible. Later on, the candidate will have ample opportunity to ask questions about the position. You can control the interview by setting the ground rules at the very beginning.

Note: A classic error in interviewing is the rush to tell the candidate about the position, the company, and so on early in the interview. This inevitably provides far too many signals to the candidate, and the result is that you will soon be hearing what the candidate believes you want to hear.

To start the candidate talking about herself and her career, the most direct and effective starter is to say, "It will help me understand how your career has been shaped if you will take me back to school and bring me forward from there to the present—in whatever form or detail you like." Most candidates will recite their history in 20–30 minutes or less. As they talk, you may occasionally ask an unloaded question, such as, "What was happening then?" "What kind of person was he?" "Why do you think that happened?" or "What did you like best about that job?" and "What did you like least about it?" Do not ask questions that can be answered with a simple yes or no.

Follow the career recitation with further probing questions. (Do not ask questions about age, religion, marital status, family, financial condition, health, or encounters with the law.) By the same token, do not ask questions of one group (such as a minority) that you would not ask of another group.

> How would you describe the perfect boss? What would be his or her characteristics? How would you describe that person's management style?
>
> What kinds of things make you angry? What do you do with your anger?
>
> What do you look for in picking people to work for you?
>
> Some people prefer dealing with others on a one-to-one basis; others like to work with groups. Do you have a preference?
>
> Some people like to set their own priorities, while others like to be in situations where the priorities are already established. Do you have a preference?
>
> Did you ever work for anyone you didn't like? If so, without revealing any names, could you describe that person?
>
> What do you think your past subordinates would say about you as a boss?
>
> If you were given a magic wand to create your perfect job, tell me what it would be.

With your questions answered, give the candidate the opportunity to ask about the positions for which he or she is being interviewed. If the candidate is clearly not the person for the job, find a way to leave the person whole. Comment favorably on any assets, strengths, or experience the person has had that could prove valuable in another position in another organization. In all other cases, tell the candidate when you will contact him or her again, by telephone or letter, and then be certain to keep your word.

As soon as the candidate has left the room, go immediately to pen and paper and write down the essence of your evaluation: the strengths you see in the person, the weaknesses, and your remaining questions.

THE EVALUATION

Cross-check what you have learned in the interview against the critical criteria on your three lists of context, position, and reporting relationship. Read between the lines to determine what this candidate has told you about his or her abilities for the position.

Measure the candidate on his or her ability to judge situations for what they are; his or her ability to assess other people; whether the candidate is a project or process person; whether she or he is an architect, a contractor, or neither; the person's level of self-worth; his or her sense of humor (and if appropriate, what kind); and if the candidate learns from mistakes.

Further, evaluate the candidate's level of self-knowledge; whether the candidate has good listening skills and social skills; if this person is a reader or a talker, a firefighter or permanent fixer, a short- or long-range thinker; the candidate's ability and willingness to delegate; his or her talent for follow through; if the person tells you what you want to hear; and whether this is a shirtsleeves producer or someone who is more effective or comfortable behind a big desk.

You are unlikely to have answers to all these questions in your first or even your third interview. But with practice, you will get the answers you need quickly and easily.

REFERENCES

It is a fact of the 1990s that more and more employers are unwilling to provide anything more than dates of employment of former employees for fear of litigation. However, that should not deter you from calling references; much grief would be avoided if more employers were to do so.

References should be called after the interview, not before. Otherwise, how will you know the most important questions to ask? Try to reach not only former superiors but also former peers and subordinates. It is perfectly reasonable to take the view that most references provided by candidates are a wee bit suspect; nonetheless, they can be an excellent starting point and can, in many cases, lead you to the names of former peers and subordinates.

The best results are obtained by saying to the reference, "John

Doe and I are talking about a position in my organization. He certainly has a lot of strengths we can use, but I want to be very careful that neither he nor we make a mistake. If we did so, it would be harder on him than on my company (or family). The position we're talking about requires someone who. . . . And it won't work for a person who. . . . I know his skills are such that he can find a good situation elsewhere if this isn't the one for him. Could you tell me what you think?" This approach does not assure results, but it works more often than not.

A FINAL CAUTION

If you are seeking a professional resource or someone to fill a key executive or managerial position, you should know the three "killer" attributes. You will meet them again and again as you evaluate candidates in the years ahead. The three "killers" are the main reasons that men and women fail as professionals or as managers.

1. The person who doesn't know himself or herself. This person doesn't know his or her own strengths and, most important, does not recognize or admit to his or her own limitations. This person can't accept that there are some things he or she is not capable of doing. When placed in a position of responsibility and authority, this person will commit the organization to deeds it cannot perform and thereby waste money and resources in great quantity.

2. The person who cannot confront others. This person can't say no. He or she will say almost anything except a flat no. In the role of executive or manager—and as an advisor—this person will be unable to present his or her true opinion and will be unable to establish or maintain standards and disciplines. He or she will soon be surrounded by a highly politicized organization.

3. The professional resource or manager who cannot read people or situations for what they really are. This person continually misjudges people and situations. This person either sees what he or she wants to see, or doesn't see at all. This person will mismatch people and responsibilities, he will cost you time and money by inadequately assessing situations, and he will prove very difficult to oversee.

We may be able to tolerate many shortcomings, but the presence of any one of these three attributes can be devastating. And do not think for a moment that somehow you will be able to compensate for the flaw!

CHAPTER

8

PHILANTHROPY

Allocation of Time, Talent, and Treasure

It is ever to be remembered that one of the chief obstacles which the philanthropist meets in his efforts to do real and permanent good in this world, is the practice of indiscriminate giving...

Andrew Carnegie[1]

Philanthropy can be the single most rewarding benefit of wealth ownership, and this synonym for stewardship serves as the inspiration for the title of this book. For a growing many, philanthropy provides a rich, rewarding vocation. For them, interest and pride as philanthropists are far more important than reaping the rewards of sound financial accomplishment. Anyone can incorporate philanthropy into his or her ongoing financial investment management and personal philosophy no matter where he or she is on the continuum from novice to seasoned philanthropist.

Some wealth holders, despite being knowledgeable, may never choose to be benefactors, and thus fall at the extreme end of the philanthropist continuum. When wealth is relatively new, an ethic, history, and family tradition of philanthropic endeavor usually are nonexistent and have to be learned. This is nascent philanthropy farther along the continuum. For more seasoned families and individual wealth managers, philanthropy might be incorporated later as they broaden their knowledge and commitment and come to see philanthropy as more than simply an estate and tax planning device. Moving along this continuum is the family that has devoted its resources to building a business and has limited its philanthropy to the corporate level. At the far end of the continuum is the fully evolved philanthropic family that is actively involved in thoughtful and wise giving and that believes and practices the systematic incorporation of philanthropy as a dedicated percentage of its ongoing asset allocation planning at all levels.

An example of living corporate and private philanthropy is that of the King Ranch family and business, long-term practicing stewards of the land and other resources under our management. Through the King Ranch Family Trust, the founding family practices the wide-ranging philanthropy that was begun by our ancestors six generations ago. The family corporation today supports local, regional, and national industry not-for-profit endeavors across a range of youth activities, education, and agribusiness and human medical research. Individually, many family members continue this same tradition in their own and joint efforts via family foundations and extensive private activities as volunteer board activists, fundraising donors, and members for a breadth of charitable interests across the country. Frequently, in cooperation with federal and state agencies and private conservation groups, a separate wildlife research foundation conducts ground-breaking research on lands owned by the corporation. Originally begun to save the endangered Attwater prairie chicken, the Caeser Kleberg Wildlife Foundation has extended its studies to species that cross the political and geographic borders between Texas and Mexico, borders that few public agencies will cross.

Although this example is not at the outer extreme of the continuum, one individual who is dedicated to including philanthropy as a separate asset class in an allocation model is Peggy Dulaney of the Synergos Institute. Peggy was raised with multigenerational philanthropic roots, and her personal goal at one time was to "give away" 50 percent of her annual income, a philosophy she learned from her family. Establishing an institute was her way of strengthening her personal goal against a fluctuating income stream, supporting her program design, and protecting both as the whims of the investment marketplace changed.[2] I share her perspective but have not been as successful in implementing it. Most advisors and wealthy families believe that philanthropic goals have no place in asset allocation decisions but readily include it in overall planning and practice.

In this chapter, we will look first at the trends developing in philanthropy today, characteristics of a good philanthropist, and the components for a basic framework for practicing good philanthropy. Finally, descriptions of various individuals and instruments will be provided to help you define and implement your philanthropic mission and objectives.

The role philanthropy plays in wealth planning and management varies according to many intangibles. The importance of the activity cannot be underestimated, particularly by those who have never viewed it as an option. Likewise, those who have given in the past can benefit from revisiting a long pattern of giving to keep current with trends and with changes in the family, group culture, society, and the law. The trends today reveal the practice of very different kinds of philanthropy from that practiced by the founding Carnegies, Rockefellers, Fords, and Astors. Their heirs and new philanthropists are redefining the terms for philanthropy and stewardship.

TRENDS AFFECTING PRIVATE PHILANTHROPY

Philanthropic trends are studied by public and private groups for many reasons, but increasingly, they are being examined in order to assess the ability of private giving to supplant government funding and to awaken philanthropists to the need for their involvement in addressing and supporting solutions to the tough issues we all face as caring human beings. Some of these trends are hopeful, many are disturbing.

There seems to be decreasing involvement in giving by the very wealthy. Two likely factors are suspected in this trend. The first is a "new" wealth tendency to prefer accumulation, as first-generation wealth, and the resultant lack of philanthropic habit or ethic. If you've never had it to give away, you haven't really thought of all of the possible ways to use it, nor do you have the knowledge about how to do it. The second is that post–World War II entrepreneurs and star managers are only just now reaping the benefits of their labor and turning focus onto the opportunities for giving.

Although there are notable exceptions, top wealth holders give away only a small percentage of wealth in their lifetimes.[3] There is some indication in a recent study that if taxes are lowered, the incentive to give living gifts will diminish even further.[4] As the window for tax-beneficial giving is closing, the ethic and value of giving is focusing on enlarging the creative possibilities in philanthropy.

Patterns and styles of giving are changing from those establishing individuals whose names are synonymous with philanthropy—Carnegie and Mellon, among others. Cause-related giving is supplanting institution-based giving. Socially Responsible Investing (SRI), which encourages political and philosophical statements by the investors, demonstrates greater activism with a conscience as an adjunct to philanthropy. Leaving a name-perpetuating legacy is becoming unimportant and has been supplanted by an emphasis on personal control, freedom to direct, and individualism. Active involvement is equally embraced along with financial giving. The character and integrity of the recipient is a key factor.[3] And as they declare their independence and learn effectiveness, women are more visible in their individual philanthropy, making independent decisions distinct from family and spousal giving. Donor networks are multiplying. Tracy Gary in San Francisco established the Women's Donor Network for women donating $25,000 or more a year to social-change philanthropy. International Skye Associates, an association of wealthy families of primarily younger-generation participants, sponsors and implements summer Habitat for Humanities projects. Gerald Freund, a philanthropic consultant, stated in a recent interview that, "Activism is fine as long as the passion lasts!"[5]

More options for giving are available with the nationwide growth of community foundations, professional management of those same foundations, established recipients competing for shrinking federal funding, and innovative planning mechanisms negotiated between donors and beneficiaries. (See Chapter 4, "Imperatives of Planning.")

The window for tax beneficial giving is closing and the ethic and value of giving is focusing on enlarging the creative possibilities in philanthropy.

Alliances between charities are forming to maximize the impact of the philanthropic largesse. For instance, the Nature Conservancy and the Nicholas School of the Environment at Duke University are jointly funding a professorship and shared research, thus giving a donor more bang for his or her buck.

Another interesting trend is the use of philanthropy as a discussion topic to pave the way for product sales to the wealthy. Because entry into the private-wealth client base is so difficult and psychological isolation from the norm is so prevalent, there are consultants forming businesses on "how to market to the wealthy using philanthropy as the hook" for entry into the world of private wealth. Charitable institutions have "planned-giving" offices, or at least an officer, or a brochure to directly benefit the charity. Many frequently use estate-planning seminars as "educational" forums to encourage giving. Financial planners, money management firms, major banks and trust companies, and family offices and family office advisory groups emphasize philanthropy in some form, many of them only using the pitch as a sales tool or "hook" to the real target—your money. The primary goal is not to help you build your general philanthropic expertise.

"Wealthy individuals, often isolated by virtue of that wealth, are being targeted in innovative ways to separate them from their money."[5] A university development office or a money management firm attempting to teach the principles of philanthropy and inform you of the ways to accomplish that goal rarely takes into account all the other factors an individual or family must incorporate into their desires, goals and management responsibilities. This really must be done in concert with other advisors with a broader view to the individual's needs.

For the philanthropist, having a working knowledge of what is being done in an area of interest and having personal goals and a mission are more important than all of the "expert" advice about what personal philanthropy might be. Specialists such as Private Funding Associates and The Philanthropic Initiative have stepped into the void where banks and others catering to the ardent giver are failing to assist with any thoughtful planning and implementation expertise.

The alarming drop in public support for public philanthropies is not being met by a commensurate increase in private giving. Large private foundations are stating that they do not have the resources to take over the programs affected by federal cuts. Smaller foundations or trusts generally focus on local and state shortfalls in public funding. A sophisticated philanthropist often focuses on broader horizons rather than on how he or she can effectively bridge the gap locally. Corporate philanthropy is being squeezed by the downsizing and restructuring occurring nationwide and it won't fill the void either. There is an opportunity inherent in this situation to encourage real innovation in private philanthropy.

TRAITS OF A GOOD PHILANTHROPIST

There are four simple but powerful traits of a good philanthropist. First, there must be a resource to donate. Personal motivation, personal involvement, and maximizing the benefits of philanthropy complete the short list.

Wealth

Wealth is the donatable resource. Wealth is in the eye of the beholder and takes many forms, including those of time, talent, and treasure. People who are less financially secure often have an enormous capacity for philanthropy, and sometimes, those with the most to give will give the least. Studies show that 51.5 percent of all charitable dollars come from households with incomes *below* $60,000. Americans of low-to-moderate income are equally as generous as upper-income individuals in their contribution of time and money, but low income benefactors contribute more by income percentage than the wealthier population.[6] Most of the contributions flow to religious affiliates close to home or into the far-flung coffers of satellite evangelists. For our purposes, we will concentrate on much larger resources—wealth that creates "insurmountable opportunities." Your first task will be to define what this donatable resource is for you and your family. The power of the philanthropic dollar and personal commitment are only limited by your motivation, vision, organization, leverage, and knowledge, and by the goals you set.

Personal Motivation

Personal motivation is generated in three ways. The motivation can be inherent in the personality, such as "a giving person." The motivation can be instilled by family culture, such as in those cases where generosity is modeled by the family or is a family tradition. Finally, motivation may come from a desire for personal satisfaction gained by doing charitable works. At significant wealth levels, the third type of motivation prevails. Power and recognition sought by some often deepens their sense of personal satisfaction. The largest donors are characterized by the satisfaction derived from a passion and conviction for what they are doing.[5] Unfortunately, an unenlightened individual or family might never come to an understanding of how phil-anthropic endeavors can enrich a life—theirs or someone else's. Some will only come to see philanthropy as a useful tool to build into an estate plan or from a purely tax-motivated perspective. Motivation helps direct how the philanthropist gets involved in the work of giv-ing.

Personal Involvement

Personal involvement results in good philanthropy, but too much involvement can be too much of a good thing. An example of too much involvement is the Getty Museum, which frequently overpow-ers art markets and creates imbalances in the museum world due to the caveats of the founding bequest. Some who believe that Lee Bass was too directly involved in the disposition of his $20 million gift to Yale University see his involvement as manipulative. Others praise his benevolence. Highly visible, involved philanthropy, although it has drawbacks, has the power to positively transform programs and institutions far beyond its monetary value.

Maximize the Benefits

To maximize the benefits of philanthropy, you need to understand what those benefits are. Aside from the enormous satisfaction it brings, giving by choice gives the philanthropist an opportunity to "invest" by satisfying the human desire to build community by help-ing others and by making a difference. A philanthropist has the free-dom to choose what benefit he or she derives from that philanthropic activity. He or she has the freedom to choose recognition or ano-nymity and the freedom to choose active or passive community in-volvement. The benefit of using philanthropy as an educational tool to learn and to teach management, research, and communication skills; respect for other's ideas; teamwork; and decision-making skills receives more attention in wealthy families today.

Philanthropy provides the opportunity to blend values and in-dividual focus across generations and genders within a family. An-other benefit of philanthropy is the ability to control where your money goes rather than giving taxing authorities the opportunity to "spread your wealth." Philanthropy is a win–win proposition for the charitable beneficiaries, and the individual doing the planning and is an effective estate- and tax-planning measure for the family. Philanthropy provides a living example of balancing work ethic with

wealth, and rights with responsibility. Philanthropy is a tool to leverage privilege into effectuating thoughtful change. Philanthropy
is a leadership and trend-setting opportunity. Philanthropy is an opportunity to give back. Caution: Using philanthropy as a means of
"bringing a family together," although it is a high-minded goal, has
its dark side, too. If philanthropy is used to forcibly keep dissident
family members in the fold, resentments can build and manipulation can result.

This general overview of what philanthropy is and the trends
apparent today is only a place to begin to shape your personal definition of what philanthropy is. Simply knowing what philanthropy
is and sending a check to the United Way in your community does
not make you a philanthropist. But designing a framework for a lifelong, perhaps generations-long, philanthropic agenda includes many
elements that can be enhanced by a better understanding of what
philanthropy is. The real work is in building the framework and then
using it creatively and intently.

THE PHILANTHROPIC FRAMEWORK

The philanthropic framework has several parts, none of which are any
less or more important to the endeavor of designing a philanthropic
ethic or plan. Use of philanthropic specialists to help define and accomplish the goals set out by a family may be helpful, and come in
several forms. At the least, you will need legal and/or accounting
advice to help you direct your giving within legal and tax planning
parameters. Another part of the framework is the definition of the
philanthropist's mission and purpose. The third part is learning what
the elements are in screening a request. The development of relevant
and effective philanthropy is derived from building these other parts
well and will lead to the development of a satisfied philanthropist,
one who will be a model for others. The client with a thorough grasp
of his or her goals and missions can talk to any advisor about implementation. In Chapter 4, Jane Gregory Rubin suggests concrete means
of planning on which to build your program.

What to Look for in a Philanthropic Specialist

Traditionally, the unbiased advisor interested and well-versed in incorporating giving into a client's broad planning has been the family lawyer—a true general counsel. Specialists in law firms are more
the norm today; general counsel attorneys are no longer common.

Legal, accounting, and financial advisory have changed dramatically in the past 10 years, creating an education gap on the part of these advisors. When making a philanthropic plan or decision, it makes sense to use an attorney who has experience with philanthropic planning that is similar to what you seek to achieve. Independent advisors not associated with traditional tax and legal advisors currently specialize in helping people define and direct their philanthropy. The Council on Foundations in Washington, D.C., has a separate staff devoted to family and other private foundations that provides general support and philanthropic education for families setting up philanthropic programs. Educational and other charitable organizations often have staff advisors who help facilitate a donor's objectives in planned giving specific to that institution or charity. With such a range of advice available, some general criteria on what makes a good philanthropic advisor are worth noting.

A philanthropic advisor needs to be sensitive to and aware of what a wealthy person wants in life. The advisor needs to understand the sense of accomplishment that can come from use of the philanthropic dollar and not simply be focused on tax- or estate-planning implications. For many philanthropists, tax advantages are secondary, but an advisor intent on the tax benefit aspect as a singular focus can divert a client from his or her primary goals. Instead, the ideal is for the advisor to encourage the good intention while providing effective planning mechanisms to achieve the client's objectives as nearly as is possible.

A good advisor can help point you in your own best direction given your goals. The advisor should not define your goals for you or put ideas in your head and words in your mouth; he or she should help guide you to your own objectives. The best advisors can maximize the impact of your giving and enhance your priorities of feeling purposeful and accomplished in those goals. A mentor rather than a director makes a better philanthropic advisor.

A good philanthropic advisor feels a real obligation to point out pitfalls and alternative ways of realizing your philanthropic objectives. A fundamental understanding of family dynamics can be crucial for an advisor involved in the formation and management of a family foundation.

Demonstration of high personal and moral standards is imperative for the philanthropic advisor to be chosen for the sensitive trust relationship as a confidant on family wealth-management matters.

As advisors who direct client philanthropy, institutions should be able to show an ability to create new methods of philanthropic advisory within the institutions of banking and their trust departments, trust companies, investment firms, and family offices by dedicating specific positions and departments or at least, make outside consultants available to address this need of their clients.

Philanthropic advisors who have direct experience with and knowledge of how nonprofit institutions work are invaluable. When a donation of a specific nature is under consideration, an advisor without awareness of whether the specific goal is attainable will undermine the success by encouraging something that may never happen at vast expense to the donor. For example, a client wished to design a program that funded undiscovered talent for the Metropolitan Opera. The donor was armed with insufficient knowledge of what was required to fulfill her wishes, and she left the trustees of the program entrusted with an unfulfillable mandate. This occurred with a bequest of $20 million left by a benefactor to fund just such a program. However noble the goal, all funds had to be redirected because the stated goal was not achievable given the amount bequeathed and the method designed by the donor to achieve the program's overall objectives. An advisor with a breadth of knowledge into how such a program could work would have been invaluable to the donor.

Advisors can come in the form of philanthropic support groups. Such groups help focus, energize, educate, and maximize a donor's interests, desires, and passions. The Women's Donor Network headquartered at Resourceful Women in the San Francisco area, the Philanthropy Roundtable in Indianapolis, Threshold Foundation, International Skye Associates (which dedicates one of its five meetings each year to this subject), and the Council on Foundations (which dedicates an annual meeting to family foundations) are examples of such groups.

Definition of Your Philanthropic Mission and Purpose

Once the family or individual mission and values statements are defined, the philanthropic mission and purpose flow out of them. In any group, there are differences in interests, focus, and participation levels. A family foundation must be formed on a strongly cooperative base to be effective and nondivisive. One of the real dangers of organizing any group, especially a family, around a common purpose or activity is the danger of squashing the individual attributes and, otherwise, very valid interests and energies of some of the participants. As in any other area of wealth stewardship, the greatest resources for good outcomes can come from the individuals, not the wealth.

When creating a family mission statement specifically for building a family foundation, be aware of the dangers of psychological tampering. A family foundation can be used as a ploy to "build a strong family tie in a wealthy family"[5] when there are no clear reasons to remain close and work together, and it can be used as an insidious form of control by family authority figures. Consequently, the best mission and purpose statements might be broad and leave the specific form the philanthropy takes to those who will administer the philanthropy based on those broad statements. Flexibility is a cornerstone to structuring and focusing your funding and for being able to respond to changing interests over time.

Honest appraisals are important when defining the philanthropic mission and purpose. You must include an honest appraisal of the family's history and values, and acknowledge all individual differences in those values. A realistic appraisal must be made of available human and financial resources as well as of the political and social motivations of the involved individuals and their individual levels of desire to personally control their philanthropic passions. You will need to look at all past giving priorities and determine whether they have been satisfactory or unsatisfactory and if you want to change any of them. Assess your current time commitments and your understanding of existing philanthropic options. It is important to make an honest appraisal of the ability to build consensus, and about governance issues such as who manages, gives, and makes the decisions if a familywide philanthropic strategy is considered. Other necessary appraisals include what external profile you wish to project, the risk profile you have (whether you prefer giving seed money gifts or outright gifts), and whether your focus is local, global, or mixed, political, individual, or institutional. Clarifying your purpose will greatly ease your decisions and increase the effectiveness of their impact. In order to facilitate this appraisal, I have included a questionnaire at the end of this chapter that is used by The Philanthropic Initiative (TPI) to facilitate the appraisal of philanthropic focus for people who are just beginning to organize their programs.[7]

Thoughtful Screening of Requests for Philanthropic Support

A stated mission eliminates the tendency to practice reactive philanthropy. The proliferation of requests and the overwhelming nature of the many social, educational, and cultural needs drive away many potential philanthropists. Confusion clouds public and private responsibility and effectiveness. Philanthropic decisions can't be made in a vacuum. In order to be effective, do your homework first. There are bogus charities with very sophisticated representatives who can and will mislead you. The shock waves created by personal mismanagement at United Way and the highly visible Ponzi scheme of the Foundation for New Era Philanthropy clearly highlight this. Even very sophisticated philanthropists have been duped. If your planning has been done, you can screen very efficiently and say no without guilt. Anonymity to preserve privacy is also an option.

Consider the following:

If an organization's request is of interest to you and is worthwhile, consider it. As a minimum, expect written information and do your own investigations rather than relying on a list of recognizable donors to lead your commitment to that organization or cause.

Review the organization's status as a qualified charity. Are its 501(c)(3) not-for-profit designation, by-laws, and financial reporting up to standard for your commitment?

Look for leadership that inspires confidence. Research the organization to assess effectiveness of the management and the viability of the programs to ensure wise use of your contribution and maximum impact for your efforts. Expect the recipient to be responsibly run—fiscally, managerially, and philosophically. Poor management and irrelevant programs squander great intentions and great resources.

Expect a potential recipient to have attainable and measurable objectives. Recipients should be held accountable for the support you give. A regular reporting to the donors is the least you should require. When the recipient falls short of the projected goals, the organization or program must be able to clearly explain the reasons to the supporters.

Composing an Enlightened, Creative, and Effective Philanthropic Program[5]

Impulse giving is enjoyable if the stakes aren't high. But giving money away well takes planning, thought, and time. For some, it becomes their business, and they do it very well. Seasoned philanthropists have learned to use the following techniques to make their work more fulfilling and fun. Think about incorporating these characteristics into your developing philanthropy.

Clarify goals openly with affected family members. For instance, in the case of establishing foundations, conflict exists between those who believe the foundation is private property and those who believe it is a public trust.[5] Decide how much control you want, and build your goals into your philanthropic activities accordingly. Be clear in your mission.

Research. Research existing interest areas and individual programs for the philanthropic entity and individuals using the technique suggested in the section on screening requests.

Get involved. Be proactive in your communities wherever they are. Working as a volunteer in a community is the best way to see what needs doing. You can take what inspires you from institutions you have admired in the past and take their lessons into new places. Talking to other philanthropists you admire and to experienced advisors will help open your vista within the volunteer work you do. The not-for-profit world is desperate for strong management. Because the pay scale is so low, top management talent is rarely drawn to serve philanthropies except through periodic, volunteer board participation. Directing philanthropic dollars toward the salaries of well-trained managers as executive directors creates a value to the target program far beyond the size of the monetary contribution. Serving as an unpaid advisor in your field of expertise can benefit the organization beyond measure. Work cooperatively with your chosen recipient to help in times of conflict. At these times, original capabilities and intent are undermined by fortune reversals, change in policy, or other obstacles to fulfilling the philanthropic mission. Investing your time and energies will not only be satisfying, it can also save a valuable organization or program that would otherwise fail.

The largest donors are characterized by the satisfaction they derive from the passion they possess for what they are doing. The Ethel Clark Foundation in Pebble Beach, California, changed its structure in order to practice involved philanthropy. Rather than just giving to educational causes, the family convenes seminars to help local nonprofits become more self-sufficient. "We spent some time talking about what to do as a family, now we are in charge of the publicity and the programs. It's more hands-on. Ultimately, we feel our money is being spent more judiciously."[8]

Look for unique and new ways. Create lasting effectiveness by leveraging your philanthropic actions. An example would be sponsoring individual talent, as in the MacArthur "Genius" Awards and Whiting Writing Awards. You could expand this concept to giving support to emerging talent that has already been identified but is not quite developed (e.g., a finalist for the Guggenheim Fellowships who does not win or a not-quite-ready runner-up for a Southeast Center for Contemporary Art (SECCA) award. Focus on the untapped talent of the youngster trapped in the social limbo of inner city educational and societal funding that is living in a "concrete" jungle. How many newspaper stories are there about inner-city ghetto children who drop out of special programming due to parental negligence and other factors beyond their control? Or what about funding a library at a school for exceptional children that has a book budget of only $1000 when a bank turns down their loan request. Investing in a school with intellectual capital that is falling through the cracks is truly an investment in the future strength of this country. A private initiative, with strong structure, vision, and guidelines, could transform a public debacle overnight. Another leveraging mechanism is replication, creating the same successful program in multiple locales without having to reinvent it each time, such as the Adopt-a-School program pioneered by the Lang Foundation.

Teach the next generation. Be a model and challenge budding philanthropists as you would challenge a recipient. Match the savings from the young person's allowance with a contribution to a favorite charity, or require that half of an allowance raise go to charity, unless they see *themselves* as their favorite charity. Be reasonable. Be open with why you are giving and invite (not coerce) them to give with you to a shared interest. Allow them to go their own way, too. The Brown Foundation in Houston, Texas, and The Lawrence Welk Foundation pass authority and involvement in the giving process over to the family children as teenagers through adjunct foundation boards. The children are gradually given more responsibility and authority, learning as they go.[9]

Consider giving your wealth in your lifetime. You will then be able to enjoy the fruits of your passions. Minimize concern that tax and federal budget cuts will undermine the incentive to give away today. A good philanthropist is not *singularly* motivated by tax planning. Just as in effective money management, "the tax tail should not wag the philanthropic dog."

Be flexible. Stay open to the future in the dizzying atmosphere of change and need in which we live. It is counterproductive to try to "dictate a vision, no matter how heartfelt."[10] The Hamilton Foundation in Wilton, Connecticut, has "opted for a grant-making agenda that will shift naturally with time and family input."[8]

PHILANTHROPIC VEHICLES AND STRUCTURES

Once your goals are defined, your research is done, and your assessments are made, you need to examine the vehicles and structures you can use to exercise your philanthropic mission. These vehicles range from simple to highly complex. The more complex they become, the more "hands on" the donor will become and the more important it becomes for you to have clear ideas of what you want to accomplish.

Socially Responsive Investing

Socially responsive investing(SRI) is considered by some as philanthropic. It often does not provide the investment returns, but it satisfies the investors' desire to "live" their community passions on the for-profit level. Socially responsive investing can force social, environmental, and political change and raise public consciousness. It is not philanthropic in the truest sense because it has a profit motive for the individual. TPI states that "Philanthropy is the venture capital of social change and social improvement."[7] SRI can be viewed similarly.

Direct Gifts of Cash

Direct individual gifts of cash take the form of annual and capital gifts, or long-term pledges. Although this technique is the simplest and most direct form of philanthropy besides volunteering, danger of abuse occurs in the case of any single-donor program or capital support that relies on only one benefactor. The glamour and impact of such a gesture can cause foolish and dismal actions to result when the recipient is needy and the donor wants to be needed and appreciated. For example, a major corporate donor, a cigarette manufacturer, attempted to force a museum to make public statements supporting the donor's corporate policy, with the implicit threat to withdraw the support for noncompliance. A positive example of wise individual support is Sallie Bingham's gesture in July 1995 to totally fund the Santa Fe Stages theater in New Mexico, but for only its first three years. She states "... I felt the community needs to show its support before five years. That's always the danger with one donor: The community feels its participation is not needed, but it definitely is—as an audience and as donors."[11]

Direct In-Kind Gifts

Direct in-kind gifts of equipment and other items useful to the philanthropy, such as computers given to schools by a computer manufacturer or donated services and personnel, are badly needed and are rarely funded by direct support.

Gifts of Appreciated Property

Gifts of appreciated property such as real estate, artwork, and the like are complicated continuously by ever-changing governmental regulation and are subject to interpretation or prior revenue rulings requested by the donor. An attorney, tax advisor, or other trained advisor familiar with your overall situation is necessary when making gifts of a substantial nature. Often, the charity itself is hampered in its goals by the nature of gifts of appreciated property. Proper research can avoid unsatisfactory outcomes. (See Chapter 4.)

Naming a Charitable Recipient

Naming a charitable recipient rather than a relative as beneficiary of your deferred, taxable IRA, Keogh, or other retirement plan, or your insurance policy changes the taxable nature of the asset at death and realizes its full use and value when it would otherwise be taxable in your estate.

Charitable Trusts

Charitable trusts in the form of remainder trusts (CRTs), and lead trusts (CLTs) are enormously useful, technical mechanisms for fulfilling philanthropic purpose and retaining income for heirs or other beneficial interests. Both types of trusts can be used as a living vehicle or as a bequest. A CLT allows a charity to receive income that is not critical to the family, and it provides for that gift to revert back to the family at a later date, giving the donor a tax-advantaged position at the time of the gift. In both instances, the donor cannot sell the asset without incurring a capital gains tax, but the charitable trust can. There is also an income tax deduction to the donor at the time of the gift. There are complicating income (Alternative Minimum Tax) and gift tax ramifications that must be considered in each particular case depending on the characteristics of the beneficiaries or recipients of the remainder and the assets being transferred. Remainder life interests in trusts can be transferred this way. Proper structuring is critical for effectiveness especially when closely held stock is the gift. (See Chapter 4, "Imperatives of Planning" and Appendix E.)

Charitable Gift Funds

Charitable gift funds provide vehicles for administering donor funds to a public charity that do not restrict the donors to a specific community or region. Unlike community and boutique public foundations, which will exhibit some or all of those restrictions, control remains in the hands of the donors. Fidelity Investments started such a fund in 1991.

Community Foundations

Community foundations and other pooled public charities, such as United Jewish Appeal and United Negro College Fund, allow the transfer and administration of philanthropic intent for many who would otherwise consider establishing a private foundation due to some of the limitations on them. Public foundations are professionally staffed, minimizing administrative costs for smaller pools of philanthropic dollars. For a living donor, greater thresholds of asset classes can be transferred to public charities as compared to private charities. In the case of a public charity, 50 percent of your adjusted gross income (AGI) may be donated as a cash gift, and 30 percent of AGI may be donated if the gift is appreciated property. For a private foundation, the restrictions are 30 percent and 20 percent, respectively. There is no excise tax liability on a public foundation, but there is tax liability on a private one. Both public and private foundations allow the donor to carry forward the excess value above his or her AGI, with some restrictions. The value of appreciated property is calculated at fair market value, unlike that for a private foundation, where *cost* basis is used for calculating estate- and gift-tax value. For a public foundation gift, the donor would *not* pay capital gains tax, but he or she would be required to pay this tax for a gift to a private foundation. Gifts of tangible personal property such as artwork are only deductible at cost if the use of the property is unrelated to the recipient's exempt purpose. (Giving a Rembrandt to an educational program rather than to an art museum is an example of a gift deductible at cost.)

Although certain IRS criteria must be met, the donor can have more control over the direction of the gifts than he or she might think. The two largest hurdles when using community foundations as gifting structures are the lack of absolute control and the limitations in directing your philanthropy to a specific region or community depending on how the particular foundation is structured in your area. You can direct your contributions to a community foundation out of your area if your philanthropic focus is in a region of the country other than that in which you live. An array of structures exists to accommodate different interests for a family or individual. All community foundation gifts are endowments and ensure ongoing good works unless the donor otherwise specifies. An investment committee of professionals manages the pooled funds.

Family or Private Foundation

There are many valuable reasons and purposes for forming a private foundation, so be clear about yours. Your mission, values, and objectives should drive the language of foundation intent and structure, and so should the choices of who participates in it, such as family, advisors, and key personnel. A foundation is another business to manage. Be sure you want to manage one before you create it. A simple pass-through foundation that requires minimal administration and excise tax compliance may be better for you unless you contemplate future philanthropic expansion. Experts believe that $500,000 is the minimum needed to establish a private foundation. Some suggest $2,000,000 to justify creating, managing, and reporting on a separate entity or subjecting it to an additional tax. But to generate enough income to pay excise taxes(1–2 percent of endow-ment income), staff it (unless you rely on volunteers), and have 5 percent to distribute as required by law, the Council on Foundations suggests a $5–10 million minimum endowment. The value of the foundation to the individual or family is singularly personal. It is a great vehicle for accomplishing multiple goals while exercising the control most public foundations can't ensure.

A family foundation centralizes the task of managing philan-thropic dollars. It gives the whole family and other involved per-sons a format to direct policy and pool and manage funds for distribution. It can be a unifying entity if it is thoughtfully devel-oped. The foundation serves as a good financial, philanthropic, and management training arena, provided that communications among participants are open and honest and goals are clear. The family foun-dation is particularly suited for those who aren't interested in, or have been discouraged from, going into the family's business, par-ticularly women and younger family members. But, utilizing the foundation as a control device specifically to insure that the children stay close or compliant will only drive a wedge into family harmony.

A private foundation shields the family from having to directly field the inevitable assault of requests for funding. It reduces income tax obligations while concurrently removing assets from future es-tate tax liabilities. Grants and scholarships to individuals, staff sala-ries and reasonable expenses incurred in the running of a grant-making program, grants to non-U.S. charities and to noncharitable organizations for a charitable purpose are, for indi-viduals, nondeductible distributions, but they become deductible if conveyed through the foundation.

Other restrictions that apply to private foundations include the tax on excess business holdings. The foundation cannot own more than 20 percent of an operating company or stock in which a re-lated person owns a controlling interest. It has to distribute 5 per-cent in *qualifying* distributions (self-dealing is taxed—you can't pay yourself more than a reasonable salary for work that must be proved to be legitimate). The board is subject to prudent investor restric-tions on funds investments, and certain expenditures made out of the foundation are taxable. These restricted activities include lob-bying; electioneering; voter registration; certain grants to individu-als, unless prior ruling has been given by the IRS; noncontractual distributions or expenditures to other nonpublic charities such as a Chamber of Commerce; and anything of a noncharitable nature other than reasonable administration expenses.

Family business and philanthropic experts advise caution when forming or changing a foundation. Many of the precepts for successful management and incorporation of family members and outsiders into the workings of the foundation are the same as in the business and family office systems. Families often don't want outsiders getting involved in their business. Good help is required to formalize governance and compliance to create the required foundation structure. Strong boards and good policies are equally as important in philanthropy as they are in business to help direct a family through the inevitable conflicts. Family conflicts arise regularly. Drs. Gersick, Landsberg, and Davis, in a study done on family foundations for the Whitman Institute, reveal that to ensure sustainability, flexibility should be built in to allow for changing focus, succession, and board representation as the foundation matures from the founder's interests and visions to those of the succeeding generations.[12] There is a founder's myth that he or she can govern and control from the grave to direct a philanthropic vision. Few philanthropic visions can remain static and survive, when the founder of the vision seeks to control the outcome beyond his or her life span.

Once the desire to incorporate philanthropy is established, planning and implementation decisions are necessary for a family group or individual to satisfyingly accomplish their goals and fulfill those desires in a satisfactory way. The TPI questionnaire that follows can get you started. But you cannot be in a hurry and still be an effective philanthropist. "To give money away well takes a long, long time."[13]

Author's note: Gerald Freund is the primary source of much of the information represented in this chapter. His counsel and wide-ranging experience at all levels of philanthropic pursuits enriches the wisdom represented here.

The Philanthropic Initiative Family Questionnaire

1. Do we understand what our family history is and agree on our basic family values? How would you express them as a family? as an individual?
2. Are your individual values different? If so, how would you express that difference?
3. The family is fortunate to have significant resources that can be used to enable family members to further important personal business and philanthropic interests. What is your view of these resources, and what opportunities, risks, and issues do they represent to you?
4. Does a family foundation seem like a good idea? If so, why? If not, why not? How do you think a family foundation should be organized?
5. Individually, we have a history of charitable giving and volunteerism. Do we know why we made those gifts of money and time? Do we feel good about them? Do we know if our efforts made a difference?
    a. Which of our past gifts have given us the most satisfaction?
    b. Which have given us the least?
6. As a donor, and perhaps as a trustee of a family foundation, what criteria would you put on proposals before they are funded?
7. What are the things about which you feel passionate? What are the things that really interest you? There are many major issues facing society, ranging from the arts to children's issues, to civil rights, to education, to environment, to housing, to hunger. They are all important, but which are the ones that you feel are the most important and why?
8. To what extent would you like to be involved in the work of exploring and analyzing problems and shaping promising solutions?
9. In order to develop a process that works for each of us, what would be the most helpful way for you to learn about what interests you?
    - Research on specific subjects.
    - Site visits to nonprofit organizations.
    - Background information to read.
    - Visits with experts.
10. How much direct contact with donees would you like to have?
11. Given your other commitments, how much time do you have to devote to philanthropy?
12. Based upon what you know about the family, do you think it is possible to arrive at consensus around giving?
13. Irrespective of consensus, should resources be made available for each individual to give and to use as they wish? If so, what amount could you effectively use in 19__?
14. What level of recognition and visibility is of interest to you?
15. How much risk tolerance do you have? (That is, are these funds to be used as seed capital, or are you more interested in building organizational capacity within existing organizations?)
16. What is your preference for geography: local, national, global, or some combination of all three?
17. Are you more interested in helping individuals, supporting organizations, or affecting public policy?
18. Any other ideas or thoughts?

Source: The Philanthropic Initiative, Inc. 77 Franklin St., Boston, Mass. 02110

ENDNOTES

1. Andrew Carnegie, "The Gospel of Wealth," in *The Gospel of Wealth and Other Timely Essays*, ed. Edward C. Kirkland. (Cambridge: Harvard University Press, 1962), p. 14. Originally titled "Wealth" and published in *North American Review* CXLVIII (June 1889) pp. 653–64; and CXLIX (December 1889) pp. 682–98.

2. *Ethics and Wealth* : A Conference, Airlie, Virginia, May 25-26, 1993, International Skye Associates, Inc., Washington, DC.

3. The Philanthropic Initiative, "Lessons from Wingspread," a report of recommended strategies for promoting philanthropy from a Wingspread conference, September 1994.

4. Holly Hall, "Taxation: Giving and the Wealthy," *The Chronicle of Philanthropy*, April 6, 1995. Reprinted with permission of *The Chronicle of Philanthropy*, Washington, D.C.

5. Gerald Freund, interview with author, 18 April 1995. Gerald Freund is president of the Private Funding Associates and Pro Bono Ventures, Inc.,

6. Independent Sector, a report, *Giving and Volunteering in the United States, 1994 Edition*, (Washington, D.C.: Independent Sector, 1994).

7. Family Firm Institute, "The FFI Interview: H. Peter Karoff," in Family Firm Institute Newsletter, Winter 1995. © Family Firm Institute, Inc.

8. Allison Wheeler, "Nurturing a Grantmaking Vision," *Foundation News & Commentary*, March/April 1995, p. 36. Reprinted with permission Foundation News & Commentary.

9. Kelin Gersick and Deanne Stone, "Family Foundations," (paper presented at The Family Firm Institute Conference, Davis, Calif., October 1989).

10. Allison Wheeler, "Unearthing 'Pictures of the Future,'" sidebar from "Nurturing a Grantmaking Vision," *Foundation News & Commentary*, March/April 1995, p. 37. Reprinted with permission *Foundation News & Commentary*.

11. "Heiress Pumps $3.5 million into New Santa Fe Theater," *The San Antonio Express-News*, 9 July 1995, p. 6G.

12. Kelin E. Gersick, Ivan Landsberg, and John A. Davis, "Family Foundations at Work," (research project report, The Whitman Institute, Los Angeles, Calif.).

13. Jane Gregory Rubin, Interview with author, New York, N.Y., 19 July 1995. Jane Gregory Rubin is a trust and estates attorney in New York.

9

MONEY MANAGEMENT

Take Time and Trust Yourself—It's Your Money

> The melancholy fact is that in the popular imagination, wealth has alchemical properties that transmute its possessor into a Jefferson-like paragon with transcendent capacities and knowledge. What's more, the richer the person, the more sweeping the capacities, the more profound that knowledge. Billionaires, in other words, automatically are wiser and smarter than millionaires.
>
> *Alan Abelson*[1]

Money—"liquid gold"—is where American individuals, families, and advisors focus first when setting priorities, spending their time, and directing their efforts . Money is tangible, desirable, alluring, measurable, and lost or used faster than it is made. Families and their appetites grow faster than fortunes. The immigrant "work and save" ethic and the agrarian "frugality and work" ethic are increasingly rare as the numbers of the affluent who own more of this country's wealth rise and the distance from our historical roots increases. The old saying, "from shirtsleeves to shirtsleeves in three generations" is not a joke. On the other hand, neither new wealth nor multigenerational, inherited wealth is any less susceptible to squandering. When asked why her contemporaries were struggling to manage a well-known, American fortune, a family member responded, "The first generation accumulates; the next one dissipates; the cycle starts over again. Count them up. We're number four." The speaker came from the second level of "dissipaters." The good news is, if you work at it cycles can be broken and patterns can be changed.

The quantitative, esoteric, and occasionally obscure vocabulary and structures of the money management world can send client-stewards begging for someone they can understand. But clear language doesn't indicate competency or commonality of purpose. Ultimately, a wealth holder must learn to trust her or his own ability to make and manage decisions about whom to trust with his or her wealth. Charles D. Ellis, in his book *Investment Policy*, states, "Clients own the central responsibility for formulating and assuring implementation of long-term investment policy... this responsibility cannot be delegated to investment managers."[2]

Money managers, bankers, lawyers, and accountants are not interested in your business out of the "goodness of their hearts." Never forget, service providers make a living off of your money. The fears, uncertainties, and false bravado around money issues create further opportunities for abuses large and small, both intentional and unintentional. One outspoken manager at an industry conference once commented, "There are only two things that are important when considering money management—fear and greed. Don't ever forget it." Those comments are pretty harsh, but they are illustrative of a powerful ethic of "the street." The Securities and Exchange Commission (SEC), which regulates the industry, feeds the common misconception that wealth, by definition, equals sophistication and knowledge when it classifies a person with $250,000 income for three consecutive years or $1 million net worth as a *sophisticated* investor who is qualified to invest in limited investment partnerships such as hedge funds. Most people at this level have no idea what a hedge fund is.

This chapter is a general resource guide. It is not meant to teach you the money management process. There are books, MBA programs, and long careers that teach you how to manage money. The assumption is that you won't have years to learn before making certain decisions. Just starting out, the most important things you need are a vocabulary, some simple tools (actions to take) to help you get a feel for the world of money management, and a basic introduction to common industrywide characteristics. First, common mistakes you will make are identified so that you can be on the lookout for them; then, the common industry characteristics are explained. Following these sections, two related glossaries are provided to familiarize you with the money management structures and instruments that drive the industry. With these basic resources, you can converse with anyone as your experience grows.

Keeping realism and dreams in balance when you have just gained access to sizable wealth is really hard to do. The surest way to achieve balance is to gain confidence in your abilities to make good decisions. You gain confidence with knowledge. Knowledge–knowledge of yourself and how your actions and decisions affect others (a child, a parent, a partner)—is power. Know what your risk tolerance is, what type of money personality you have, and what your limitations and advantages are. Know also what your personal interests and concerns are and how they support or complicate your money management plans. Knowing what you want for others in your life gives you personal power to make confident choices. See how it goes?

You gain knowledge two ways: by your own study and research and through communication with others who have the information and knowledge you need or want. As explored further in Chapters 2 and 3, the most important communication you can have about money management is with your significant others. The second most important communication for you to have is with people who have been or are in your shoes, followed by dialogue with well-chosen advisors. In this way, you are provided with knowledge from three perspectives. Asking questions, as many as you need to get comfortable with the advisors you choose and what you choose to do, helps you process what you learn. Stating opinions and objections and seeking compromises and consensus helps others gain knowledge about what is important to you so that they can better advise you and help implement your policies. Finally, financial decisions are always emotionally charged for the private investor. Communication between your head, your heart, and your gut makes them work in unison. Relying on one of these to the exclusion of the others undermines your equilibrium and can lead to costly mistakes.

MISTAKES PEOPLE MAKE

Mistakes in managing large amounts of capital are exacerbated by volatile emotions (measured on Wall Street as "investor sentiment"). These emotions play a much larger role in money management than most individuals and advisors acknowledge or realize.

Mistake #1: Crisis Management versus Planning and Education

"Hip shot" decisions that put money to work without education and planning to implement the long-term policy can sabotage personal security and flexibility. Crises or unforeseen circumstances can't always be averted (inheritance of a mattress stuffed with $1,000 bills or winning the lottery), but many changes can be foreseen (a trust vesting, an aging or highly successful spouse or parent, ownership succession in a family company, etc.). Too often, advisors and investment institutions are hired and money placed without consideration of the interlocking requirements needed to manage them.

Solution: Take time to grasp the fundamental elements comprising the industry and to learn its basic vocabulary. Plan first before you even think about taking decisive action. Decide what you want or need. Education and experience take time. Trust your abilities to learn, care for, and protect yourself. You can learn everything you need to learn for confident decision making in good time.

Design a flexible, workable investment policy and stick with it. Patient investing is always best. It is hard to think clearly in a crisis. Include in the policy the key elements of time horizon, risk tolerance, performance expectations and measurement guides, asset allocation guidelines (constraints and strategy), rebalancing guidelines, manager selection and characteristics preferences, process, expectations, and monitoring guidelines.[3] (For a review of these concepts, see Chapters 4 and 5.)

Mistake #2: Abdicating Responsibility

You can abdicate your responsibility by blindly trusting in advisors, family members, friends, and retainers. Lack of self-confidence causes you to give up the reins to your assets, sometimes to questionable advisors. Lacking personal responsibility for the wealth you have will ensure that it won't be with you for long. Denying the weaknesses of familiar or comfortable things and people around you carries great financial, psychological, and emotional costs. Circumstances can change gradually or dramatically. (See Chapter 7, "Picking People and Choosing Professional Resources," and Appendix C for more information.)

Solution: Take responsibility; overcome belief systems of either entitlement or helplessness. Be proactive. Keep learning. Look after your interests. Charles Ellis states, "Clients should assert their responsibility for leadership in policy formation... and while responsibility for it can be abdicated, it really cannot be delegated."[2]

No one needs to be a sheep among the wolves unless he or she chooses to be. Emotional attachment to others can hamper wise choices. Due largely to inexperience, inattention, misperceptions, sheltering, or spoiling, women and younger people are more subject to these pitfalls. The benefits of taking responsibility are personal confidence, empowerment, and modeling for others in your sphere of influence.

Mistake #3: Shortsightedness

Formulating and sticking with a long-term investment policy doesn't come naturally to most individuals and families, unless they are very comfortable with risk. Focusing on fashionable, labyrinthine "benchmarks," daily trading, and market timing in an attempt to maximize performance every quarter or every year over time has proven to be a faulty approach to personal investment success in comparison to committing to the long-term view. Market timing is not for the faint of heart or for anyone but a minority of investors that possess a gambler's sensibilities and risk appetite. You won't be missing that much if you say no to an idea that has to be executed immediately with no prior warning. For instance, a broker calls and tells you that XYZ is going public and that you will miss the narrow window of opportunity to gain on the initial rise in value. Unless the broker has proven to be a great stock picker over a consistent time (10 years), either don't blame your loss on the manager or don't take the bet to begin with.

Solution: Set long-term investment policies and horizons and stick to them; this is the key to preserving and growing capital to outpace taxes, fees, and inflation. No matter what the market does in the short term (less than three years), cycles need 3 years minimum, but ideally 5 to 10 years (assuming no changed circumstance that interrupts personal plans), to work their magic.

MONEY MANAGEMENT FRAMEWORK

When a carpenter builds a framework, he has to use different tools to accomplish different tasks to get one result—a frame to use. These tools (actions) might not be directly related to one another, but they have one goal. This toolbox of actions is designed to build a foundation for understanding money management and to begin a long-term, comfortable relationship with making financial decisions. You won't be able to go out there and manage a $10 million portfolio on your own yet, but you will be conversant and comfortable with how portfolio management works.

Investment Vehicles and Structures

Acquaint yourself with what investment vehicles and structures are, the benefits and complications associated with them, and their suitability for your purposes and for others affected by your choices. A glossary of investment instruments at the end of this chapter gets you going. Chapter 13 describes alternative investment vehicles and structures. The reading list in Appendix D and the glossary in Appendix E are both resources from which to draw while you are learning about the industry. For instance, assume that your parent just left you an interest in an individually managed account at a money management firm. Do you know the difference between an individually managed account and a mutual fund or a money management account? Why does it matter that you know? Pretend the answers are "no" and "because I have to tell them what I want done with it or leave it up to them." You next have to ask, "But who are *they*? They don't know me and I don't know them or what they do." If you don't care, then you really don't need to go any farther with this exercise. If you do, get busy learning before you leap.

Research Available Institutions and Individuals

Acquaint yourself with institutions and individuals that manage the mechanics. A basic glossary of money management resources is provided later in this chapter to help you get started. The specific research into individual firms will be up to you. In taking action, you will be more likely to choose those who respond to you and your needs. Don't just take their word for who and what they are. Do your research. Techniques are provided in Chapter 7 and Appendix C.

Revisit, Review, and Manage Expectations and Intuitions

Your expectations and intuitions about money and how and who you want to have manage that money will change. Are they still relevant? Are they realistic? Are they progressing in the manner you had hoped? If not, redefine your expectations or change your personal direction. Get real, but don't lose sight of your vision. Keep emotions in balance without denying them, and trust your intuitions. Recognize the difference between the two. Use the resources in this book for review information.

Familiarize Yourself with Basic Investment Terms and Measurements

Don't erroneously assume that something irrelevant to you as a measure of risk or return is a useful benchmark for you. Customized portfolio benchmarks are used increasingly as the preferred method of measurement to provide a greater level of understanding, relevance, and comfort. Use measurements comparing apples and apples, not apples and oranges; that is, compare growth managers against growth managers and the market performance of growth managers over time. You can't get a fair picture when comparing a value manager to a growth manager, because their fundamental assumptions are too different. Don't be intimidated by mind-bending terms used by the profession, such as Sortino and Sharpe ratios, alpha, beta, standard deviation, and market neutral, that can either impress or confuse you. Even veterans of 20 years or more admit the incomprehensible and intimidating nature of these terms. Use the information in Appendixes D and E to expand your knowledge. Comfort comes with familiarity, time, and experience.

Learn the Essentials for Interviewing, Engaging, Monitoring, and Terminating Managers

Even if you will never perform these tasks yourself, it is important to master the skills. Sit in on manager reviews and interviews. If you have a comfortable working relationship with a manager and your staff or advisor recommends termination, you will need to have a working knowledge of what went into the choice in the first place so that you can understand the recommendation and know whether to object or not. This can result from your advisors misunderstanding of your priorities and desires. It is tough to be honest with yourself and to admit that you might be staying with an advisor for all the wrong reasons. If you are comfortable with the manager choice from a place of general understanding of the essentials learned in the search process, and you understand the options, then the action won't leave you bewildered.

Know Your Priorities

Different investors value different qualities in an advisor or institution. Common objective and subjective considerations are fees, taxes, inflation effects, performance (returns), risk tolerance, personal chemistry, trust, priorities (does wealth, family, or security, come first?), accountability (reporting), availability, age (of portfolio, investor, and manager), liquidity needs, and asset allocation (within the portfolio itself and in concert with other asset classes). How involved in or divorced from the process do you want to be or can you afford to be? How involved are your children? Do you protect them, prepare them, spare them, or control them? Develop an investment policy, however broad, using Chapters 4 and 5 as aids. It is too late to address these questions when you need the answers on the spot, so be prepared.

Monitor and Review the Process

Regularly examine variables such as reasonable responses to market fluctuations and volatility; what constitutes clear reporting requirements; refactoring changes in circumstance, age, and liquidity needs or pressures; cost effectiveness; and qualitative requirements (communications, expectations). Ask for what you want. Don't be dissuaded without weighing potential consequences.

Build a Model Portfolio

Carve out an amount as "fun money" and try your hand at portfolio management in a small way, going a step farther than simply doing it on paper as Lou Leeburg suggests in Chapter 5. Read the daily and weekly financial papers. Pick two, three, or more companies to follow. Visit the companies. Buy the products and try them. Talk to others who have studied the company. Do your own research. Read works by Peter Lynch and other successful investors to help set a personal portfolio strategy. Check out specific stocks in *Value Line* and other special publications. Decide what you can realistically afford to lose. Take the leap and learn by doing. You will have a great sense of what it takes to be a good money manager and to get your money's worth out of the professionals you hire. It can be challenging and fun for you.

Decide How to Manage

Will you manage using a personal family office or by farming the work out to another office? Will you use a hands-on style or will you use an institution; in-house, unrelated (to you) management; or an investment consulting firm? Will you give it away and move to a desert island so you don't have to think about it? If the latter is the choice, then consider the cost of the Averell Harriman heirs, who ended up with almost nothing. Their $35 million inheritance dissipated to an estimated $3 million due to lack of oversight by the beneficiaries and several trustees over the trust managers.

GLOSSARY OF COMMON MONEY MANAGER CHARACTERISTICS

All money management resources have common characteristics. Before you can understand their differences, you must recognize the similarities. Familiarity with industrywide structures, billing policies, and so on helps newcomers to familiarize themselves with money management terminology and how money management entities look and operate. This glossary should help remove some of the mystery for you and help you better understand the money management resources list that follows. Refer to Appendix E for other unfamiliar terms. For example, specific types of money management entities that share these characteristics are defined in later sections of the chapter, moving us from the general to the more specific as you become comfortable with the language. Let's take a look at characteristics shared by money manager resources.

History, Staff, and Asset Size

All money management institutions have a history, including a founding date; certain transitions as their fortunes have changed and grown; and current staff size and type, including how many are investment professionals, what their investment expertise is, and how many of these are support staff. Assets under management tells you how big a firm is, which, in turn, gives you a good idea of how successful it is or what its range of motion might be in the marketplace. Those who are too big can't be very flexible. Their visibility in the markets is high, and the positions they take can really change the face of the market. A young, aggressive manager who is just starting out might have a short work history with another firm—most usually do—but no history at all where he or she is now. The opposite end of the history spectrum is Merrill Lynch, an obvious example of a firm with a long history.

Portfolio Size Limits and Requirements

Generally, high net worth managers will not manage individual accounts below $1 million. Exceptions to this rule are in larger trust companies and banks, and with start-up managers eager for new business. But the number and variety of flexible managers are shrinking as they direct their marketing and management efforts toward larger pools of liquid wealth due to the economies of scale and resulting higher profit margins for the managers. Unless you work directly with a broker who has no minimum requirement and who also isn't a portfolio manager, mutual or pooled funds will be recommended for accounts smaller than the stated minimum. Naturally, anything less than $1 million will send you to a bank, mutual fund company, or boutique firm with hefty fees.

Strategies

Every type of management has a strategy, which will include a philosophy, such as growth or capital preservation; a process, such as "top-down" or fee-based trust management service; and a style, which defines what type of investments they look for, such as growth companies or real estate investment instruments. These managers have an aim, such as those participating defensively in market cycles with periodic reallocations or market timing, and they use some articulated form of risk control, such as hedging, rebalancing, or quantitative analysis, or some other tool that further defines their strategy. You might want a value-oriented hedge fund manager who does only bottom-up research. This will limit the scope of your search.

Range of Services

Services vary from a single-niche product to full service. Fully diversified services include money management, ancillary, and nonfinancial planning and management services for trusts, individuals, and related entities.

Style

Traditional managers use growth equities, value equities, fixed income (taxable and tax exempt), balanced, foreign and domestic, and combinations of these styles. Limited partnerships (LP), more commonly used by nontraditional managers exclusively, are available in some traditional managers' product lines. LP, nontraditional managers use hedge funds with macro, long/short equity, and equity/bond portfolio strategies. Other LP alternative strategies include commodities, currencies, distressed securities, risk arbitrage, short selling, market timing, and sector- and industry-specific management techniques.

Structures

Depending on the firm or individual, varying structures are available, including limited partnerships, characteristically employed by hedge funds, individually managed accounts, managed pooled accounts, brokerage accounts, wrap accounts, fund of funds in wrap and partnership form, and mutual funds.

Registration and Oversight

Varying levels of oversight exist based on which agencies direct the compliance. The securities, banking, and commodities industries are tightly regulated, but abuses are common. Designations to look for are Chartered Financial Analyst (CFA), Certified Financial Planner (CFP), registered investment advisor, and a corporate affiliation (brokerage houses and money management firms require licensing of all personnel who trade, sell, and do research, while banks and trust companies have internal compliance departments and codes regulated by federal banking authorities). There are specific standards to which the industry professes to adhere (Association for Investment Management and Research or AIMR), some enforceable, some not. The Prudent Investor Rule (Third Restatement) will play an increasingly important role in regulating actions. Limited partnerships are favored by many managers for their lack of registration and regulatory requirements.

Reporting Methods

Reporting methods vary and are frequently inadequate or too complex for the taxable client. Clients should acquaint themselves with the methods and scope of reporting they can expect from a manager or institution, and they should be willing to ask for what they need to know. Because the bulk of funds under management come from nontaxable, institutional sources, most firms are familiar with nontaxable client requirements but have been slow to address taxable client needs and demands. That is changing, and it is placing pressure on the management firms to change their reporting methods. Annual and quarterly reports that include after-tax, net of fee, real, and total returns, are not too much to expect unless the firm manages funds in a complex limited partnership structure. Actual tax effects of transactions cannot be determined until a year-end audit is completed for the partnership return (if it is unaudited, don't invest with that manager). The partnership return form referred to as a

K-1 is often delayed well into the first quarter of the following year due to certain accounting and investment instrument complexities, and portfolio turnover characteristics. Gross numbers, however, should be readily available from most firms and managers on a daily basis. If not, internal controls and back-office accounting and reporting systems are faulty or suspect. As pressure from the growing wealth-management sector increases, firms and managers are being forced to effectively address this "need to know."

Fee Structures

Fee structures are variable depending on the form of money management used. Some managers disclose fee structures readily; others must be asked to clarify the negotiable arrangements they have with their traders and brokers if they don't transact their own trades. These are what constitute the base fees charged by the manager. Many brokerage firms often have separate discount subsidiaries to transact their trades. Expect fees that include management fees (based on hard and soft dollar measurements), commissions, trading costs, execution costs, incentive (performance) fees, custodial charges, consulting fees, and administrative costs and are based on the amount of money under management, the type of account being managed, the type of structure used, and the services being performed. Quoted fees paid for money management often don't include trading costs. A recent study shows that the typical $100 million equity portfolio generates $410,000 in commission costs and from -$513,000 to + $359,000 in execution costs. Total trading costs for the portfolio range from -$103,000 to + $769,000. Median transaction costs are approximately $250,000 (25 basis points).[4] Investment managers apply institutional investment techniques on a private client account but charge substantial private client fees for same-size accounts. Recently, as large, influential private clients become more aware of the existing double standard, considerable pressure has been placed on these managers to treat taxable and non-taxable clients equally in their fee structures. In mutual fund parlance, the fee is referred to as a "load."

Tax Considerations

Although an investment strategy should never be solely tax driven, consideration of how a manager's strategy and operations affects your tax position can play a key role in a choice of managers. With all other variables equal, a high-turnover (85 percent) portfolio will erode real, after-tax (federal) returns over a 10-year period by 50 percent before fees and commissions are applied. Most hedge funds cannot be expected to be tax sensitive, but it is important for the investor to understand that an aggressive manager may not measure up to a more conservative one on an after-tax basis. Also, mutual funds with high portfolio turnovers are notorious for year-end surprises in their attempts to boost pretax return figures. Mutual funds do not report net-of-tax returns, and the limited partnership incentive (performance) fee is not deductible as an investment expense against federal income taxes. The deductibility of other expenses is limited by law.

Account Sales and Management Characteristics

Unless they are an independent or new business, very few money managers are their own sales representatives. This presents inherent problems for the investor who wants to deal directly with the person managing his or her money. Money managers are not where they are because they enjoy sales or relationship management. They are there because they enjoy managing and making money. Some firms have highly trained financial advisors who serve as client liaisons to the managers. Others have only sales representatives with little or no expertise in financial advisory. Know what to expect in communications with your advisors. There are very good managers who are quite willing and open to maintaining communications as long as demands from the client don't adversely affect daily management. The more successful they become, the less they need you with them. The best money managers remain loyal and in communication with those clients who started and stayed with them throughout their careers. In time, you will decide what communication links you prefer with a manager—direct or through an intermediary. This can greatly impact the type of manager with which you choose to work.

Substance versus Style

For the uninitiated, recognizing the substance beneath the style is tough to do when making your investment decisions. The way a representative is compensated will tell you a lot about what their role should be in those decisions. For example, a "fee only" planner or CFP is clearly not benefiting from the sale to you of any underlying product. Fee- or salary-based compensation with a sales incentive attached usually indicates that sales, not client service, are the priority. Frequently, you will see incentive sales personnel in larger institutions such as banks and money management firms, and in insurance-based CFPs. These people are a layer or more away from managing the money, yet they are charged with gaining your confidence and your capital.

Debt: Leverage and Margin Accounts

Know how you personally feel about debt. There is low- and high-risk leverage. Ask the manager about his or her philosophy and use of leverage. The outsized returns of many hedge funds are due to creative, speculative, and active use of leverage. Margin purchases in a brokerage account allow a client to purchase up to twice as much of the stock as they have capital invested. It must be paid back some-time. If you bet right, you win big. If not, then... Ask yourself again, "How much am I willing to lose?"

Qualitative Considerations

Some considerations are tangible, while others are not. For example, experience and reliable staff (low) turnover is a qualitative measure-ment tool and should be given great weight when making decisions to hire managers. Most people look for a manager and/or strategy with which they can stick. This is not to say that a manager who never changes is all good. On the contrary, you want a manager who has experienced market cycles and demonstrates humility balanced with self-confidence, not arrogance—a trait that is endemic to the profession. You are also looking for a manager who displays wis-dom, coolness under pressure, vision, and a reasonable willingness to communicate. Managers aren't known for great interpersonal re-lationship skills. Anyway, you want them to tend to the business for which they were chosen. Curiosity, energy, integrity, and a willing-ness to admit mistakes and shortcomings and to learn from them and go on are other qualitative traits of a good manager. If your manager's investment style changes, it is to your advantage to ex-plore his or her reasons why and feel confident with the answers. Otherwise, it is time to leave. And what do their surroundings say to you? Is too much compensation spent on management's personal and work environment, or is it being spent on managing and re-searching for the investors? If personality compatibility matters to you, assess it. Is there rapport? If you don't care, this isn't an issue for you. The bottom line is to be comfortable with each manager's style and to know why you hired him or her. You will want to review these premises annually.

GLOSSARY OF MONEY MANAGEMENT RESOURCES

For the layperson, besides the baffling vocabulary, the most confusing thing about money management is sorting through the titles and what they mean. There is no uniformity in terminology. So often, a title means whatever the individual wants it to mean, except for a few required certification titles, such as registered investment advisor. These designations separate out the types of money management suppliers and products you will most likely deal with as you are practicing wealth stewardship. General terms in the previous section are applicable to all of the following resources.

Money Manager Resources: The People

Investment Consultant

When the term "consultant" is used in the money management context, it refers to a person performing a fee-based service for recommending and sometimes monitoring the investment performance of portfolio managers to address diversification requirements. Consultant implies the existence of varying degrees of a due diligence function. The following are typical consulting types in the industry.

Independent Consulting Firm or Individual   An independent consulting firm or individual provides fee-based manager searches and monitoring for individuals, institutions, and family groups. Depending on your requirements, asset allocation models, customized benchmark design, and portfolio measurement are available. Callan Associates is an example of such a consulting firm. Comparison shopping between firms is a must. Consulting firms are exclusively interested in the portion of the portfolio dedicated to money management and liquid asset allocation. Most consulting firms are traditionally biased to institutional, nontaxable clients. The first question to ask is, "How many private client searches have you done?"

Securities Firms   Securities firms provide soft dollar and/or straight-fee- or wrap-fee-based manager searches and monitoring. This service can be found in larger retail money management firms. Lee Hennessee's Hedge Fund Select in New York City provides this type of specialty service in the hedge funds universe.

Financial Planning Consultants   Financial planning consultants provide straight-fee or wrap-fee manager searches and monitoring. These consultants are more likely to work other considerations into the financial management, such as rebalancing accounts and account reporting. They are typically small to medium-sized firms. Brinker Capital in Pittsburgh is an example.

Institutions as Managers

An institution can be viewed as any large, publicly traded or private partnership (Goldman Sachs, and Neuberger & Berman) that trades and invests, such as large institutional money managers, banks, and trust companies.

Brokerages   Brokerages are discount and full-service firms providing discretionary, discount retail, short-sale, long, hedged, and derivative equity investing. Some have expanded to provide limited partnership, fund of funds, convertible bond, mutual fund, and balanced account investments. Don't expect a small account to be actively managed unless the broker is busy churning your account to boost his/her commissions. Monitor any brokerage account closely, especially with regard to costs. Charles Schwab and Smith Barney are examples.

Investment Management Firms   Investment management firms are publicly traded or private partnerships with money management specialties, predominantly for large accounts. Their primary function is often investment banking and trading for their own institution's account, which generates heftier firm revenues than managing private accounts. Individual account minimums range from $1 million to $5 million to $10 million, although exception is made when there is some assurance that a larger sum will come in at a later date. There are scores of investment styles, preferences, strengths, and weaknesses within this grouping; for example, Morgan Stanley has a strong identification in foreign markets management and measurement. Retrenching and restructuring abounds in the industry. Stay current; old information or reputations might be irrelevant.

Trust Companies

These companies come in several forms and differ from retail banking and money management firms, although those institutions might also be chartered to provide certain trust services. The quality varies enormously in expertise, range of service, firm commitment to the business, and motivation.

Private   These trust companies provide special-interest or narrowly focused fiduciary management for clients and are owned by investment firms such as Neuberger & Berman, or Fidelity in Boston. These trust services departments are generally very narrowly focused in their commitment to clients, providing first money management and then trust services. Distinctive from companies that are extensions of money management firms are those independent, private trust companies, such as Legacy Trust in Houston, that provide professional, personalized, trust management services for one or various families as their primary function. These are usually unaffiliated and have been formed to provide a broad range of fiduciary duties to a small group of private, often related, clients. Their greatest benefits are stability of focus, personnel, purpose, ownership, and access to investment policy decision makers.

Public/Institutional   Large trust companies (U.S. Trust, Fiduciary Trust International, and so forth) offering a full range of investment, trust management, and private banking services are most clearly identified with trust services by the general public. Some institutions are limited in their client focus by size of accounts, but they are adding services never available before, such as individually managed portfolios and manager monitoring, and venture capital opportunities created through in-house investment strategies designed to attract upwardly mobile and mega-wealthy clients and complex family groups that are no longer being effectively served by local private banks. The drawbacks of this type are distance from a policy center, the absence of personal loyalties, frequent personnel turnover, limited personal service, broad variation in quality of service, and inflexibility in investment management.

Selective   Bessemer Trust in New York, an example of this type, originally served as a single-family office, but it redirected its focus to include other family groups and their investment management and trust capital management. This type of company is not full service and usually carries very large minimum account requirements. They have a limited investment style that is frequently reflective of the philosophy of the founder rather than the client.

Commercial Private Banks

This category includes J.P. Morgan, Citibank, Chase Manhattan Bank, and Banker's Trust. These multilayered banks have a special division that provides trust, private mortgage, and conservative investment management for wealthy families and individuals. Many have global private banking offices.

Commercial Regional Banks

Banks such as NationsBank, Bank One, Wells Fargo, and so on supply services similar to those provided by private bank services. Regional banks have a penchant for impersonal service and long-distance management with a lower capacity for customizing to meet the needs of families and individuals with complex investment policy management requirements. Many lack global custody services for large private clients and suffer considerable turnover in client service personnel.

Family Offices

This is a relatively recent term, although it is not a new institution. There have been family offices for several generations, but since 1990, there has been an explosion of new ones, creating a whole new industry that is dedicated to providing specific wealth management services to families newly organizing themselves. Within the family office classification there are several types. All of them manage money in one way or another, but they can also provide other services. Only the money management feature is highlighted in this section. (See Chapter 6, "Foundation Constructs for Management.")

Single Family, Multigenerational, Free-Standing, Full-Service Office   In this office, one family shares the overhead costs. The Rockefeller family office expanded its services to bring in families with assets of at least $100 million. That minimum has since been lowered. Others, such as the Pitcairn Trust Company, also invite outside families, but the minimums and the range of service vary with the amount under management and services required by the client family. The single-family offices, not open to outside families, such as the Bass Family operations, tightly manage their own investments outside the view from the public arena.

Single-Family Investment Management Office with No Ancillary Services   In this type of office, one family pays the management fees, manages the portfolio internally or externally, and farms out all other service needs.

Multifamily, Multigenerational, Full-Service Office   This family office type charges on a "bundled-services" basis, a set-fee basis, or a combination of the two and may segregate other fees for services from money management fees based on portfolio size. The Perry family enterprise, Asset Management Advisors, Inc., orchestrates family meetings, and educational and other services included with the money management function. No one family dominates the investment policy and strategy profile.

Multifamily, Multigenerational Money Management Service with Limited Ancillary Services   Portfolio size determines qualification and fee for this type of office. Ashbridge Investment Management, a branch of the Grace family in Philadelphia and Milbank-Winthrop in New York are examples. There are more forming every day, especially in the Midwest, Southwest, Florida, and California.

Family Office Cooperatives   These loosely associated cooperatives pool assets and services of unrelated family groups to negotiate lower fees on custody and brokerage and to share services in other areas of mutual interest. CCC of Boston, a cooperative formed by members of the Pitcairn and Corning families, is an example.

Money (Portfolio) Managers

The most commonly recognized professional money management structures used by wealthy individuals and families come with several titles and various forms. They are generally recognized first for their investment style and their performance record. (See the discussion of general characteristics in this chapter.)

Investment Counselor/Advisor   Often referred to as boutique firms, these range in size and character—small, medium or large, independent or partnership management structures—and have varying account minimums (from $100,000 to $20,000,000) and individual and firmwide investment strategies frequently available in the same shop. Tweedy Browne in New York is an example.

Manager of Managers   This investment advisor type manages a stable of other managers or funds (fund of funds) for individual clients or partners in a pooled investment management arrangement. He or she might manage individual accounts or partnership interests. A number of family investment offices are structured this way. Ashbridge Investment Management in Philadelphia, and LJH Alternative Investment Advisors in Naples, Florida, are examples.

Money Manager   Equity, fixed-income, and alternative marketable instruments and funds are all used by managers. Depending on needs and preferences, the private investor can choose from a universe of managers across the world, new or experienced, specialist or generalist, brilliant or stupid, ethical or sleazy. Attracted by the challenge, the game, the sex appeal, the excitement, the compensation potential, and the gamble of the markets, every conceivable personality type and competency can be found here.

Global managers diversify or specialize their strategies either country specifically, globally, domestically, or in combinations of all or some of the above. More traditional investment advisors and institutions increasingly seek to offer exotic strategies in equities, global investments, venture capital, and real estate partnerships to attract clients. The money manager characterized by a single strategy, style, or core of strategies better maintains competency and effectiveness over time. Pinnacle Associates in New York is an established global equities specialty firm.

Insurance Companies

Historically, insurance companies have the least professionally specialized money management firms; they are slow to respond to markets, conservatively managed, invested in illiquid assets, overpriced as managers due to high fixed costs, and are not recommended as investment managers. Their businesses are insurance sales and money lending. Investment strategies are predicated on risk management and asset growth for their own accounts to fund future payouts to subscribers and beneficiaries. Although they sell money management products such as annuities (which are not insurance policies but are touted as such and are unjustifiably costly except for very long-term investors) they are insurance companies, not money managers. Insurance companies have strayed far from their core business into real estate management, venture capital, and other investments, such as long-term debt, to protect and invest the capital they collect from premiums. Unless you purchase a large policy ($10 million), you have no choice of investment managers overseeing your account.

Money Management Resources: The Hybrids

A hybrid is something that is a blend. The following are two blended money management vehicles that combine structure and vehicle.

Treasury Direct

These include bill and bond purchasing locations. This is what is referred to when you personally direct your own account with the Federal Reserve branch nearest you to buy, sell, and deposit U.S. Treasury instruments free of fees. You manage your own bond account with them. They take care of the technical details, but you have to monitor them for yourself. (See the bond section of *The Wall Street Journal Guide to Money and Investing* for a description of the procedure.)

Mutual Funds

This hybrid refers to pooled, professionally managed accounts offering every conceivable type of index and arrangement to the investor who wishes to spread his or her risk. Mutual funds are a painless, impersonal, and simplified way to manage large and small sums. Because of the rising minimums for individually managed accounts by other management forms, many large investors are turning to the mutual fund industry to diversify and manage trust, personal, retirement, and executive compensation accounts. Figure 9.1 offers interesting comparisons between mutual funds and individually managed accounts.

FIGURE 9.1

Mutual Funds and Individually Managed Accounts: A Comparison

Characteristics	Mutual Funds	Individually Managed Accounts
Control for tax purposes (turnover and timing)	None over timing	Can direct turnover and timing
Control of investment strategy	Annual distributions required by law; no turnover control	Can buy and hold
Relationship with manager	None; no obligation to inform of manager choices	Direct manager communications
Information accessibility	None; no list of positions	On demand but discouraged by many; can take manager away from task at hand
Performance tracking/comparisons	Semiannual reports; fund comparisons in daily financial newspapers	Difficult to measure against like managers; information not readily accessible
Fees	125–150 basis points/year	50–150 basis pts.; downward sliding scale; avg. $1,000,000 fee is 100 basis points
Diversification	Yes; buy several or buy index funds	Yes; infinite within the style and by manager
Information flow/reporting regularity	Semiannual or quarterly consolidated statements	More than you might want to know; individual transaction confirmations and monthly statements
Entry requirement	$1,000	$1,000,000, $5,000,000, or $10,000,000 depending on manager reputation and policy; $500,000 is rare

Copyright © 1995 Sally S. Kleberg.

Money Management Resources: The Instruments

Investment Instruments

Because this a primer of sorts, I won't attempt to characterize all of the ways you can invest because of the complicated nature of many of them. Instead, some broad categories are defined here. More terms are defined in Appendix E and in books listed in Appendix D.

Equities   A term for common stocks or units of ownership in publicly traded foreign and domestic companies. These may be further defined as to sector, industry, characteristic (growth or value; large, medium, small capitalization), by index (S&P, NASDAQ, Dow, Russell, etc.), and by type (common, voting, nonvoting, preferred, ADR, restricted, 144).

Fixed Income   This is the general term applied to a family of instruments, including bonds or other instruments, that generate a known income stream. These vary in usefulness according to their taxability or tax-exempt character, risk (the higher the risk the higher the coupon rate or yield), or issuing agent (local, state, or federal governments; public companies; or private institutions). Bonds of publicly traded companies range in type from investment grade to junk (high risk/high yield). Convertible bonds are a quasi-fixed-income instrument prior to and regardless of conversion but are also convertible into common stock at a stated price.

Derivatives   A derivative is a financial instrument, often referred to as "risk management," whose value is derived from another underlying security. Although the term has acquired a sinister connotation, simple derivative instruments are important risk-management tools for any sizable money management strategy. Options (put and call) are an inexpensive form of leverage (borrowing) to maximize return and hedge price fluctuation risk. Currency futures are used by individuals, money managers, and corporations to spread risk of currency fluctuations affecting their foreign investments. Others, such as mortgage-backed securities, are unreliably valued.

Commodities   Commodities are bulk goods such as grains, energy products and food animals traded on a commodities exchange. The trades are regulated by their own agency, the Commodities Futures Trading Commission (CFTC). The instruments used are referred to as futures and are sold in the form of a contract with a set delivery date. There are a number of "exchanges" through which trades can be implemented, such as the Chicago Commodities Exchange (COMEX).

Alternative Marketable Securities   These are real estate investment trusts (REITs). Although considered by many as real estate plays, their characteristics more closely resemble common stock than real estate investments. The art of researching the stocks as marketable securities requires a slightly different type of knowledge and sleuth work of the real estate industry. (See Chapter 11, "Real Estate.")

Author's Note: Named managers and institutions are illustrative as examples only and are not in any way preferred or recommended by the author.

ENDNOTES

1. Alan Abelson, "Bank on It," *Up and Down Wall Street, Barron's,* September 1995, p. 5. Reprinted by permission of *Barron's.* © 1995 Dow Jones & Company, Inc. All rights reserved worldwide.
2. Charles D. Ellis, *Investment Policy: How to Win the Loser's Game* (Burr Ridge, Ill.: Irwin Professional Publishing, 1985 and 1993).
3. Donald B. Trone, William R. Albright, and Philip R. Taylor, *The Management of Investment Decisions* (Burr Ridge, Ill.: Irwin Professional Publishing, 1995).
4. Donald B. Trone, "The Hidden Costs of Securities Trading," Family Office Exchange Newsletter, Oak Park, Ill., fourth quarter 1991.

10

VENTURE CAPITAL
Investing in New Ideas

Nor is he the wisest man who never proved himself a fool.

Alfred Lord Tennyson[1]

Nowhere else in the investment world have I found the above Tennyson quote more applicable than in venture capital (VC) investing. Although some will argue, more fools are suffered here than in any other field of investment. Nevertheless, there is irresistible appeal in trying to discover the next Apple Computer, a device to save the ozone, or the recipe for "new" Snapple because of the tremendous financial rewards if the guess is right .

The rule of thumb is that every 10 new venture ideas spawns 1 marginal success. Skeptics submit a formula of 100 to 1. Whatever the chances, when investing in a venture capital fund, single idea, invention, personal start-up, or fund of funds, always determine in advance two things: (1) How much am I willing to lose (because you will)? and (2) Do I have an exit strategy (sometimes that won't work either)? Known also as "risk" capital, VC risk can mean either losses of 100 percent or gains as high as 5,000 percent—a mighty swing in extremes.

I actually never invested more than 5 percent of income in any one year in VC and other special situations combined. Ultimately, I lost all or a portion of every VC investment. We reviewed a range of deals from seed money in huge amounts (too rich for my blood) to restricted stock participation in amounts as low as $30,000 in start-ups. No venture capital fund required less than a $250,000 per unit participation minimum. Consequently, most of my brushes with VC came in the form of entry-level restricted stock in new companies (a short-haul railroad with car leasing and tracking) and technologies (a smokeless cigarette invented by a man dying of lung cancer and a video telephone technology developed by Datapoint alumni). The one VC fund we purchased as a family group is now liquidating after an 11-year holding period, resulting in a tax bill for two minor distributions and losses of 75 percent on the original capital.

Today, "megafunds" are the face of venture capital investing due to large-scale entry into the field by institutional investors acknowledging the advisability of diversification and the value of asset allocation as prudent investment considerations. The capital is rarely start-up, but rather later stage equity capital. The due diligence of fund investing should be just as thorough as if you are directly investing in the product or technology. The lock-up period (an average of 7–10 years) precludes any prior exit strategy if things go south on you. The typical management fee is 2 or 2 ½ percent of invested capital for the duration of the fund. Even when the fund is losing value, management collects their hefty fee. In addition, venture firms collect 20 percent or more of profits on a deal-by-deal basis. Because you are a limited partner, your flexibility will be limited. Only the best venture funds have historically returned 13 percent over the life of the fund.[2]

The advantages of indirect fund of funds investing are the spreading of risk among as many as 20 venture funds for the same amount of capital, limiting the lock-up period to as few as three years (instead of 7–10 years) and having access to otherwise inaccessible investments. As in money manager fund of funds, tax reporting is delayed due to dual partnership reporting (K-1), and there is an extra layer of fees between you and your potential return. Beware of fad investing with players not historically knowledgeable or proven in this asset class.

The art of venture investing is being lost except with entrepreneurs themselves and in investor groups such as Investor's Circle headquartered in Chicago, which was formed to help women learn the business by reviewing deals.

When you invest in anything, your assets are at stake. Expect abuse if you leave decisions to others without doing your homework. Even if there is nothing you can do, at least stay informed so that you understand why and what your options are. If management changes, find out what that means to you as an investor. If the focus of a fund changes from the original prospectus or partnership agreement you signed, ask why and what the ramifications might be. Don't roll over and play dead.

Graeme Henderson has worked in the venture capital arena at every level and ultimately concludes that to be "in" venture capital, a private investor must work in venture capital, not merely invest in it. It is not a passive endeavor. "One of the outstanding dividends is its experience."[3] The principles for VC investing imparted in the following pages are relevant to any kind of investing that you do.

VENTURE INVESTING

Graeme W. Henderson

Venture capital has been a part of human social and economic activity since recorded history. While today the manifestations of VC investing can be immensely complicated, the principles are exactly the same as when primitive humans offered up capital goods for use in someone else's enterprise in exchange for a share of the outcome. I can envision a young hunter at the entrance of a smoky cave requesting the loan of an elder's long-proven spear, promising that, should he live through the foraging expedition, he would compensate the elder with a fresh sloth's haunch. The secret of success is risk assessment for both hunter and elder, or entrepreneur and capitalist, as it were.

The lure of venture capital lies in the expectation of disproportionately large investment returns. VC's "leveler" lurks in the limitless ways in which some or all of each investment can be lost. How does a prospective VC investor sort through the relevant factors in order to make sensible decisions? How does the prospective investor even determine what the relevant factors are?

At another conceptual level, and very basically, why should a person step into a risky investment arena like venture capital if he or she has enough inherited or earned money to be securely comfortable without having to be employed? Risk is, after all, by most standards, the antithesis of "comfortable." Why not practice pain avoidance and stick with Prudent Man, diversified, high-quality liquid securities? What's the benefit of vast investment success—to be doubly or quadrupally comfortable—whatever that may mean?

If the objective is greed, more power, castles around the world, elevated social position, or building a worthy institution, inviting risk into one's home may be worth the price of exposure. One of the nice aspects of risk is that, to some extent, it can be sized and shaped by those dealing with it. Unlike predestination, ministers skilled in the art can affect events to shrink risk and improve outcomes.

Risk, like opportunity, seldom comes with a label, a set of instructions, or a roll of blueprints. Like addressing the Almighty, one is unable to gaze directly into the face of risk in order to gauge its appearance, size, shape, attitude, dynamics, and so on. One can only postulate, extrapolate, and speculate about current and future risk characteristics. Risk consists of a series of evolving factors, only coming into some degree of focus after the fact. This aspect is educationally valuable but not especially practical as a guide for action because one invests today to achieve outcomes from largely uncontrollable events in the future.

Knowledge, experience, creativity plus a daredevil flair, and the willingness to use these skills and attributes assertively are key in attempting to domesticate risk. Probably the most overlooked benefits of VC investing are the maturity and skills one develops in learning techniques for coping with risk. Anyone, even the dopiest and laziest of individuals, can cope with prosperity. Dealing well with adversity and serious trouble, risk's first cousins, is entirely another matter. Sooner or later, everyone faces a severe adversity. It is obviously wiser to confront a tough situation with foreknowledge than with innocence.

Pursuing a regimen of regular and challenging exercises is correctly accepted as an appropriate way to enhance one's physical condition. A similar approach toward strengthening one's mental abilities, self-confidence, and maturity is valid. Wrestling with risk and adversity in a dynamic but nondamaging environment in unfamiliar surroundings is a fine approach for any but the faint of heart to accrete the mental "muscle tone" that adds power to one's ability to make decisions—not merely decisions relating to business, but to all aspects of life. For the introspective, few better paths exist to lead someone in his or her 20s and 30s with a conventional education, upbringing, and initial business exposure toward the pinnacle of self-understanding and taking full responsibility over one's own life.

Conventional education consists largely of being exposed to compressed experience. Receiving the benefit of education can only come through one's absorption of vicarious and lived experiences. Education is expensive. (If you doubt this point, ask anyone who is paying tuition at top-grade secondary and collegiate institutions.) Likewise, experience is expensive in all the ways we know. Here is an important rule to live by: Gain your education and experience on someone else's money!

Accepting this rule is common sense to many, as is the flip side of the admonition. In venture capital investing, avoid letting others learn on your money! They would have gained something, but your lost money is unable to earn itself back.

There are, however, two ways such an approach (giving your money to someone else to use or lose) makes monetary sense. One is for you to have learned valuable lessons otherwise unavailable without the association with the other participants. The second is for you to secure a long-term association with those learning in the trenches and let their enriching experiences lessen your collective investment risk in the future. In that way, you stand a chance of earning disproportionately high returns on the money remaining at your disposal and being better off financially than if you had invested conservatively all along.

A seemingly plausible approach to VC investing constitutes buying small interests in a number of VC syndicates in order to lessen one's aggregate risk. To me, that is silly. If risk invites you to the dance, show off your fanciest terpsichorean steps. Don't sit out the waltzes with the wallflowers beside the punchbowl. If it's timid you want, stay home.

Venture capital investing at its most basic level is an active, not passive, pursuit. Unlike making the majority of your portfolio decisions between nine and five in your own office as can normally be done with most publicly traded securities, with venture capital placements, one needs to be out in the world where businesses actually operate. The word sedentary is not in the VC investor's lexicon, neither for the portfolio manager nor the investor behind the portfolio. If he decides to lend his spear, the elder would be wise to tag along on the hunt. After all, a good sloth is hard to bag, especially for a young hunter working alone.

TODAY'S VENTURE CAPITAL LANDSCAPE

The 1994 annual review of the National Venture Capital Association (NVCA) states that in the United States, about $35 billion of venture capital is currently under management. That number is impressively up about tenfold over the last 15–20 years. Evidently, half of the fresh capital comes from pension funds. The $35 billion is spread over approximately 600 portfolios, the majority of which are limited partnerships. About 30 percent are under $10 million in size, while 6–8 percent are over $200 million. Their appetites for individual investment positions would appear to range from $100 thousand to $50 million for the largest capital pools.

The bulk of the aggregate funds' growth has been in the larger funds. Their size dictates such jumbo individual placements that rarely are those pools involved in start-up or near start-up companies. More likely, they are seen to specialize in leveraged buyouts, which, while many times proving lucrative, suggest a type of investing more in the nature of merchant banking than traditional venture capital. The latter typically associates with the growth of products, concepts, and services, not facilitating of ownership changes of stable business enterprises using leverage to elevate risk and potential return. In many ways, explosive growth of these funds resulted from the unwillingness of banks to take expansion capital risks in the 1980s banking crisis. Many entrepreneurs had to bow to this situation, giving up some ownership to the funds to ensure growth of their companies.

Impossible to count are the individual pools of active money going into small ventures all around us. Tallying their total economic value is also impossible. A comfortable speculation takes the sum to

a multiple of the earlier stated $35 billion. Add to that private acqui-
sitions and privately syndicated leveraged buyouts and the multiple
probably grows into double digits.

Venture capital industry composite investment returns reported
by the NVCA on portfolios they follow averaged 11.5 percent annually for the 20 years through 1993, and 10.0 percent for the 10 years
through 1993. For the effort and risk involved in VC investing, these
results are hardly impressive and are probably not out of line with
returns from more liquid, institutionally managed portfolios composed of old, large international companies with household names
such as GE, P&G, and 3M.

Like all averages, the laggards offset the winners, and some of
the winners have been spectacular. Their successes obviously buoy
the reputation of the industry. Skill, hard work, and luck trump a
plenitude of resources shackled by bad luck.

If there is any common denominator to VC portfolios, it is di-
versity. Almost any kind of business, goods, and services can be found
among the commitments made. While many VC firms tend to specialize in industry specific companies such as technology, there are
more who are opportunistically oriented. Such widespread differences in businesses demands broad investment knowledge plus an
ability to learn quickly.

Properly applied, venture capital can create many new jobs as a
by-product. For those licensed as small business investment companies (SBICs), and closed end investment companies, paperwork and
rule-following seem also to be by-products. The bulk of VC portfolios, though, are unfettered by tight government regulation and hence
are more able to approach investment opportunities and challenges
flexibly.

There does not seem to be any rule of thumb as to whether VC
investors usually take financial control of the business in which they
invest or leave the majority of stock ownership with management
and prior investors. There are so many different issues and aspects
of each investment that no formula could be devised to derive the
proper equity balance between investor and management. Experience, judgment about relationships, instinct, and a clear crystal ball—
and luck—furnish the answers.

THE ACTIVIST VENTURE CAPITAL EXPERIENCE

Unless you are terribly lucky, one of your first realizations will be that losses tend to turn up early. Profits normally require longer to develop. The natural outgrowth is early stage discouragement and doubt as to whether to make future investments. One must recognize, accept, and plan around the initial round of disappointments. Unless you are prepared to persist and build a fair-sized portfolio, you will deny the law of averages and your own judgment a reasonable chance of working for you.

If your entry into VC is via only one or two local investments, emotional well-being is better served by sticking with enterprises, management, and partners that you know. Your objective should be to minimize risk while gaining experience in the new investing endeavor. With confidence, you can step up the risk and targeted rate of return as you see fit.

What results can you expect from 10 typical investments out of an average portfolio of at least several dozen positions acquired over a 10-year time period? One big winner plus a couple more that show moderate to attractive capital gains. Several more will return their investments and a little interest or dividends along the way. Of those remaining, two or three will be wipeouts and the other(s) will be losers.

One of the best ways of earning a substantial multiple on your initial investment in an operating company is to stick with it indefinitely so long as it continues to perform. Normally, one should expect growth rates to taper off as a company hits its stride and achieves a certain degree of maturity. A doubling of value over a six-year period equates to a compound return of 12–13 percent. If you have already achieved a 20/1 value ratio over the original investment, taking it to 40/1 in another six years and perhaps to 80/1 over the ensuing six years should not cause the Financial Analysts Society to toss you out for nonperformance. Assuming the risk level for the investment runs less than 12 percent, which suggests that the position should remain a "hold," consider that you are merely banking an enlarging pool of cash to redeploy into higher risk VC placements sometime in the future.

Similar logic applies to the non-VC investing world. San Francisco's redoubtable Philip A. Fisher, author of *Common Stocks and Uncommon Profits,* has practiced for over 60 years the art of managing an equity portfolio of few holdings with turnover measured in decades. His research on corporate managements might be termed as intense; his investment results are unchallenged.

An important caveat to remember: Letting an investment roll because of an aversion to paying capital gains tax is a pernicious trap. Tax planning over the short run makes sense. For the long run, investment judgment must be the dominant factor in deciding the retention of the portfolio position.

VC investing is an active discipline, a rolled-up sleeves activity. The action happens out where the operating companies function, where they make their sales calls, and where they produce their goods and services. That's where one needs to be. Expecting to run a VC portfolio while sitting in an executive tower office in downtown New York is a mistake. Introverts do not generally make successful VC investors—nor do the sedentary.

As in the other aspects of life, one should not enter a VC situation without first considering how to get out of it. Usually, the really large VC portfolio gains come cyclically with strong IPO markets and aggressive corporate acquisition trends. With both financial and emotional staying power, one can time liquidations with superior market conditions. Many dispositions occur as part of strategic moves that are unrelated to general economic cycles. Although the bulk of visible VC money has sunset provisions because of partnership arrangements and thus bears self-induced pressure to liquidate, long-term VC investors functioning with their own money should not hobble themselves with pressure to liquidate positions prematurely. Admittedly an extreme example, Capital Southwest Corporation has retained a position in TCI since 1969, despite many opportunities to take a profit from selling the stock. Current value of the position exceeds $3 million; the cost was $68.

One of the most difficult decisions in VC investing revolves around the expression "throwing good money after bad." It's obvious that doing so is foolish. But how does one know what is foolish? Is success just around the corner or two corners? Who really knows? So many evolving companies have required round after round of financing, many times with a wolf at their doors. Some have succeeded; many have not.

One always has an array of reasons why fresh money should be invested, plus a host of reasons why the rat hole is real. Tangible factors never rule those decisions. What really rules are subjective elements: how the investor feels about management and their performance, and about the prospects for the product and the industry; what people believe competition may be scheming; where the next round of financing will come from (if the availability is not probable, kill the project now!); and so on and so forth.

Two major elements combine in enhancing one's subjective powers. The first is how well you are in touch with your own feelings, and derivatively, how well you understand the character, mental processes, and qualities of others involved in the investment. The second is how closely you have followed the company, the principals, the industry, and the various other factors relating to the possible success or failure of the business. Knowledge and clarity of vision lessen risk and enhance the quality of judgment. Properly applied effort on your part can improve both.

On the subject of decision making under conditions of uncertainty and ambiguity, seasoned judgments seldom come from callow MBA graduates. A plausible, well-organized rationale for a decision has only marginal value if unreinforced with pertinent experience. Rely on your own instincts.

Making sharp deals runs counter to sound VC investing. Squeezing your future partners, the management of the venture you are preparing to fund, is patently counterproductive. If management has an excessively high opinion of their enterprise's value and the only way to get it into line is to negotiate management's back to the wall, decline the opportunity and move on to something else. How would you feel if an investor put the squeeze on you? As you operated the business, would you think about getting even? Bad feelings lead to unhappy investments. Remember the Golden Rule and live by it, even if you get shafted more times than not. If management capitulated because they knew that the quality of their business was less than they were leading you to believe, you may unwittingly be receiving a free lesson about deficient analysis on your part. Why turn the experience into a potentially expensive lesson?

A continuing challenge in life is to decide how much to discount what people tell you. Anyone presenting their company for investment is going to exaggerate. That's a given. Instinct will guide you. It is up to you whether to accept the amount of exaggeration or to reject the exaggerator. Where does a hopeful opinion or a wish phase into a lie? Determining that point is one of the delicious challenges of VC investing. You can never ask enough questions from independent sources who know the people presenting the deal.

A common phenomenon you will encounter is the high estimation of the founder's own value held by many young, creative engineers and computer geniuses. Egosphere makes their idea of a fair equity split of their concept as being worth 80–90 percent to your total risk of $5 million as worth 10–20 percent. In fact, that might be a fair arrangement, but let someone else with the money and time to waste make the investment.

The term "vulture capitalist" primarily comes out of these very high self-valuations. But by and large, inexperienced entrepreneurs misinterpret the market's valuation of their positions and become incensed that prospective investors refuse to buy into their fantasies.

Prospective investments are everywhere all the time. To be a successful VC investor, being continuously alert to opportunities is a major advantage. Even small farm towns have surprisingly large and sophisticated companies engineering and manufacturing equipment for the world market. Some of the largest specialized metal grinding equipment in the United States, for example, is located on the banks of the Missouri River in Atchison, Kansas, owned by a company formed through a leveraged buy-out. Not all nifty small companies are located in the Chicago suburbs or Silicon Valley.

Supply and demand play a role in VC investing. Too many venture capitalists with fresh cash to invest will tend to worsen the terms available from attractive companies in search of capital. Those are the times to align yourself with borrowers (ideally someone you have already invested with) and take advantage of investors competing to get their money working rapidly. If you have a natural adversity to competition, spreading your contacts over a variety of industries and locations should produce some nonmainstream prospects undetected by the VC herd.

There is a lot to be said for going in a different direction from the majority in almost any business. Consider a thoughtfully analyzed and understood course that runs across or against the conventional grain. Explore some of the more respectable literature on the subject. Your perspective (accompanied by your portfolio) will be enriched. For example, some of the best areas to find interesting start-up companies are near dramatically downsized large companies (leading to a weak localized economy) where energetic, qualified people are laid off. Ideas created in an unaccepting environment are strikingly mobile. When Datapoint reorganized in the early 1980s, small, brainy technology start-ups sprang up all over San Antonio, Texas, led by research scientists with empty pockets but heads full of good ideas.

One of the most valuable contributions a VC investor can bring to an operating company is an understanding of the changing management requirements as a business grows. All too frequently the power and vision of a small business exists in the genius of one person. Knowing what kinds of pressures form in a company as it goes to market with its first product, adds staff, moves across borders, sets up delegated decision making, or prepares for an acquisition or major diversification can activate early warning systems, suggesting key issues for discussion and decision among the directors and management group. Stephen Jobs was the right person to start Apple computer, but John Scully was the right one to take it to the next level.

In a competitive VC environment, your solid reputation of constructive relationships with current and past investee companies can be the determining factor in inducing prospective investees to select you as a financial partner and advisor instead of all the others. Being a patsy in negotiations and passive as a board member is not supportive of the enterprise nor of your reputation as an investor. Behave as an active, fair-minded, and consistent partner to broaden your reputation.

A huge proportion of the success of any business enterprise depends upon management. Striding into the unknown, as is the characteristic of most small and rapidly growing businesses, enlarges the dependence upon management and generally upon the CEO alone as prime visionary and motivator. The VC investor's ability to make sound judgments about management will directly translate into portfolio performance.

Your task is to rapidly enhance your ability to a better than satisfactory level of assessment and judgment without the experience costing you too much. The way to gain experience is simply to step up and make judgments, invest your money, and take ongoing responsibility for your decisions. If you are in the operating company loop, you will have a continuing ability to affect corporate directions and management's approach to handling those directions. Correcting your mistakes on the fly is your finest classroom. Remember the truism: Every solution bears the seeds of another problem. The classroom holds a never-ending series of lessons and quizzes. Boredom is not a factor.

Always set up checks and balances in the operating entity between members of management, between management and the directors, and between the company and its investors. That is as prudent as having the controller report to the board of directors. Having disagreements bubble up to the top is critically better than allowing them to be choked off under the corporate mantle out of view of the full group of partners, including directors and investors. Bringing broad perspectives to important decisions is infinitely superior than the opposite approach. Many, if not most, CEOs will normally gravitate toward calling all the shots, letting the directors assume the role of rubber stamp—not smart for the business.

Success in the VC business can cause some unpleasant headaches. Assuming that your investment entity has some younger participants with carried interests, portfolio profits can build reasonable net worths for them. Wealth leads to independence. It also enhances appetites, so the staff you have paid to educate themselves may be able and desirous of leaving to start their own VC firm, perhaps in competition with yours. Staff turnover may or may not be a positive factor. When it happens, be prepared for the fallout of steep learning curves with new staff members.

Departures of young, recently enriched staff members isn't inevitable. If they have become close to the "family," enjoy the work environment, have been encouraged to stretch their wings, and are able to invest with the partners in the next round of placements, the probability of the solid ones remaining goes up substantially.

Another interesting phenomenon associates with a burgeoning

portfolio. Assume the good fortune that in 10 years an initial $20 million VC investment has grown to $120 million. Your per investment range would be something like $0.5–1.2 million, suggesting 30 fully invested positions. With $120 million, you really don't want to expand the portfolio to 180 positions. You are then forced to allocate larger amounts per investment, increasing your range from $3 million to $8 million to maintain the manageable position balance. Investing in those amounts is a thoroughly different business than that in the original plan. Assuming you want the same equity position in each company, the size, maturity, and characteristics of investee companies won't be in keeping with original strategy.

The question is what to do when your original approach has been so successful. Do you throw away momentum and shift to the next level of VC challenges? Are you as comfortable placing $5 million bets as $0.5 million ones? Have you found that stepping into larger positions is more profitable? Is there more competition from other financing sources at that level? Are you prepared for a new learning curve with the larger dollars associated with that educational experience? Are you about to break in a new, untried staff on these larger positions (the old staff having cashed in their chips and founded their own firms)? Should you pare off $75 million into a conventional equities portfolio and continue your VC operation with the same investment policies as before?

Letting your changed perspective suck you into a different investment area can be inadvertently foolish. Yet people fall into the trap. It's like pledging the last fraternity that asks you. Don't let prosperity change your behavior. That's adversity's job. Prosperity says, "Congratulations, you are doing things right." So there must be some compelling reason to consider changing. And there might be. In the meantime, it isn't wise to fix what doesn't appear to be broken.

Boredom occasionally creeps into one's life despite the pleasure of success. If boredom is driving your need to change the nature of the business perhaps unwisely, look outside the business for stimulation. Take up flying, or painting, or leading seminars in archeology. Enrich your mind and create satisfactions from new and different directions. Tossing away a major asset wrapped up in knowledge, momentum, and success is goofy. Rebalance your life so the asset business assumes a lesser focus.

One of the perverse balances in VC investing is that people spend multiples of time working through a troubled investment over that spent on a successful one to make it better. That may not be cost effective, but it is human nature. Be prepared for the uncovered overhead and look upon it as valuable experience. At the same time, heed the sound of warning bells. In our age of litigiousness, spare yourself grief by maintaining a sharp, street-wise attorney at hand (but not on staff) when dealing with trouble.

Another very natural trait lies in failing to unbundle motives. Muddy decision making and troublesome portfolios are usually the outcome. Distill all your motives down to singular, indivisible motives. Assess each one. Apply a value to each. Line them up neatly and look at them honestly. Making an investment because it looks like another you had success with before, because it will enhance your image in Rotary or at the country club, because other prominent VC firms are taking lead positions (so why bother analyzing the situation from your perspective?), because the industry is currently hot in the IPO market, and so on, may skew your portfolio toward the direction of charity unless you are graced with a celestial amount of luck.

TAKING ACTION

Shun passive VC partnerships unless managed solely by an experienced and successful relative or old friend in whom you have a huge amount of faith. Even then, controlling management should have been in the VC business at least 15–20 years, enough to have been through at least one major trough in the economic cycle. Research their background carefully and thoroughly. Your money will go into a blind pool, which is to say that you have no idea what investments will be made until after you have ceded control of your cash for 10 years or so. If your prospective investment is substantial both in amount and in percentage of your total net worth, you will make a jumbo commitment. Be exceedingly cautious. You are moving in an exceedingly high-risk area.

If you simply have to have a part of a VC portfolio, buy a few shares in one of the publicly trading VC firms, such as Capital Southwest Corporation. Most are fully invested, and you are able to assess not only the portfolio behind the stock but also how seasoned management performs. This feature eliminates several layers of risk. Besides that, you aren't locked in contractually for a decade, more or less.

You might be a person who thinks long term and multigenerationally. Your wealth came from a successful entrepreneur father or grandfather. You would like to build extraordinary wealth in somewhat the same way for your children and grandchildren, but you don't see yourself running an operating business, making sales calls, negotiating with unions, going to trade shows, and the like. The role of a participating investor in a number of different kinds of enterprises would be more to your liking.

Start by doing your own research. Secure all the literature on the subject you can find and absorb it. Buy a respectable block of stock in each of several of the more interesting publicly trading VC firms. Then go to visit the managements of each. Learn from them. Meet other VC investors and limited partners managing VC pools and learn from them. Determine to your own satisfaction what qualities are successful in a VC investor and what qualities inhibit success.

Follow your nose. If you become sincerely comfortable with what you are learning and feel as though venture capital is an area for you, determine what your active or, at least, semi-active role would be in directing your VC investment program and keep moving ahead. If the way to proceed is at all unclear and uncomfortable, back off and avoid venture capital as a major commitment.

Almost invariably, moving ahead will be accomplished only in conjunction with one or several partners who are experienced with venture capital. Choose them well. You will be sharing a lot of time and wild experiences with them—perhaps even champagne every now and then—or barbecued sloth.

ENDNOTES

1. Alfred Lord Tennyson, *Locksley Hall Sixty Years After,* St. 124.

2. Gene Bylinski, "Who Will Feed The Startups?" *Fortune,* June 26, 1995, pp. 98–106. © Time Inc. All rights reserved.

3. Graeme W. Henderson, letter to author, 24 November 1995. Mr. Henderson is a venture capitalist in Pasadena, Calif.

11

REAL ESTATE

The American Dream

Personal experience taught me the inside meaning of "land poor"—having too much land to the exclusion of other, more liquid assets with which to pay the associated costs of keeping and tending it. When the core asset is based on land ownership and the income must support the family as well as the land, production costs, and taxes, seeking additional investments in raw land doesn't really make a lot of economic sense. I've heard it referred to as a twist to "the golden monkey trap." You stick your hand into the trap to get the gold, but you can't pull it out without either losing your hand or letting go of the gold. Owning other classes, such as income-generating real estate, will have to offset a lack of liquidity if real estate is the primary asset class. But presumably, if you are reading this book, especially this chapter, you do have at least some resources that you might want to devote to a real estate investment or two. For the purposes of this chapter, the emphasis is on *direct* investment in the asset class, not passive investing in real estate investment trusts (REITs).

Real estate comes into a life in several ways. You can inherit it, you can win it in a property settlement, you can get into it because you think you would like to do so, or you can approach it from a process that begins with a financial plan and a targeted investment policy. There is no straightforward way to describe real estate investing in a short chapter. Instead, I assume that you want to get some fundamental information about the subject because people are approaching you to invest, because you have financial, legal, and tax advisors that suggest you consider acquiring some investment real estate, or because you don't know anything about some that you already have.

When you evaluate any specific deal, especially when entering an unfamiliar asset class, you need several resources from which to draw. Ideally, you should have a basic education in the field you are considering. If you don't have that, you need really good technical advice from trustworthy, independent advisors. By that, I mean that you need to talk to someone who does not have a vested interest in seeing you buy into the deal. Real estate attorneys with technical evaluation skills can be very useful and worth the expense over the long term. Two perspectives are better than one because there are so many ways to enter this investment field. If you have already done your investment planning as suggested in earlier chapters, you have a grasp of your overall investment goals and of your risk tolerance. Presumably, you have some comfort level with the investment type or else you wouldn't be considering it. To eliminate much of the guesswork, you will have done a background and due diligence check on the reputation of the fellow venturers.

To begin, jot this down: Investing in a real estate deal is like opening a box of Whitman Samplers and finding no labels in the top—it will not be what you thought you were getting into. Depending on the market, you can basically expect any real estate investment to be long-term, cyclical, more expensive than you originally expected, and to be situated somewhere within a broad spectrum of available opportunities ranging from the extremely conservative to the highly speculative.

The real estate business has changed in the past 10 years. The 1986 tax act closed many loopholes, making speculative real estate ventures and historic preservation and rehabilitation projects less attractive. The bank and S&L failures further tightened available credit, putting thousands of real estate projects into play, thus glutting the market in many regions of the country. Also, in these years of controlled growth and low inflation following years of high inflation, land as an inflation hedge is a failed expectation. The factors that affect us are global and thus more distant from our spheres of control. Weighing return on underlying asset value is less reliable and accurate than ever before. The economics of change force land developers, stewards, and managers to be more efficient and cost-conscious producers.

Today, projecting real estate returns or expected rent increases, land values, or turnover rates in a given sector, such as apartments in Western states, is not like shooting fish in a barrel. Rather, it is more like shooting craps in Las Vegas. If anyone claims to be able to predict these with certitude, suggest that they take a large chunk of Rockefeller Center off of your hands and see how fast they leave the room. Even though the potential for success is affected by many factors, you must first investigate local, investment-specific market conditions. In 1995 alone, the return on REITs (the most liquid and most comparable to other tradable investments) was 8.8 percent versus a return of 28 percent in the equities markets, a reflection of vast differences in location, quality, and market segment of the underlying assets.

As in the oil and gas industry, ardent commitment to real estate investing often goes far beyond the economics of the industry. If that were not so, the cyclicality of the business would have ended many real estate careers. As a nation, our attachment to the land is deep. Love affairs with the wilderness that national parks cannot satisfy also feed the passion. But by and large, for the individual investor who is seeking only to add diversification to his or her portfolio to offset cyclical and systemic risks in their other asset classes, real estate is generally not well understood or as profitable as other assets over time. It is simply the oldest asset there is. Now if you are planning on going into the business as a business, not as an investment, then it can be very profitable for you. The purpose of this chapter is to discuss real estate as an investment, not real estate as a business.

A friend's entrance into the real estate development business grew out of an off-hand investment request. Enjoying Lake Travis as a college student, Beth Robertson Morian was interested in buying a lot on the lake. Instead, her family's financial advisor found the 1,200 acre Davenport Ranch on Lake Austin—neither a single lot nor on Lake Travis. It was purchased through the Robertson Family Trust for her and her four siblings in undivided interests.

Their story is not unusual. Decisions about land are often random and circumstantial, even visceral. As a result, many investors approach the real estate market without a discipline for hard research. More than 30 years later, after many twists and turns in her own life and the economic life of the state of Texas, Morian has made a career of developing that ranch land for herself and her family. She didn't set out to do it that way, but by honing her powers of observation, trusting her instincts, and having basic information-gathering skills, she increased her knowledge base and learned from her mistakes. She now carries on in her work, developing the land as a good model for anyone investing in the business who chooses to make it a business.

On the other hand, if you have a stomach for risk you can be comfortable as an active investor even if you are behind the learning curve. The real estate business is particularly prone to market risk (see the discussion of the Prudent Investor Rule presented in Chapter 4). The last bust, which occurred over 10 years ago, is only just now beginning to fade. Most successful people in the business didn't come into it as clairvoyants, able to predict the cycles, and even the most experienced have been knocked down at least once in their real estate careers. Trammel Crow, Gerald Hines, the James Rouse Companies, and many others have learned equally from their failures as from their successes. But there is a big difference between being in the business and investing in the business.

My assumption is that you have little or no knowledge about real estate investing and that you have no intention of going into the real estate business. What you need is very basic information to begin a more targeted education process for potentially becoming an investor. I am not going to describe the business or how it works; it is too multifaceted and diverse to do that in a small space. I approach this chapter as a skeptic because my background is one of having had too much tied up in agricultural real estate, over which I had no control for too long. I am not a real estate developer nor do I put deals together. As a result, I am an investor who went into real estate to diversify my portfolio at a time when the Texas real estate scene was on fire and nobody was losing.

Understanding the common variables that impact the nature of a piece of real estate other than cost would have led me to decide differently (to invest in income-producing, low-risk projects with industry partners) about when and how and if to enter the field at all. My inherited, land-poor portfolio greatly influenced my choices.

General measures can be taken of all real estate investment deals, some to be performed in advance, others only when you are already in an investment, that will classify a deal for you but will not help you decide one way or the other about it. Because real estate is local and has to fit your goals, specific advice is not going to help you much. Knowledge of the fundamentals of real estate investing comes from defining and measuring the deal with these aids.

REAL ESTATE VARIABLES

Location, Location, Location. Location *is* real estate, and investment real estate is always local. The most important factors you need to know are locked in a real estate location. Explore the environment of the location—economics, politics, demographics, climates, esthetics, traffic patterns, market desirability, and so forth. The list is long and is rarely truly complete. Regardless of whether it is raw land, a shopping center, an apartment building, or a duck pond, you can never know enough about the location. If you are not reviewing your own deals, you still need to know everything you can about the location if you are considering throwing your money into it. If you haven't done this, you might as well stop now and forget about investing in real estate.

Consider the following simple deal. Then, apply the variables from Figure 11.1 to the deal. Let's call it paper practice.

A real estate broker, a personal friend you have known for several years, comes to you with a deal (simple deal) to invest in 210 acres of agriculturally classified land on the edge of a smallish (population 25,000) town (Smalltown). On one side of the near perfect square is a frontage road of a major interstate highway, on a second side is a small river, on the third is a farm-to-market road, and in the back is more farmland. The land is not cheap to buy, but the growth of the whole region is brisk. The taxes are low because it has a firm agricultural lease on its surface; thus, it enjoys agricultural exemption on the local tax rolls. Two major growing cities are located on either side of the small town along that same highway. One is within 20 miles (Northcity) and the other is 40 miles away (Southcity). People are complaining about the congestion in both of them and are voicing desires to move to a smaller place within commuting distance of the opportunities these cities afford them. The highway frontage between these two cities is dotted with light industrial installations like WalMart distribution centers and the occasional mega car sales lot, but mostly it is rolling farmland with the occasional small creek or river running through it. The rivers are prone to flash flooding once a year or so from upriver downpours, but some years they don't flood at all. The parcel is too big for you, but not if there are other partners to share the deal. Your children can also participate, if the risk is deemed low enough. Based on current trends in the region, land of this type is expected to turn over within two to five years. Although priced at the upper end of the market, if marketed properly, the after-tax, cash-on-cash return, annualized over two to five years, should range from 10 to 15 percent. The broker doesn't even want a commission at closing. He says he'll take it plus a net-profits interest only when the land is sold.

Now, look at the variables that influence Simple Deal viability. Your investigation might look something like this. Assess the variable according to what you do know, and then consider a possible unknown that might change that variable.

The location sounds good. What is the location? Well, it is on a river. It is just off of a highway. It is near two growing cities with lots of opportunity. It is across the road from a light industrial installation and half a mile from a huge Wal-Mart regional distribution center. See how it goes? There is much more to divine about location, but that is how you start. At this point, it sounds really promising, doesn't it? Can you think of a downside for this location? The city could condemn the land to build a highway interchange; as a result, you couldn't sell it off in parcels to realize the return. At least you will get what it is worth at the time. The downside of location appears to be limited.

Look at the people variables. Population levels appear to be strong. This is a good-sized, growing town that is near growing cities where young families are having and raising children. It is not stagnating or shrinking. There is no downside here. The unknown might be an unforeseen economic downturn, but all of the prognosticators call for the highway corridor region to continue booming for the foreseeable future. Warning: Always question anyone with clairvoyance, especially real estate people.

There is no information about the prevailing interest rates for financing the purchase, nor have you paid much attention to the banking climate. That is something you will have to explore. After you do that, you should review the location factor again in that context. Are they lending on land in this location? The downside analysis has to wait.

FIGURE 11.1

Some Expected Variables that Affect Real Estate Investments

- Location
- Demographic and employment shifts.
- Population levels.
- Interest rates.
- Location.
- Investment quality.
- Investment structure.
- Holding period.
- Type of real estate.
- Environmental impact.
- Location.
- Saturation and vacancy rates (supply and demand).
- Staying power in a lengthy downturn.
- Government policy.
- Weather and natural disasters.

The investment quality is pretty straightforward—land is good in this area. It is good-quality land given what you are buying it for—resale with a short time horizon. There is one minor problem caused by location near a flooding river. You wonder how much is useless due to flood plain exposure. On the surface, there are no hidden costs, at least according to what you have been told so far. But you will get more information if the other criteria hold up and don't tube the deal for you in the meantime. Mark this one down as "needs further investigation."

This type of real estate—raw land—has flexibility. All you will have in it is land cost and taxes for the holding period, which will be low because of the agricultural (ag) exemption. You can decide later about whether to add infrastructure costs to make it more salable. The risk of that is low if the turnover period is short. Even if you have to put more money in to make it more salable, you can just take it out of the sales proceeds. Your up-front costs might be big, but you will have the cash from the sale to handle them. You would have to wait and see about this variable.

The investment structure, at this point, is simple—cash. You will have to figure out how you want to pay for it. The options are borrowing it, partnering with others, or some other way. (Borrowing is good if done right and if the banks are fair.) Interest is tax deductible as an investment expense. There are no brokerage commissions. That might fit into your tax and cash-flow planning just fine. Partnering might be a problem if your individual objectives deviate, so getting good partners will be important. The downside is limited by good partners.

The holding period is two to five years. That is a reasonable time period to be without that capital for other things. The downside would be if all the assumptions fail and the land is still sitting there 10 years later, long after you need the return for liquidity.

The type of real estate is raw agricultural land of a reasonably marketable size and location with development potential. Will anyone want to buy it without you changing the character of the land, such as by investing a whole lot more in it to situate it as a development property rather than raw land? Do you risk changing your purpose? The city might change the zoning. You will have to monitor the political climate.

The environmental impact of the property is minimal. The fact that it is on a river that floods means it will need to be analyzed for runoff contamination possibilities. This might require a study and the associated costs. The downside is that the land could be condemned if the impact study warrants it. You don't think that is very likely, but is there a field office for the Army Corps of Engineers in the region to which you could direct your questions? Another piece for further investigation.

Now you know what is meant by location, location, location.

The saturation and vacancy rates don't apply unless the land is zoned commercial office or residential. You need to look into that. A potential buyer might want to put up a planned community or an apartment complex here for all of those young commuter families, but there might be plenty of those already around here. This isn't the town you live in so you don't know it that well. You should talk to the broker and find out what he knows about this.

You have staying power. You will, if you can, lay off part of the deal and do your cash-flow and investment planning. Even if the land doesn't sell in the expected time, or if you have to negotiate an unfavorable loan, you think you can stay with it for at least 10 years. Surely the land will sell in 10 years. You should find out what the "worst case" evaluation might show.

Governmental policies in the town are favorable to growth and development. You also know that the city north of here has a strict no-growth city council. It is a university town, famous for its changing mind and its liberal city council. That will be good for this property. Pent-up demand in Northcity seems to have people wanting to stay close but out of that strict jurisdiction. The downside is that the government policy could change again in Northcity in the election two years from now or that the friends in high places that the real estate broker has in Smalltown could be thrown out of office, requiring him to make new contacts to keep you informed. But you can't imagine that happening.

You know that the weather can be unpredictable around here. Those flash floods can really be a problem. You will get a survey to tell you what percentage of the property is unusable due to flooding. Then you will have to see what the cost might be for bringing in landfill to make it more attractive to a buyer. The broker should be able to tell you both the high side and low side of the cost for fill.

CLASSIFYING THE INVESTMENT

Assume that you like what you know about Simple Deal but you want to know how it will specifically fit into your plan for you and your children. You still don't have all of the details, but using these measurements, you will begin to formulate a palatable investment. This set of measurements can be applied before you buy or can be used for monitoring an investment you already have. It simply tells you if a deal satisfies your investment goals and objectives—if you have set them. Not all classification measures apply at all times to all investments, but as an investor, you will use them all at some point. They are a starting place. They are in no particular sequence. All of the measures give you fundamental information to decide if you choose to venture beyond the scope of this chapter into sophisticated deals.

Classification Measurements

The Spectrum: Conservative to Speculative

All real estate deals line up along this spectrum. Knowing the difference between what is considered conservative or speculative comes from experience, from getting advice, and from listening to your gut. A spectrum test is differentiating between buying a leased-up building in excellent condition with credit worthy tenants who have long-term leases in a healthy region in a growing Sunbelt state, and investing in raw land with no improvements on which to build a new office building in an untested or depressed market such as a shrinking suburb of Detroit after the auto industry has downsized. Find the differing ranges of risks between buying and flipping raw land in an overheated market (such as Denver during the oil boom of the early 1980s), and buying low for a long-term hold in a solid growth area (a growing retiree state like Florida). There are many options between the extremes. Comparing opportunities with different levels of risk is not wise. Apples should not be compared with oranges, even when many variables might be similar. Much of this you can get from talking to people in the business or to advisors. As an example, Simple Deal, as presented here, is relatively speculative for the price even though the location seems ideal because there is a lot of vacant land where it is located and a lot of speculators in the contiguous market region. There is also no plan for whether to develop or prepare for development. You don't know enough about its prospects to consider it anything less than moderately speculative, especially for the children's trusts. That would require trustee approval.

Risk Level

The lowest risk, most passive approach to real estate is owning stock market positions in land-rich companies such as Wal-Mart and the rail companies, such as Union Pacific and Burlington Northern Santa Fe, who globally own their own stores, distribution centers, and rights of way respectively. Almost as passive, but not risk free, are REITs, which act more like common stocks in the marketplace. You can better control your time horizon and downside risk in the event of a market downturn. You have a quick exit strategy available. However to make it worth the risk, the potential return must be exponentially greater on a speculative investment than on a conservative one. On a basis of lowest risk being a 1 and highest risk a 5, Simple Deal is around a 3 ½.

Stated Goals of Involvement

Are you planning on ranching or farming a property; being a passive, limited investor; or being active in development or commercial properties? What are your goals? To bind a far-flung family together in a shared activity? To manage a company or individual project? You have to first look at Chapters 4 and 5 and do your planning to use this measurement on an investment. The goals and philosophy should inform and define the direction your activity takes. If you choose to be a limited partner, it is essential that you know your partners (including your family partners) and what their personal and professional agendas and areas of expertise are. With sizable amounts of your money at risk, being a passive investor requires high levels of trust and the ability to choose trustworthy partners. Only you can say what your goals are with regard to Simple Deal. But because there are several unknowns in the variables yet to explore, there is a high probability that you will be drawn into more involvement after the fact without having planned it.

Familiarity with the Marketplace

If you are a doctor who knows hospitals and community health care criteria well, this can help define where to concentrate your efforts in the places you know about and understand. You are better served by real estate investments that draw on that knowledge, such as investing in a community clinic location in a thinly served but growing area of a major city rather than in an apartment complex in another state with which you aren't remotely familiar. Having a knowledgeable person recommend possibilities to you shouldn't preclude your further independent research. You will learn the hard way the true meaning of "absorption rates" if you don't stick with what you know. If you don't know an area, the risk level of your investment will skyrocket beyond the economics of the deal.

Measuring Simple Deal on this basis is easy. Simple Deal isn't even in your own town. What do you know about real estate investing? You are just getting your feet wet on this one. You will have to rely heavily on other people's advice and trust that they are good people.

Types of Real Estate

There are infinite possibilities: raw land; producing ranch, farm, and timberland; residential development land; commercial development land; resort, leisure, and hotel development land; single or multi-family and mixed, urban, or suburban residential land; inner city, urban, suburban, and resort commercial property; malls (suburban, waterfront, urban, outlet), retail, strip center, high-rise office, industrial park/warehouse specialty commercial property. Simple Deal is a straight raw land investment.

Leverage Requirements and Tolerance

Most real estate investments carry a certain level of debt. It is a prudent business practice to a point. Can the project carry the debt service after operations costs? The S&L failures in the 1980s were directly attributable to rapid inflation in land values, high interest rates and return, and cash flow expectations coupled with ridiculous leverage levels of 90 percent or more that occurred in the late 1970s and early 1980s. The 1986 Tax Reform Act further squeezed the speculators.

Debt will range from a very small percentage of net cash flow (after operations costs) to 80–90 percent of that amount. If you expect 100 percent of the net cash flow to be a safe bet, you deny certain contingency and cost overrun protection. Reserving 10–15 percent or more for contingencies is an effective rule. Ranchers and farmers are the most debt-averse real estate investors, although they have had to learn to live with production and equipment debt to create return from the land, earn a living, pay the taxes, and repay the operating and land purchase costs. Partnering with debt underwriters such as insurance companies and pension funds is common practice to lower leverage risks in long-term projects. Autonomy is sacrificed, but few go it alone. For Simple Deal, this is yet to be determined, and you haven't even thought about any costs beyond the asking price; but will there be a lender to help you finance the deal, on what terms?

Operating Costs

You can easily analyze the costs when you compare the actual annual return on your investment and what you receive after expenses (including management fees) are paid. The double edge of the REIT is the promised consistency of returns and cash flow and the underlying promise that the managers will always receive their fee before you see a nickel, even if the projects lose money. In direct investments, count on cost overruns on development properties and on the annual costs of carrying an investment to maturity, such as taxes, insurance, management costs, assessment challenges to local authorities, and environmental impact and surveying costs incurred readying a property for sale or development. Partnership assessments never stop, even when a property is paid for. Be realistic in your calculations. Insist on limited partnerships and limited draws. It is too soon to tell for Simple Deal. You will learn this if you invest.

Not for the Lone Ranger

This type of investment is not for the Lone Ranger, and even he had Tonto. Work with cohorts and partners, property and project managers, lending relationships, accountants, real estate attorneys, and investment advisors with real estate knowledge that assist in portfolio design. The most trustworthy advisors come from those with field experience. Use your own deep knowledge of the community to build advisory relationships. If they are known to be professional and thorough, use them. But don't assume another investor is looking out for you. Review their recommendations from *your* perspective. You've already thought about partners for Simple Deal. Good thinking.

Turning raw land into developed lots or transforming any other property into something it isn't requires a multifaceted team of planners, engineers, attorneys, and project managers. The Davenport Ranch began by hiring a seasoned, Houston-based developer, a local land planner, an attorney for city lobbying, an attorney to form the Municipal Utility District (MUD), an investment advisor for the MUD, and an engineering firm. Today, 20 years after active development began, the project staff in Austin and the consulting team expands and shrinks as the development changes. The owners reside in Houston. Outsourcing specialty services keeps their costs in check and broadens their exposure to industry information.[1] The only thing a Simple Deal owner will have to worry about in this area is a good broker, a property manager, and, as needed, appraisers and marketing help because there is no current anticipation of developing the property.

Although some of these measurements and variables are useful to critique a large, private, limited real estate partnership, these alternative investments form a class unto themselves, which is described for you in Chapter 13. These limited partnerships, with multiple partners, can have a lock-up period of 2–8 years and will extract fees ranging from .5–1 percent and an acquisition and sales fee equal to a percentage of the property value of 1–3 percent. Who you partner with can ruin your sense of humor if you pick incorrectly. Being a minority limited partner is okay if you know your general or managing partners. It's a great way to limit your risk. Because of the limited control that you exert in all nonliquid investment partnerships, these criteria differ somewhat from the measurements you use for single-parcel or project investing structured with partners with whom you are closely aligned. Applying the variables and measurements in this chapter and reviewing the due diligence section in Chapter 13, "Making Investment Choices," will give you an introduction to real estate limited partnership evaluation. Simple Deal will be structured as a joint ownership agreement so partner due diligence is important as is your liability—whether joint or several.

Matching Management and Partners to the Deal

Even the largest active real estate investors have professional managers and outside partners. Stress the importance of knowing the value and appreciating the difference between a detail-driven, conservative manager and a creative, idea manager, and emphasize the need for both in a complex project. You will always need someone who can see the forest, and someone who can see the trees. This is particularly important if you are an uninvolved participant in a direct investment.[1] Even in the Simple Deal, someone is going to have to manage the property if you buy it. This measurement tells you if you believe enough in the management and the partners to stay in it for the Simple Deal projected term of 3–5 years or longer.

Doing Business with Friends as Partners

One school of thought says, "Who can you trust if you can't trust your friends?" Another says "I never do business with close friends. I want to keep them as friends." Only if you don't mind losing whatever money you have in the deal should you say yes to making the investment, particularly with friends. If it's your grocery money, it will change your relationship with that person if it goes sour. Understand the difference between a friend and social acquaintance. The latter is less likely to stick with you in the tough times. If you do Simple Deal, you might need partners. Measuring the deal by the company you keep can be deceiving. You will have to play this one as the deal evolves.

Time Commitment

When you decide to be actively involved, even with sound partners and a great staff, the time you have to devote to that involvement may be disproportionate to the size of the asset in relation to your portfolio. Morian's interest in Davenport Ranch comprises a small part of her investment portfolio, but as president of the development, it has at times demanded 90 percent of her time. Be careful; if you make bad choices in property managers, you might have to step in to protect your investment. You could end up being the property manager of any real estate investment. Do you want to manage Simple Deal?

Investment, Philanthropy, or Both?

Call it what you will. In downtown Fort Worth, the Perry Bass family and Ray Hunt, both from oil fortunes, have made oversized commitments to revitalizing the city's downtown area. In Maine, Elizabeth Noyce, the former wife of the founder of Intel Corporation, the largest maker of chips for personal computers, focused on commercial real estate as a way to revitalize Portland's declining downtown. Is this philanthropic, does it make investment sense, or does it do both? Carefully studied and chosen, an investment can serve multiple personal and public interests and provide great satisfaction. For example, an investment group in downtown San Antonio in which I was involved rehabilitated an historic building near the Alamo and served as a model for other projects. It provided a unique and comfortable environment for our offices and a two-story McDonald's restaurant and served as a challenging and creative outlet for me. This real estate deal was a profitable growth investment that carried its costs and provided sizable tax advantages for nine years before it was sold, and it added value to the restoration of downtown San Antonio, which helped sustain the city's tourism business during the worst of the Texas recession in the 1980s. Since Simple Deal isn't anything more than a raw land purchase and potential sale, you will only measure it by investment standards. Philanthropy isn't an issue.

Ownership Structure

Each type of ownership structure has its benefits. The structure needs to fit the stated goals of the investor, whether it is a simple or limited partnership, tenancy in common, a corporation, a trust, a joint tenancy, or an individually owned or pooled tradable form, such as an REIT. Measure Simple Deal against the value the ownership structure provides if you enter into it. Good legal advice on structuring will make this measure more valuable.

Owning Property with Family

When is the point of diminishing benefits reached? When there are too many generations, owners, and diverse interests invested in one property? Negotiating buy-outs and managing a plurality of interests for trusts, partnerships, and individuals can be unnecessarily costly and aggravating. Minor interests can torpedo even the best offers to develop or liquidate a real estate asset. The nonquantifiable effects of binding ownership can easily nullify the quantifiable benefits to diverse family members. You can measure Simple Deal's value as a family asset before you invest. Pay attention to the cautionary note at the end of the chapter about real estate as a family investment.

Liability

There are several liability considerations. The first is personal liability. If you are wealthy or even perceived to have "deep pockets," you are a vulnerable target for litigation, however unfounded it might be. Owners are also subject to environmental liabilities. Insurance coverage limiting liability via corporate or partnership structure, and preempting governing authorities by implementing environmental impact mitigation actions are effective liability controls. Learn what liabilities are inherent to your investment and seek legal advice on how best to address them. Measure Simple Deal against that environmental liability you looked at before and on the possibility that you will have to hold onto it for awhile. You have all of that river frontage. There is risk in trespassers using your property for all kinds of activities that are enjoyed in and by the water. Further debt liability is also an important consideration depending on financing terms.

Predicting Future Value and Income

For long-term planning purposes, real estate investments have made fools out of savvy, long-time investors. (Review Figure 11.1.) Cycles, interest rates, rent projections, and employment trends are notoriously unpredictable. To be attractive to an investor family or individual, real estate can require a 5–20-year hold to manifest acceptable returns on the original commitment. Insist on knowing when the payback starts—evaluate *current* return on investment. Now this is where Simple Deal is really unpredictable. It is hard to predict the future. That is what speculation means.

Investment Horizon: Timing

How long do you want to be there? Can you get out when you want to? If not, do you have the wherewithal to see it through? The Davenport Ranch was purchased in 1967. With the advent of Loop 360,

Austin's outer loop, planning and permitting in Austin's restrictive development climate commenced in 1978. The first residential slabs were poured in 1982. By mid-1995, through the best and worst of Austin's economic cycles, Davenport Ranch was two-thirds complete and home to over 470 families—a 30-year investment coming to fruition.[1] Measure Simple Deal against the longest imaginable holding period, such as into the next generation. That is always a possibility. What is the likelihood of that? Just in case, if you get into the deal, take this into consideration in your estate planning.

Don't Get Greedy

Don't get too enamored of any investment. Be prepared to sell. The more successful investors have a knack for selling early, before a downturn snatches away their opportunity. Timing the market as different types of deals become more viable is a reasonable strategy. For instance, buy into built, underleased office buildings in a rebounding market area with an early exit strategy. Reportedly, the senior Mr. Rothschild, when asked how he became so wealthy, replied, "By selling too early." A more modern turn of phrase heard in the business is "Pigs get fat. Hogs get slaughtered."[1] Measure your greed factor in relation to Simple Deal against a willingness to sell early.

Diversification

A diversified and nimble operation rides cycles less fitfully. Howard Hughes amassed a diversified business empire that included oil field equipment (Hughes Tool), movie properties, Las Vegas casinos and hotels, and other Las Vegas and Los Angeles real estate. Thirty years after his death, his heirs agreed to sell his tracts of undeveloped land and buildings, concentrated in the western United States to the Rouse Company, one of the largest shopping mall developers, which operates primarily in the eastern part of the country. One massive transaction, valued in excess of a half a billion dollars, accomplished instant diversification within the industry by type and geography. The value lies in spreading risks across uneven markets and in insuring flexibility. Does Simple Deal satisfy your diversification goals?

Financial and Pro Forma Review

Begin by doing three pro forma estimates—best case, worst case, and probable case. Evaluate each one for every place that assumptions can break down. (See Figure 11.1.) I walked away from a "sure bet" in an attractive market with a major prime tenant and leading industry partner because of the inconsistencies in information I was given in a prospective deal. The industry partners had stubbed their toes before, but the prime tenant was a leading bank and the promoter was a bank board member and a financial advisor to many knowledgeable individuals. I was uncomfortable with the advisor's proximity to the outcome of the deal and with the results of an independent assessment of the pro forma information done by my real estate attorney. Within six months, the bank was hit by the Mexican peso crisis and it decided against expanding. The proximity to Mexico soured the local economy. The industry partner filed for bankruptcy, but I still had my capital. Simple Deal has no pro forma yet. You need to get some help running the numbers from three angles—worst case, best case, and somewhere in between. Then you can measure the economic upsides and downsides.

Exit Strategy

Real estate is an inexact science. The best laid exit strategies often go awry. As Mr. Rothschild suggests, sell early or plan on being surprised at how long it takes to actualize your expected rewards in real estate. In some cases they will have to be realized by your heirs. With Simple Deal, you have a way to go to get to this point. The deal has to be structured first. Right now, your exit strategy would be to walk out the door.

Now that you have assessed Simple Deal by applying variables and measurements, ask yourself if you would buy the land only knowing what you know so far. If you have answered yes, this is what happened to your money and the deal.

The Outcome

In 1983, investor family group joined in a co-owner's (the group) agreement to purchase 25 percent of Simple Deal. Another family group and four other single partners purchased the other 75 percent. The environmental impact study by the Corps of Engineers was declared inadequate shortly after the deal closed. The group learned that another study could take a "couple of years" to complete. Any potential buyer would have to be told of the delay. The asking price would suffer. Eighteen months later, the price of oil dropped from $40 per barrel to $7.50 per barrel in a matter of months.

As a result, Smalltown area banks with climbing loan defaults were redlined by Federal bank examiners. The banks began to fail, so the regional banks moved in. The regional bank that took over the co-owner's loan compressed the payout schedule (from 10 years to 3) and imposed 200 percent joint and several liability. Overnight, the real estate market in the entire region collapsed. Land values fell 30 percent. Owners began defaulting on their loans. Two of the group's partners went bankrupt increasing the remaining partners' liability and loan payments for Simple Deal. A philosophical split moved the management of the property from one partner's office to another. A second management change came when the lead investor family pressed for independent professional management when the bankruptcies interfered with effective administration and marketing of the property. The loan was paid off in 1989.

In 1996 Simple Deal is still unsold, but a potential offer surfaced for the first time since 1985. The Smalltown region is slowly rebounding from the real estate bust in the 1980s, but not enough to move the property. The original purchase price is the current offering price pending the buyer's review. Legal fees to structure a sales contract have been paid. The potential buyer will not agree to the owner's restrictive terms, which have been designed particularly to protect the various trustees and executors of one estate from future liability.

The estimated 2–5-year projected holding period has stretched to 13 years. The owners continue to pay the maintenance and upkeep and taxes. Costs for improvements to keep the land sale-ready are partially offset by the rental income from the farm lease to grow corn there. The river still floods every year or so, and the Army Corps of Engineers still hasn't completed its environmental study. The broker's contacts at City Hall tell him that there is talk that the Corps might condemn 30 percent of the property as unusable due to the drainage and contamination that flows through the land from upland farms.

Real estate investing is not for everybody. It is not like buying a house in which to live. It might not be for you, but most diversified investors have it in their portfolios. This is a place to begin considering it for your portfolio.

Caution: Real estate holdings of a long-term nature can transcend several generations. They can unwittingly end up in trusts and estates that have poor management to steward them on behalf of the beneficiaries until they are sold. When managing properties in trusts and estates, it is important to appoint knowledgeable trustees. For families experienced in ongoing real estate management, a bank is rarely the preferred choice for this role. Other long-term considerations when investing in real estate are what the disparate portfolio risk profiles and needs are and binding children to illiquid assets to accommodate estate planning for the elder generations. Undivided interests with no exit strategies make it difficult to transfer real estate for liquidity requirements or charitable purposes. The planning suggestions in Chapters 4 and 5 are important when committing to a project of an expected long-term nature, such as the Davenport Ranch. Even though Simple Deal was expected to be, in real estate parlance, a short-term deal, the investor family groups, particularly for the children's trusts, suffered due to a lack of adequate preinvestment planning. The two bankruptcies and the death of one of the partners have subsequently muddied sales potential.

As in all other asset classes, understanding the language of real estate, the real estate industry, and yourself prepares you to make the best decisions you can with little or no regret.

ENDNOTES

1. Mrs. S. Reed Morian, interview by author, Houston, Texas, 16 June 1995. Mrs. S. Reed Morian is president of Westview Development Properties, Inc.

12

OIL AND GAS

The Oil Patch

Texas is a trilingual State: English, Spanish, and oil patch speak.

Jett Rink (the swaggering, get-rich-quick, James Dean character in *Giant*) and Spindletop (the East Texas elephantine oil discovery depicted in *Giant*) notwithstanding, I find it remarkable that anyone who hasn't been exposed to the culture, or as we call it on the street, "the awl bidness," would dare sink a nickel in any venture in minerals without a lot of learning first.

Raised in an oil patch and exposed to the vocabulary from an early age, I made every conceivable error when I actually had the capital to try my own hand in the business. I might as well have been in kindergarten. My college degree was useless. An example of what I succumbed to after a few successes was to buy into a lease promotion (I'd never done a pure lease deal before) brought to me by a college acquaintance with whom I had previously invested with some success. According to him, the leases were "presold," all I had to do was finance the package for us to keep the leases from expiring while he finalized the lease sales. The leases, in fact, weren't presold. They expired, and I lost 100 cents on the dollar. Ten years later, I'm still sitting on a promissory note from that "friend." The last time we talked, he tried to trade me penny stocks to pay off the note. He has since left the state, "forwarding notice expired."

The smartest thing I did was to hire the man who wrote the following chapter as an industry advisor. He models the very qualities sought in any business, though never noted in any resume, unshakable honesty and integrity. The second smart thing I did was to take a four-day intensive course from the Independent Petroleum Producers Association in geology and geophysics. It was through Tom's wisdom and the course that I gained an understanding of the terminology, how salt water and oil can look exactly the same on a log, and other useful tools for measuring risks and making decisions.

I made enormous mistakes as well as good decisions and choices along the way. Debt was new to me but became a regular visitor. You have to borrow money to create a future revenue stream in this business. Knowing that 1 in 10 successful ventures would be the overall odds in the portfolio, I had to ask "How much am I willing—or able—to lose?" I grew up in a ranching family. Ranchers quake at the word "debt." Bankers lend them too much money. That's how ranchers get into trouble. Debt is synonymous with oil and gas investing.

The rationale to invest at all had everything to do with replacing a depleting income stream from a 50-year-old oil and gas field in which I shared ownership. I felt my family group had to diversify from dependency on family assets while we had the ability to do so. At the same time, the prevailing marginal tax rate was 70 percent, but thankfully, preference was available for depletion considerations associated with natural resources and their deductible intangible drilling costs. As a result, staying in the oil and gas business was a wise investment move at the time. Nothing else had the upside available to replace a 20 percent per year declining production curve. Today, after restructuring some years ago, only a few outside interests in oil and gas remain in my portfolio.

Today, the business has a more rational and cleaner face. It's an industry like any other—downsizing and ever bottom-line vigilant. The flushing out in the oil-bust years taught a lot of unethical operators and amateurs a lot of painful lessons, and many of them were sent packing. That isn't to say that slick operators and fly-by-night landmen (deal promoters) have disappeared. Every business has its promoters and wheeler dealers. But even the good times in "the patch" are hard these days, and an investor needs to want to be there. Allow Tom to enlighten you from the perspective of a "lifer."

OIL AND GAS INVESTING, AND OTHER MINERALS, TOO

Thomas B. Henderson, Jr.

Why all the excitement? Yesterday there was no gusher, there was only barren rock, just the same as the day before that, and probably the year and the years before. Suddenly, it's a gusher! Gold! We've struck gold! Visions of instant wealth and Hello, Easy Street. The rush of ego justification, "I knew it was there all the time," and the deep in the belly knowing that "Just maybe I'll be able to eat enough to have to let the old belt out a notch" are the cap for the instant explosion of hard earned joy. Life is going to be different!

Why do people put themselves through often severe stresses to pursue wealth? Perhaps there are many answers. Let's think about how the oil and gas exploration and production business works and see if we can find an "answer gusher" or two.

To begin with, we have to be aware that all wealth comes from the earth. We have nothing until someone takes the economic, and often physical, risk of capturing something from the earth through mining, farming, or fishing, and introducing it into commerce. Once a commodity is captured and made available, people can do things with it. They can eat it, weave it, burn it, or work it into a tool of utility or beauty. This capturing is the beginning, essential step, upon which our complexly intertwined economies absolutely depend, and it takes place under the dark star—risk. In the *De Re Metallica*, which chronicled mining in Europe during the Middle Ages, Georgius Agricola referred to the industry as "mining, a calling of peculiar dignity." To be involved in the continuing responsibility of keeping civilization alive sounds overly dramatic, but no matter how plainly or grandly the capturing process may be described, that is what is going on.

One more bit of philosophy before we grab for picks and shovels and drill bits. The idiom "to make money" is strictly an American concept. Other languages, and civilizations, look at the process as "earning" or "gaining" money or wealth, that is, changing the ownership of something that is already in the economy. The English use the word "win" to describe mining, the capture of coal or a metal from the earth, as in a great contest of strength and wits. But the idea of creating something of value that was not there before is purely American, and I think that this element is also part of the mystique of the oil business.

That the oil and gas business is full of risk and uncertainty is no news to anyone. Risk is the defining ugly gene that is carried by all members of the mining family—every sister has the wart on her nose, but they are all great dancers. There is something fascinating about these gals, and if the light is kept low, and a lot of powder is applied, the warts don't show. But they are still there. Many of the things said in this chapter about the oil and gas business apply in general to the other minerals. No exception, moreover, is granted to the dictum that central to economic success in the business of finding and extracting minerals are understanding and accommodating risk.

The lure of wealth. Ah, yes. Gold! Our histories are brim full of tales of the pursuit of wealth (mostly stealing it, an enterprise not without risk), and our language is blessed with references to our fascination with the successful accumulation of wealth, such as "rich as Croesus," "richer than Ben Gump," and the Fortune 500. Regardless of how it is accumulated, wealth is the reward for taking a risk. The bold chaser of wealth thinks first of his wealth goal and second of the risk that must be taken and how it can be kept at a minimum. The conservative chaser of wealth thinks first of the risks and then sets his wealth goal according to his appraisal of what the risk might justify. The return on dollars put at risk in winning wealth from the earth through farming and fishing is modest at best when compared with the potential rewards for the much higher risk of exploring for significant oil reserves.

CONSIDERATIONS IN OIL AND GAS INVESTING

As an opportunity to make money, the "awl bidness" will get the job done. In conventional terms, you can realize rates of return on your capital ranging from 5 percent (not considering the growth potential) on NYSE integrated, international giant corporations, to 20 and more times 5 percent on a participation in a single wildcat. The school teacher's retirement funds invested in Exxon or Shell, for example, are just about as risk free as T-bills; you can't say the same for a single-shot partnership unit. Risk is present in both venues: Exxon and Shell keep the overall risk low by balancing the higher-risk exploration portions of their budgets with almost risk-free development drilling and their refining and marketing activities; the wildcat driller puts it all in a single hole in the ground. In between these two extremes, there are as many variations of investment opportunities as there are models of 1996 look-alike automobiles.

A defining characteristic of the oil, and other minerals, business is that the value of the asset is greatest on the first day of production, and it goes down as the reserves are reduced. This depleting aspect is in sharp contrast to the increasing value of, say, a start-up manufacturing company that expands in response to sales success and is worth more each year. There is no way that more oil can be added to a reservoir. Fortuitous and/or anticipated market price increases may keep the net income from oil production level or allow it to rise, but sooner or later the income stream is going to decline and come to an end.

Just as there are many real and personal reasons for the purchase choice of a particular automobile, there is a similar range of choices of the vehicle for oil investments. These choices allow for the personality and wealth level of the individual investor. To what degree does the investor want to be involved? Is the investment made to round out a portfolio and have some oil stocks just because everybody needs to have some energy stocks? Or is the investor a thrill seeker with a need to talk big at the club bar? If putting money into oil is really a form of venture capital investing, we are really talking about the control of risk. The investor in Exxon stock would be at the low end of the risk curve, and the bar talker would be at the high end. In between is where the bulk of the real oil business dollar action takes place. The investor's spectrum of choices has many colors. Which one is the most flattering for you? Which one do you wear best? Let's look at the rainbow and see if we can find your pot of gold.

WHERE OIL AND GAS ARE FOUND

Where is oil found and how is it found? In answering these questions, the goal will be to simply tell you what time it is, not to try to tell you how to build a watch. Oil is found in sedimentary basins, such as the Gulf of Mexico, where the crust of the earth has sagged and where sand and clay, carried by rivers to the sea, form deltas that advance into the basin. And, perhaps, on another margin of the basin, where the sea water is clear and warm, reefs may grow with associated limestone deposits forming in the shallow waters of the protected lagoons, and evaporites (salt, for example) may precipitate where the salinity is high. The basin may be as large as the Gulf Of Mexico, or it may be only as large as a county, and it may accumulate sediment thicknesses of as much as 30,000 feet or as little as 5,000 feet.

Oil and gas, which are hydrocarbons (made up of hydrogen and carbon), are formed from the recombination of hydrogen and carbon from plant and animal cells that are buried in the sediments. As the muds, in which the hydrocarbons are formed, are compressed by the weight of additional overlying sediments, the oil and gas are squeezed out; some of it is then trapped in sandstones in the pore spaces between the sand grains, or perhaps in the pore spaces of a reef. Being lighter than the sea water that saturates the sediments, the oil and gas rise to the tops of the reservoirs, where they segregate into gas over oil over water. Sometimes there may be only gas, and other times only oil, and many times wells find that nothing but salt water is present.

The reservoirs where oil and gas are trapped, which are the targets for drilling, can be found by mapping data from previously drilled holes and by the use of seismic and other near- and remote-sensed geophysical data. Only within the last year or two have computers made possible the analysis and mapping of seemingly infinite bits of geometric data gathered by 3D seismic (a geophysical mapping method), and the risks of drilling a dry hole have been significantly reduced but not eliminated. In spite of all the advances in technology, it gets back to what Mr. Wallace Pratt said, "Oil and gas are found first in the mind of man."

VOCABULARY OF OIL AND GAS

All industries have their own special vocabularies, and the oil business is no exception. Many of the terms find their origins in English common law, and many others find their origins in American common men. The farm boys and laborers who became the roughnecks and roustabouts of the oil field utilized their farm and workplace words, homey and almost never salty, to name the newly invented tools and processes developed for the new industry. Here are enough basic definitions to keep you from sounding too much like a weevil (a beginner). The order is pretty much as you would run into the words in a drilling deal.

oil and gas lease   The legal instrument reducing to words the agreement whereby the owner of a mineral interest grants for a period of time (months to years) the exclusive right to explore for and produce oil and gas.

lessor   The owner of the mineral interest who grants the leasehold rights.

lessee   The person to whom the lease is granted.

bonus   The consideration paid for the lease, usually in dollars per acre, which might range from $5 to $1000 or more.

rentals   Also called delay rentals; the annual payment to keep the lease in effect in the absence of actual drilling.

royalty   The percent of the recovered oil or gas reserved by the lessor. This word is from the time when the king owned the minerals. In the early days of the oil business, the "standard" royalty was one-eighth, but times have changed, and as lessors' sophistication has increased, so has royalty increased to three-sixteenths and one-quarter. In exceptional cases where a lease may directly offset production, the royalty may be one-half, or even more. Royalty is taxed as ordinary income.

depletion allowance   A break from the government to allow for the depleting nature of the asset. This was only available on older properties and declines with time.

overriding royalty (ORR)   A royalty interest that is carved out of the leasehold interest, which may be assigned to a geologist or a landman for services.

working interest (WI)   All or a portion of the ownership of a lease, which carries with it the right to pay the bills.

net revenue interest (NRI)   The decimal interest in the production from a well that is owned by the royalty and working interest owners.

lease operating expense (LOE)   The monthly cost of operating a well, generally deducted from the monthly revenue stream.

authority for expenditures (AFE)   The well always costs more than you think. The AFE is the itemized list of all additional expenditures, capital and otherwise, to be spent in drilling or working over a well. AFEs come with greater regularity than you can imagine and often eat up any income you might realize off of older wells.

before federal income tax (BFIT)   Designation seen in revenue projections on oil and gas deals.

title opinion   A letter from a title attorney stating who owns the minerals and who owns the lease. Usually a drill site title opinion is first obtained for the lease, or portion of the lease, where the well will be drilled. If the well is completed as a producer, a division order title opinion states who owns all of the interests represented, the royalty as well as the working interest.

division order   The schedule of net revenue interests in the well, signed by all parties, authorizing the distribution of proceeds from the sale of the oil and gas.

landman   An oil and gas lease broker.

operator   Usually an owner of working interest who is responsible for the drilling and day-to-day operations of the well. This function may be contracted to an operating company.

joint operating agreement   The contract between working interest owners that designates who is going to be the operator and identifies the rights and duties of all of the working interest owners.

drilling rig   The derrick, drill pipe, draw works, mud pumps, and the thousand tools and bits of hardware needed to drill the hole.

pusher   The toolpusher; the supervisor of the operation of one or more rigs.

driller   The boss of a crew of three, four, or five roughnecks; the man who actually has his hands on the drilling controls. The day tour (tower) driller has seniority over the evening/night tour and morning tour drillers, and may relieve the pusher.

roughnecks   The crew of floor hands and the derrick man, who seem to get dirty all of the time. Roughnecks owe fealty to the driller, who hires his crew. Eventually everybody working on a rig is related one way or the other—brothers, brothers-in-law, nephews, cousins, wives' cousins, plus relationships our English language is too poor to name.

spud in   To begin drilling. Originally, a special "spudding" rig was used to drill the hole for the conductor pipe that lined the first 50 feet or so of the hole. The spud rig was then moved off and the drilling derrick was built over the hole. Today a tilt-up rig is set up over the location and does all of the drilling.

drill   To bore the hole with a bit fastened to the bottom of a string of drill pipe, through which mud is circulated through the bit back to the surface, mud that lubricates the pipe as it rotates in the hole, washes the drill cuttings up to the surface, and prevents gas and oil that may be encountered from flowing into the hole.

core   To cut a cylinder of rock using a special bit that may often be faced with industrial diamonds.

mud logger   The person who monitors the stream of mud returning to the surface for shows of gas and oil and who catches and describes samples of the cuttings. Typically, the mud logger's trailer contains a complex of computers and gas analysis equipment, microscopes, coffee pots, junk food, a TV, and a spare bunk or two.

electric log   A generic term for a variety of recorded electrical, acoustic, magnetic, and radioactivity properties of the strata through which a well has been drilled. These are measured by equipment lowered into the hole on a multicircuit-electrical cable and are recorded and processed by computer in the logging truck. These data, usually presented as curves on long strips of paper, are used to help determine whether oil or gas may be present in a reservoir. The invoice from Schlumberger, the giant of this service industry, for logging an 8,300-foot wildcat was over $40,000 for a full suite of logs; a plain vanilla logging job on a 2,700-foot well would be closer to $5,000.

sidewall cores   Thumb-size samples of rock punched from the wall of the hole by a tool lowered into a hole on a wire cable. The oil, gas, and water content is measured, as well as the porosity and permeability (how easily fluid can flow through the rock).

formation test   A sampling of the fluid content and pressures of a reservoir by a tool lowered into the hole as part of the logging operation.

casing   The string of pipe, cemented in place, from the surface to the bottom of the hole, which is perforated at the face of the producing reservoir to allow oil or gas to enter the well.

tubing   The small diameter pipe lowered into the cased well through which the oil or gas flows, or is pumped, to the surface.

christmas tree   The assembly of valves and gauges affixed to the top of the casing and the tubing of a well through which flow rates are controlled.

pump jack   The rocking beam that looks like a jackass's head that pumps oil from a well. Some oil wells flow by themselves in response to liquid and/or gas pressure in the reservoir and do not need to be pumped.

separator   A connection of small and large tanks to separate produced oil, gas, and water.

meter run   The meter that measures the pressure of a gas flow stream. Knowing the size of the pipe through which the gas is flowing and its pressure allows the volume to be calculated.

tank battery   Tanks near an oil well in which oil, and water if it is also produced, is stored before being picked up by trucks for delivery to a refinery. Oil production from a well is measured by a gauger (also called a pumper), who measures the level of the oil in the tank with a steel tape through a hole in the top of the tank.

severance tax   The tax imposed on produced oil and gas at the wellhead.

ad valorem tax   The tax imposed on the market value of the remaining reserves.

A SIMPLE DEAL
Version One

A simple deal works like this. A geologist studies an area and compiles the data about the existing wells and reservoirs on a map; in so doing, he sees some indications that another reservoir may be present on an edge of the field where no wells have been drilled. The geologist has a seismic line that confirms that the fault, which is critical for the prospect, is where it is shown on the map. He shows his findings to an operator, who is familiar with the area. The operator likes the prospect and agrees to pay the geologist $15,000 for his idea (payable when a lease is taken) plus a 3 percent of 8/8 overriding royalty interest in the production from the lease.

The operator asks a landman friend to see if the minerals under the 640-acre tract are open. The landman learns the identity of the land owner, who informs him that the acreage is not under lease. The landman further learns from the owner that when he bought the farm, the seller kept half of the minerals. The owner agrees to lease his half of the minerals for a term of three years for a $30 per acre bonus, but he insists on a 20 percent royalty instead of the offered three-sixteenths. The seller also agreed to lease his half of the minerals for the same $30 bonus, but since he hasn't kept up with drilling activities in the vicinity of his old farm since he retired to a cabin on a fishing lake, he agrees to the offered three-sixteenths royalty. The lessors get $9,600 apiece ($30 per acre for one-half interest in 640 acres), and the geologist gets his $15,000 and an assignment of his override. The operator is now exposed to the tune of $34,200.

A drilling contractor gets a call from the operator, and the next day he submits a bid to drill the 4,000 foot hole on a turnkey basis for $48,000, including clearing the location, digging the pits, building the road into the location, setting the surface casing, and supplying the drilling mud. Schlumberger bids to log the well for $4,200, and the operator budgets $3,600 for plugging and cleanup in case of a dry hole. Total costs to test the idea will be $90,000; if it is successful, another $50,000 will be required to run casing and complete the well.

The operator contacts three parties who have invested with him in the past and offers each of them a one-quarter working interest in the deal for $30,000 (one-third of the total cost) to the casing point in the event of discovery or through plugging in the event of a dry hole. This is the standard third for a quarter promote. In return for finding the deal, doing all of the organizing, and banking the advance costs, the operator's 25 percent working interest in the well gets carried to the casing point free of all costs to date. In the event oil is found, all working interests, including the operator, pay their proportionate shares of the completion costs. When contacted, one party says that his boat is presently loaded and he has to pass. The other two look at the geology and agree to take a quarter each. One of the two asks if he can show the deal to a wealthy heir, someone he met last month while fishing for bonefish at Ambergris Key. Permission given, he calls the heir, who gets all excited about getting into the oil business and agrees on the spot to participate. The deal is now all sold, and the operator tells the drilling contractor to start clearing the location for the Operator No. 1 Lessor well.

Drilling proceeds with only one delay for rig repairs (replace the clutch on the draw works). The mud logger reports a good oil show at depths of 3810 to 3820 feet, and now everybody gets excited. Wealthy Heir flies down to Houston, rents a car, and heads to the location. He subsequently gets lost, calls the operator, who redirects him, and they all end up at the location in time to tell war stories while the crew finishes coming out of the hole. Then they all crowd into the logging truck to watch the log appear on the computer screen as the logging tool is slowly pulled up the hole. The sand with the oil show looks good on the log, they all get giddy, the operator tells the pusher to order out the casing, and then they all go to town for steaks. After dinner, the operator reminds the group that completion is going to cost $50,000, and asks everybody to please put a check for $12,500 in the mail first thing in the morning. Wealthy Heir's total cost for his 25 percent WI in this first well is $42,500.

The well is successfully completed for 80 barrels of oil per day (BOPD), and a location is selected for a second well. In this new well, the operator will have to pay for his full 25 percent share of the costs, and the three other working interest owners will pay only 25 percent each instead of the promoted one-third that they paid on the first hole.

Before the proceeds from the sale of the oil were distributed, the operator's lawyer prepared a division order based on the title opinion, which was sent to owners of interests in the oil produced from the well, including the lessors, the geologist, and the working interest owners, for their concurrence that their interests were correctly stated. This is what each has:

FIGURE 12.1

	Royalty	NRI
Lessor–seller	1/2 of 3/16	.09375
Lessor–owner	1/2 of 20 percent	.10000
	Overriding Royalty (ORR)	
Geologist	3 percent of 8/8	.03333
	Total R and ORR	.22708
	Working Interest (WI)	
Promoter	25 percent of .77292	.19323
Partner 1	25 percent of .77292	.19323
Wealthy Heir	25 percent of .77292	.19323
	Total WI	.77292
	Total	1.00000

What did working interest owner Wealthy Heir get for his $42,500? He now owns a .19323 NRI (19.323 percent) in the oil that will be produced from the No. 1 well and the right to participate in the No. 2 well for $13,050 (his 25 percent of the $52,200 AFE to the casing point), plus another $10,000 to complete. The lease cost and geologic fee paid as part of the first well were for the entire 640 acres, so those costs are not repeated for the second well.

The estimated oil recovery from the 40 acres assigned to the No. 1 well is 120,000 barrels (40 acres X 10 feet of sand X 300 barrels per acre foot recovery), of which Wealthy Heir can anticipate selling 23,188 barrels credited to his 19.323 percent. If oil prices stay at $18, he may net $14 after severance tax, ad valorem taxes, and lifting costs, for a gross of $324,632. That is a 7.6:1 return on the $42,500. The second well, if it is like the first, would generate a return of 14.1:1 because of the lower cost, and the combined project will return 9.9:1.

Although the initial production is 80 BOPD, the rate will decline, and it may take 20 years to recover this oil. The first year, the well might average 60 BOPD for a total of 21,900 barrels, with 4,232 barrels and $59,248 BFIT credited to the investor, roughly a one-year payout. Not bad.

So much for the mechanics of A Simple Deal, Version One. It worked the way all parties hoped it would work, and the numbers are real world numbers. If it happens to you once in 10 tries, you are doing things very right; twice in 10, you're charmed.

As for Wealthy Heir, what did he do right? Or wrong? I'll meet you at the end of this chapter and we'll talk about it there.

Version Two

A bird dog, a real talker, meets Wealthy Heir at a cocktail party in Gotham and regales him and a pair of his old classmates from St. Prep's with tales from the oil patch. Within 15 minutes the three are already mentally spending the money they are planning on making as oil men, and when Bird Dog offers to try to get them into a deal, they can't say yes quick enough. Bird Dog calls his buddy who operates Quick Rich Oil Company in Houston and tells him that he has three mullets lined up who are good for $50,000 apiece.

The next morning, Quick Rich is on the phone looking for a deal that he can do for $100,000, and don't worry if it doesn't have any seismic. A lease hound friend has a lease offsetting a discovery well in deep South Texas, about 10 miles from the border, that looks like it should not have been completed, and Lease Hound is afraid that he might not be able to turn the lease before the well dies and that he might have to eat the $30,000 he paid for it. Quick Rich has found a deal where he can accommodate Wealthy Heir and Wealthy Heirs 2 and 3, and he and Bird Dog agree to split the $50,000 profit, a 5 percent overriding royalty, and a quarter carried to the tanks.

Border Drilling contracts to drill the well on a day-rate basis (the working interest owners take all of the drilling risks), the investors sign trade letters and send checks, and the well is spudded. The evening before the rig is anticipated to get to the objective sand, the relief mud logger tells Joe, the evening tour driller, that when he was leaving town about 15 minutes ago he saw George, the day driller, going in Conchita's Cantina with Joe's wife. Joe tells one of the floor hands to take over the drilling, and as he roars off into the night, they hear him shouting something about kicking some gringo's ass.

Nothing happens at the rig for about an hour; then, the drilling penetration rate abruptly increases. In about 15 minutes, the mudlogger, who doesn't speak much Spanish, rushes over to the rig floor and tries to tell the substitute driller, who only speaks Spanish, that they are cutting a good sand, they are getting a strong gas show, and they had better stop drilling and condition the mud. By the time they have communicated, the mud is beginning to kick, and the crew closes the blowout preventers. The mudlogger calls the pusher, who immediately heads to the location, but too late to keep the pipe from sticking, ultimately the reason that the hole and the string of drill pipe have to be junked and abandoned. Remember, the drilling contractor is working on a day-rate basis, not a turnkey, and the risk is all on the Wealthy Heirs.

They end up moving the rig to the other side of the location, where they can use the same mud pits, and drill a second hole without any excitement. Wealthy Heir and Wealthy Heir 2 fly to McAllen, where Quick Rich meets them and takes them to Mexico for drinks, dinner, and a bit of night life before going to the location to witness the logging. The jolly three arrive in time to see the logging truck rigging down. Mercifully, they do not have to watch the log as it appears live on the computer screen, showing that the objective sand is faulted out and that they have a dry hole. The trip back to Gotham is sobering.

What did this adventure cost the three Wealthy Heirs? It cost them each about $150,000 for two dry holes. And they never did find out what happened when Joe walked in at Conchita's Cantina.

Again, as for Wealthy Heir, what did he do right, or wrong? I'll meet you at the end of this chapter and we'll talk about it there.

INVESTMENT POSSIBILITIES

All investing beyond the no-brains point of just turning assets over to a manager requires time and effort, and even surrendering all decisions to a manager requires decisions leading to the selection of a manager. The oil business is sufficiently broad and complicated that large numbers of investors are able to specialize, and make money, in single aspects and combinations of aspects requiring varying levels of time and dollar commitments.

Each of these branches of specialization in the oil business requires a level of expertise and experience that cannot be achieved overnight. Either the investor gets into the business full time or he has to find someone who is knowledgeable and who can be trusted to look out for the investor's interests. Each of the following areas has the potential for making lots of money, and each requires lots of work.

Purchase of Producing Wells

When done right, the purchase of producing wells is perhaps the least risky oil investment. Used car dealing may be the closest equivalent. You have to know what you are doing. Reserves are priced on a risk-weighted, rate-of-return basis plus a boot for the romance of future possibilities. The appraisal of the extent and recoverability of reserves is based on a combination of geologic and engineering data that is far more accurate than future prices seen in the finest crystal ball. An operating company can be contracted to assist in the purchase and management of the production, and the investor is free to place his or her own efforts elsewhere. Risk can be partially managed by owning undivided interests in multiple properties, but at some point, you are so diversified that you might as well be a partner in a syndicated pool.

Mineral and Royalty Ownership

Mineral and royalty ownership can be either a long-range speculation on future discovery, with your money tied up for practical purposes forever, or a rate-of-return purchase of presently producing properties. Recent years have seen the revival of royalty buying, which was a popular activity in the early days of the oil business. Typically, a royalty broker will watch wildcat wells, and if one is completed, the broker will attempt to purchase part of the lessor's royalty before the division orders are sent out. Lessors are sellers for one or more reasons: They are ignorant of the probable size of the coming income stream; they want to hedge against early depletion of the well; or they may be just plain dumb and the thought of a new TV or pickup turns them on. A royalty broker often buys on the basis of a 6-month payout and sells half of what he has bought to the investor on the basis of a 12-month payout, clearing the half that he keeps. In playing the royalty game, quite obviously it is better if you know and trust the broker.

There is another interesting aspect of royalty buying: its use as a way of participating in wildcat wells. The reason money is put into working interests in exploratory wells is not to participate in the exposure to all sorts of risks but in the hope that the acquired net revenue interest may be worth something. The object of the game is to create or acquire an income stream. If net revenue interest can be bought cheaper, or at less risk, in the form of royalty, that is a better deal than buying promoted working interest. Logical pricing has to be based on a risk-weighted present value of the anticipated income stream. Geologists to whom overriding royalty has been assigned as part of the compensation for the sale of a prospect are often good sources, but beware if the geologist seems real eager to sell—the prospect might be a little on the shaky side.

Lease Trading, Buying, and Selling

Lease trading, buying, and selling is a working-capital intensive game, but one with grand potential if you have an in with a big operator. Major plays tend to come along one to the decade, and if you have an inventory of leases, or options to lease, when the play breaks, you can make big money. It is probably safe to speculate that inside information, or a commitment to buy a package of leases, may be involved whenever somebody cuts a fat hog. And it may also be true that more than one person may share the bacon. This game might best be played by remaining available to a professional lease hound to bank his deals, but remember, you may have to eat a lot of leases if something goes wrong.

Deal Generation

Deal generation is the first, and the essential, step in the exploration for oil and gas, whether done on the level of the independent geologist or on the level of a major company. Typically, geologists, either independent or on retainer, come up with an idea of where a new field might lie or where a known field might be extended, as was the case in A Simple Deal, Version One. The idea may be confirmed by seismic data, and then leases are acquired. At this point, the project becomes a prospect that is ready for drilling. Investment opportunities lie in funding one or more geologists and paying a landman's expenses to check lease availability, perhaps buying leases and seismic data for the geologist to use. In practice, the management of deal generation is perhaps best blended with the next step, promotion of the deal, and success is closely tied to the experience level of the person who runs one of these companies.

Promotion and Operation

Promotion and operation are a two-phase couplet, the first of which is the recruitment of working interest partners to put up some or all of the cost of the exploration risk. The promoter recovers his out-of-pocket investment in the geology and the leases and his intangible time and expertise in exchange for a carried interest in the well, generally to the casing point. Operations begin once a well is completed. The day-to-day management of wells is typically done by a petroleum engineer, who has a staff of field supervisors and an office full of bookkeepers and clerks to keep up with mountains of paper. Reports go to and come from the partners who own the well, accountants, state and federal regulators, gas and oil buyers, the pipelines and oil truckers, and environmental agencies. Even the smallest of oil companies has to cover all of these functions. For a single person operating a couple of wells, it is a full-time job.

Partnering

Partnering is usually done by investing with one or more small companies that perform the deal generation, promotion, and operating functions on an ongoing casual or formally structured relationship. The company will have half a dozen or more investors who participate across the board in everything the company does. In many cases, with successful operators, the only way into the investor circle is by inheritance.

Investment Products

Wall Street offers investment products ranging from the major integrated oil companies—Exxon, Shell, and so on—through a myriad of large and small companies that specialize in exploration, production, refining, transportation, pipelines, logging, drilling, services, and supplies of all kinds. As the size of the company decreases, the risk increases. The ownership of common stock in an oil company really doesn't put you in the oil business—you are just passively investing. You are not in the oil business unless you are involved in the management of your dollars. This can happen at the least involvement level in the specialty fund categories, in contrast with the greatest involvement level when you call on independent geologists in the quest for a prospect to buy and promote. The many oil and gas industry investment vehicles available through the traditional financial markets provide opportunities for your perceived role, whatever it might be. Remember, the more layers of promotion, the less left for the investor.

ADVICE
Things to Consider

1. Think about yourself and what your goals are. (Remember the earlier discussion of mission statements and the Prudent Investor Rule?) There are risks in almost every investment, and you have to know what level of risk you feel comfortable handling. Ask for advice. Then think about it. Ask questions. Meeting people, making contacts, and exchanging thoughts and ideas is extremely stimulating. It is almost a sure thing that what you end up doing will be different, in at least some degree, from what you thought you were going to do in the beginning.

2. Oil and gas is a complex industry. And so is most every industry. Do not think that a casual level of involvement will get the job done. A lot of wells have been funded by the naive Wealthy Heirs of the countryside, and by doctors and lawyers and real estate developers and thousands of other folks who haven't gotten their money back, much less made a profit. And in general, these investors have known almost nothing about what they were doing. Don't be in a hurry, and don't let money burn a hole in your pocket. A favorite come-on for an oil deal is, "The worst you can do is get your money back." That's where you are right now, risk free.

3. Invest for the long haul. When you work with risk, you are working not only with chances for failure but also with chances for success. You have to have enough exposures to allow the odds to work for you. The best operators drill dry holes, in spite of best intentions to the contrary. In oil exploration, you will be working with an incomplete set of data. Drilling just adds more data; it seldom provides the full answer. Try to have a participation in at least 10 exploratory prospects, even if it takes 3 or 4 years (here, again, don't be in a hurry). Traditionally, only 3 or 4 exploration wells out of 10 pay out, and only 1 of those will be better than 3 or 4 to 1. Fabulous discoveries don't come along very often.

4. Do not invest your capital in oil and gas exploration. Invest your income, but keep the seed corn safe.

5. Beware of the paradigm trap. Some companies set a minimum acceptable rate of return for drilling or production projects that is based on the project as a whole. If a well logs a reservoir thickness less than the calculated minimum needed to produce the set rate of return, the well will not be completed and will be plugged and abandoned. You must never forget that you are in the business of making money. Whatever you can do that will generate a profit moves you farther down the road to wealth. If you drill a well that has less sand than you wanted, and if you can make money on the cost of running pipe and completing the well, do it, and forget the lower-than-target rate of return on the entire cost of the well. Look at it this way: The reason you drill a well to the casing point is for the opportunity to run a string of casing and make a well. Mentally write off the cost to the casing point of your wells as the cost of doing business, just as if it were additional rent. If you are fresh to the oil business, you have a great advantage in that you are not burdened with old concepts of the way it is always been done. Don't be intimidated.

6. Work at managing risk. It has been said before, but here it is again in slightly different words. You cannot avoid it, so make sure that you have plenty of exits and opportunities to elect not to participate.

7. Know the people with whom you are working. There is more than one application of this bit of advice, beginning with the people from whom you are asking advice. You have to know where they are coming from, what baggage they are bringing, and what they may hope to gain from talking to you. In the College of Engineering at Duke, a special American history course was taught for the freshmen. The principal message to be learned was that nobody does anything without a reason. In politics, everybody has a special interest, and the authors of history texts all have axes to grind, and if you want to understand what really happened and why, you have to know what somebody is trying to do to your head.

With this in mind, be wary of the specialists you rely on to advise you in how to spend your money. I promise you, the woods are full of slick talkers who will see to it that your money goes bye-bye. Some will have evil intentions, and some can get the job done in all innocence, and you really won't realize what is happening until late in the game. The best good fortune that you can have is to work with people who care about you and who work for your benefit.

Along the way, you will participate in deals with other investors. It won't do you any good to have made your plans and to have budgeted to cover your commitments when your partner fails to deliver. You can be severely damaged, perhaps even fatally. This is one thing that a good lawyer will help you defend against, but every strange turn of events cannot be covered. It is easier to deal with people you know and trust. Good friends making money together through the years is really satisfying, but there is a difference between good friends and old acquaintances.

What Did Wealthy Heir Do Right, or Wrong?

You already know the answer. When Wealthy Heir invested in A Simple Deal, Version One, he was working with good people and good things happened. The most that he can be credited with is perhaps the instincts to recognize integrity in a casually introduced fellow fisherman. For sure, he did not go through the process of verifying the safety of his investment. He was just flat lucky. As to A Simple Deal, Version Two, the only right thing that Wealthy Heir did was choosing his parents; after that, he did everything wrong.

By now, you should have the feeling that the oil business is not an easy game, and you probably have doubts about whether you really want to get into it. If you are prepared to devote a lot of time in an active oil investing role, or even if you just wish to participate lightly, establish relationships with good people and let them hold your hand. You can do it the right way. It's an exciting business. Go, find some good advisors, and make money!

13

MAKING INVESTMENT CHOICES
Stewardship Alternatives

The terms "alternative" and "nontraditional" are overused in today's financial world, creating a certain confusion for the investor. Both terms can refer to (1) any type of investment *other than* traditional portfolio management, or (2) all investments structured as limited partnerships, whether they are hedge funds, venture capital, or other niche strategies such as derivatives. Other alternatives are risk arbitrage, distressed securities, and real estate partnerships; investing might include investing in sports franchises, movie and theater projects, and commodities trading. Even art and other collectibles are considered by very serious investors as an alternative investment class.

As alternatives increase, an orderly means of classifying them diminishes, as does a grasp of the variables within them. One person might refer to a hedge fund as nontraditional. Another might classify it as an alternative class within equities. Some people look at art collection as an asset class; others warn against seeing it this way. A typical investment conference agenda lists alternative investments (used interchangeably with nontraditional) as including private equity, real estate (the oldest form of investment is now called nontraditional?), natural gas and oil, timberland and farmland, REITs (aren't these real estate investments?), buy-outs, venture capital, emerging markets (aren't these equities?), mezzanine funds, asset-backed debt, international private equity, and others. You will have to come up with your own understandable terminology. This chapter is designed to illuminate your ability to achieve that goal. This is not meant to provide an exhaustive encyclopedia of investment alternatives but to serve as an introduction to alternatives.

First, we will look at the alternative classes in a general way. Following the descriptions of these categories are explanations of due diligence tasks that will help position you to decide whether you want to further involve yourself in investments of this kind. This is a place to begin to look at and think about these types of investment options.

SPECIALTY ALTERNATIVES
Art and Other Collectibles

Neither Christie's nor Sotheby's ever encourages its clients to buy art for the purposes of investment... Because art and collectibles are about fashions and tastes, you can never know whether a particular category will remain in fashion or become more valuable in the long term.[1]

Supply and demand rules the strength of any collectible as an investment grade asset. No one can predict taste and style. There are 20–30 markets within the art market alone, including Impressionist art, contemporary art, Old Masters paintings, prints, jewelry, furniture, and coins. The value cycles of art and collectibles measured by the major auction houses indicate a general upward trend in an unpredictable and volatile, spiking pattern, with the spikes denoting frenzied speculation followed by a bust, then a long period of value building back to the last higher plateau of the previous 10-year cycle.[1]

Objects such as rare books and English portraiture were extremely expensive in the 1920s. In 1996, the same number of 1920s dollars can buy those objects. This is an embarrassing return on investment, if you indeed dare to consider it as one. Impressionist art, on the other hand, has been extremely lucrative and overshadows the overall market perception. But the range has varied dramatically even within this field in a short period of time, with the focus on the upward spikes almost exclusively made by the van Goghs. The Japanese passion for the Impressionists drives today's boom. Conversely, contemporary art, whose high values were driven up by real estate developers, was hurt most in the art market bust in the 1980s. When the real estate business went south, the value of the art market dropped 50 percent from the peak. It is all a matter of taste.

Being realistic about your involvement is important. For many, it is the game of hunting, finding, buying, and curating. Expertise gained over years of collection, study, and a discerning "gut" enable a collector to make fewer mistakes in judgment and gain greater satisfaction in collecting. Collecting and investing are rewarding and interesting work, but they are seldom mutually inclusive activities, and require study, interest, good instincts, and due diligence. When huge fortunes are made, people go shopping, many times throwing their money away without thinking.

An example highlights the necessity for caution when buying art as an investment. In the early 1980s, an investor purchasing original Audubon Havel prints via auction experienced two separate valuation outcomes five years apart. Nine years after purchase, two of the prints resold (to raise capital in a divorce settlement) at auction for their original purchase prices. Five years later, an estate sale of three prints from the same collection resulted in a "fire sale" to a retailer who bought them for half of the original cost of *one* of the prints; two very different outcomes in a relatively narrow time frame—different valuation methods, same collection. In the due diligence section, we will look at the different ways to value an asset of this kind depending on the purpose of an action taken with these types of investments.

Noncollectible Investment Alternatives

Investment alternatives range across asset classes, borders, and type. General classifications follow to introduce you to unique peculiarities that defy generalizing. If nothing else, you will have a sense of how niche investing requires special attention, diligence and knowledge before you can make an investment commitment.

Global Investing

Global investing, or expanding into international markets, requires a keen sophistication and judgment to understand and maneuver through the variables. The same basic methodology for domestic investments applies in many foreign countries, but the differences in currencies, foreign laws, political vagaries, and cultural and market idiosyncrasies complicate personal decisions and require specialized research and advice.

Commodity Investing

Commodity investing takes several forms and is subject to global and domestic politics and economics. For example, a working knowledge of both is necessary when dealing in commodities that are affected by climate and are also traded in world markets. Sugar and other agricultural products, oil, gold and other metals, and commodities that are historically used as barter and currency are most affected by these larger forces and cannot be understood from a domestic or otherwise narrow knowledge base or understanding. For example, territorial conflicts erupting in Iraq will spike the price of domestic crude oil beyond the power of the domestic economy to regulate its local market prices.

Investing in Timberland

Investing in timberland without understanding or researching the paper and packaging industry and real estate and agricultural markets raises the already inherent risks and volatility of an alternative investment of this type. Since exposure to these many alternatives need not be direct to be included in a portfolio, when understanding is limited or risk level precludes direct participation, passive, protected levels of involvement are prudent ways to expand a diversifying portfolio. (See Chapter 11, "Real Estate.") Follow the industry in *The Wall Street Journal*. Look for expert sources to help you evaluate the options in this category, beginning with the basic due diligence techniques set out later in this chapter.

Hedging and Derivatives

Hedging and derivatives have received a bad rap as investment alternatives. The decision to directly commit large sums to these management activities should be made only after weighing more easily understood methods, such as purchasing stocks and bonds in companies specializing in management of or exposure to the resources underlying these same investments. Another way is to invest with a reputable and knowledgeable dealer in less-costly commodities options and other derivatives by which you can partially hedge against volatility and limit your cash exposure to downside risks. Certainly, novices should not attempt any direct or indirect investment without realizing that they could lose large portions of their interest no matter what the sales material might claim. Perhaps nowhere else is

healthy skepticism a more useful attribute than in alternative investments. (See Chapter 9, "Money Management," for further details on
hedge funds.)

Over a five-year period, a comparison of alternative investments
of commodities traders, the S&P, and hedge funds shows the S&P
500 gaining 17.2 percent annually at a much lower risk and far lower
fees (if owned as index mutual funds) than managed commodities
accounts, which gained a 19 percent compounded annual rate of return, and hedge funds, which returned 20 percent. Even so, a sobering estimate from the Commodity Futures Trading Commission
(CFTC) claims that 75 percent of its investors lose money. Needless
to say, a minuscule number of experts are making all of the good
decisions. The rewards can be so high because the investor puts down
only a fraction of the total cost when buying or selling a contract, but
the investor can also lose several times his or her original investment and may have to come up with additional cash in short periods of time. As in money management, excellence and expertise is
found in only a small number of practitioners. The best ones don't
have to advertise.

This last fact is one reason that due diligence is complicated
and difficult when looking for advisors and advice in these narrow
market areas. The following general hints specific to performing due
diligence into specialty investments are designed to help you begin
gaining a grasp of the choices you will be offered.

DUE DILIGENCE FOR INVESTMENT ALTERNATIVES

Before considering an investment of a nontraditional nature, you need
to learn the components of due diligence for specialty investing. First,
you must know the principles of general evaluation for any field of
interest. Then you can begin to use a series of general measurement
techniques. In the case of art and collectibles alternatives, you will
need to know and use two evaluation tools specific to this area—(1)
appraisal criteria for property purchase or transfer, and (2) an understanding of how and why to determine value for specific purposes. The latter has a greater impact on whether you purchase,
collect, sell, plan for, and gift these assets wisely and well. You will
benefit from using the principles of evaluation and certain measurement techniques applicable to the noncollectible alternative investment classes as a foundation to the valuing and appraisal measures.

Principles of Evaluation

Because investors are less familiar with investment alternatives, particular care must be used to research their place in any wealth management scheme.

The investor must first commit to researching an unfamiliar asset class before investing in it. Begin by revisiting the principles of the Prudent Investor Rule (The Third Restatement), general planning imperatives (Chapter 4), and asset allocation parameters (Chapter 5).

The investor must keep in mind that there are two sides to investment analysis: qualitative and quantitative. Much of what you will be asked to review is based on speculation rather than fact. This is particularly true when faced with first-stage ventures and other alternative or nontraditional opportunities, such as new sports franchises, real estate pro formas, and hedge fund investment partnerships with narrow and arcane niche strategies. In these cases, the power of the qualitative review outweighs that of any speculated performance from a quantitative proposal or prospectus.

Private equity investments and many other alternatives are not subject to regulatory scrutiny. Without oversight, vast opportunities exist to take advantage of novice investors. This is truly an example of buyer beware. Ask about what you need to know. There are far fewer successful managers than there are investment opportunities. In particular, be realistic about the systemic risk in each alternative investment class. For other acquisitions, such as art and commodities, only some of the review process applies.

Measuring for a Perfect Fit

To begin, find people who are successfully involved in the personal investment area at which you are looking and who have a history of doing it well. Learn from them. Learn from more than one person. Don't just take someone else's word. In every instance, use "due diligence," a term you will tire of but will hear and use again and again if you want long-term financial health. It is an especially important exercise for alternative investments, and it is recommended for all investment classes. Use the following measurements to form personal conclusions:

1. Check to see if this type of investment idea and strategy fits your given goals, your values, and your guiding mission statement. If you received this opportunity in some other way (inheritance, gift, divorce) besides by choice, do you still want to participate? Do you still have to participate, and why? If you do, what do you need to know about it to understand its overall impact on your current and future situation? For instance, does your acceptable risk level allow you to consider the volatility of a hedge fund investment with an unproven manager? If not, don't even begin the conversation.

2. Be skeptical. Is this a realistic strategy for you, for anyone, or is it just a packaged exotic to make someone else wealthy at your expense? Can it be explained so that you can understand it? If you understand it, do you even want it in your portfolio? Theoretical business plans and computer models can play to a base vice—greed. Are the assumptions only based on creative hindsight, or are they structured to take realistic advantage of current and future trends in the special market represented? For example, am I sophisticated enough to understand that if I invest in repackaged home mortgage derivatives, I can lose my entire investment overnight when government interest rate policy changes as happened to many investors in the early 1990s?

3. The most important questions you will ask are personnel questions. Are the managers qualified to manage on your behalf? (See the Chapter 7 and Appendix C for applicable considerations.) If there is an ongoing business venture involved, is there an effective board of directors? Do the managers of the investment have the power to generate deals described to reach stated objectives? (Caution: Due diligence requires you to meet and to get to know the principals personally and via several references. Don't buy on past performance and reputation alone.) You might be partners for a long time, possibly 20 or more years, no matter what the original assumptions. If a manager has changed from a traditional investment strategy to venture capital investing, past performance is no guide in the new endeavor.

4. Determine if the structure of the deal reflects, enhances, or hampers your interests. Although investment partnership agreements are standardizing to a degree, many give inconceivably wide latitude to managers (a nifty way to avoid returning to the investors too frequently for approval of unfamiliar strategies). Never agree to anything too broad without review. Manager accountability is the strongest safeguard for your interests. Hedge fund and venture capital prospectuses often ask for broad latitude when the managing partner might have expertise in only a narrow range. Don't agree to anything outside the partnership's known field of experience unless your heart monitor is on snooze.

5. In the case of a limited partnership, find out who the partners are, who the advisors are that drafted the documents, and who will be reporting the results. The larger investors set the terms for the smaller limited partners. A large union pension fund that pays no taxes will have more clout in the partnership than an individual, taxpaying partner with a smaller partnership interest. Find out what the depth of experience and integrity is of the larger partners.

6. Determine how active you want to be in the deal and find out if the structure allows that. The balance sheet practices of the entertainment industries, especially the movie industry, are adversely skewed for the passive investor. Everybody else gets his or her money first. As in venture capital or oil and gas investing, there are a lot of "dry holes" before you hit a gusher.

7. Determine how much you might lose and what potential there is for future capital calls. Expect to periodically review the investment to ensure against unexpected calls. Never pour good money after bad.

8. Don't underestimate the length of the investment term. It often proves longer than originally speculated in the prospectus (offering memorandum). Remember: exit strategy.

When you gather this information and feel comfortable with what you have learned using these measurement techniques, you will be prepared to review a nontraditional investment opportunity with advisors, family members, or potential partners. Ultimately, decisions you can live with will flow from this exercise. But these will not serve you as well when trying to measure the soundness of acquisitions in the asset class of art and collectibles. There are separate due diligence measures you need to apply when stepping into these investments.

Valuing the Asset

When investing in a work of art or other rare item, you are doing it for one or two reasons: to enjoy having it near you and/or to collect or build value. There are three ways to place value on special assets. The first is to determine its fair market value (FMV). The second is its insurance appraisal value. The third way is similar to the justice who tried to define pornography when he said, "I don't know how to describe it, but I know it when I see it." You value it because you like it. You need to at least be familiar with the first two when purchasing for resale, when insuring it for replacement or protection, when doing your asset allocation, and for gift and estate planning purposes. There can be as much as a 300 percent differential between the two values.

FMV is used when valuing for resale, estate purposes, charitable contributions, bankruptcy pleadings, property division, collateral for loans, and divorce settlements. This is the real value a seller could get in the secondary market as a private person selling to a buyer (not in selling to the primary market of antique dealers, galleries, jewelers, or other retailers). The insurance appraisal value is usually based on estimated replacement cost given ample time to replace it, not a "fire sale" value. In other markets there may be no difference between the two. Full retail replacement value might even be set by the auction houses if there is very little market for certain items at the time.[2]

No one value is "correct." The IRS argues that there is only one value for purposes of appraisal—FMV. But an estate appraisal will be low due to the lack of control of sale timing. For gifting purposes, the same appraiser would place a higher value. The caveat is that there must be a fundamental agreement about what valuation purpose you have, and the values must be a reasonable reflection of the varying market reasons for selling at the time of appraisal. Research and market analysis must be defensible to the IRS for tax purposes when selling, trading, or giving away a collectible, and to an insurance company replacing a lost or damaged work. Appraisal of the piece before purchase, sale, or gift is done using the following tools.

Appraisal Criteria

Knowing what you are buying comes from years of study, buying what you like, and enlisting professional or other knowledgeable assistance. These include the following measurements.

Authenticity

Is it real? Most appraisers won't authenticate a purchase or sale unless they see something very wrong. An international auction house was hired to catalog and sell a large and diverse estate of collectibles amassed by a wealthy Texas oilman. The representatives (and subsequently the heirs) were appalled at the amount of reproduction Chinese porcelain collected by these very sophisticated, ostensibly knowledgeable investors. It turns out that the authenticator they relied upon was less than reliable, and they "bought what they liked." Due to dubious authenticity, the china was removed from the sale, and the value of the estate devalued accordingly. At the other extreme, these same collectors, who had a very practiced eye and a reliable authenticator, had acquired a near complete, extremely valuable collection of original porcelain Boehm birds from the artist's earliest years. These commanded premium prices from serious collectors at the estate auction. Regardless of an article's authenticity, if its condition is counter to what the collector's market demands, the value will falter.

Condition

American furniture collectors are fanatics about original condition. To protect the investment value, they want every scratch and every original oddity to stay with the piece. Collectors of European antique furniture place value on restoration. In the case of porcelain, the smallest disfigurement greatly diminishes the value to a collector and a retail purchaser. In many cases, a crack or chip renders porcelain almost worthless for resale. Serious investors and collectors must know the idiosyncrasies of their chosen markets just as they must appreciate the impact of supply and demand on the value of the item.

Rarity: Supply and Demand

Competition creates value in art, antiques, and jewelry. Understand that markets can be manipulated by suppliers to increase value in commodities underlying collectibles tied to those markets. The rarity of a piece is often increased by how a potential buyer values the previous ownership or provenance.

Provenance

Provenance is the history of something. Value can be created by the nature of the original source or the value placed on previous ownership, such as the jewelry of the Duchess of Windsor and the possessions of Jackie Onassis and other important icons as measured by history or celebrity. The provenance can create greater value than the actual quality of the piece. The Duchess's precious gems brought much less at auction than Mrs. Onassis's triple strand of fake pearls, but nonetheless, quality does matter.

Quality

What else is in the marketplace that is of comparable or greater value? Van Gogh's *Sunflowers* was the best painting of its kind ever to come on the market. Although not guaranteed, an object of that kind can encourage others to bring near-comparable objects out for sale, creating greater volume in quality to take advantage of upward value spikes. But even high-quality items can lose their value depending on the timing of a sale or purchase.

Timing and the Fashion of the Time

Timing and the fashion of the time impact the price and future value of the purchase both upwards and downwards. Remember what happened to the value of rare books and English portraiture over a 75-year span of time. Nothing. Contemporary art is "out" in the 1990s, but it was "in" in the early 1980s. But even if it is "in," will it fit in your living room?

Size

Oversized art has a limited market. On the other hand, two Picassos of comparable quality will result in the larger one selling for more than the smaller one (unless it is oversized).

Measuring more than the dimensions is all a part of sizing up an investment. Taking the plunge into any investment alternative is a matter of taste, style, fashion, interest, and knowledge. Your personal comfort level with risk; your awareness of global economies; national politics; fads; personal taste; circumstance; and most importantly, a sound effort at due diligence determine your satisfaction and success with alternative investments. Branch out. Check them out. Enjoy the learning, but be aware and beware.

ENDNOTES

1. Marc B. Porter, panel presentations, *Fine Art: Acquisition–Protection–Recovery*, The Second Annual Wealth Management Forum, Institute For International Research, New York, N.Y., September 1995. Marc B. Porter is senior vice president of Christie's, Inc., Estates and Appraisals.

2. Richard S. Wolf, *Fine Art: Acquisition–Protection–Recovery*, The Second Annual Wealth Management Forum, Institute For International Research, New York, N.Y., September 1995. Richard S. Wolf is senior vice president of Sotheby's, Trust and Estate Services.

14

SECURITY AND INSURANCE

Safeguards, Replacements, and Protections

Because insurance is an investment that covers broad areas of need, is highly individual, and is often not used except in the ordinary course of business, I have left a basic discussion of it to the end of this book rather than dealing with it as a core planning matter. Wealthy families treat many of their insurance needs separately from their planning, except in the case of life insurance. And even then, families rely on life insurance primarily as a liquidity generator with a short-term purpose, much like one would use flower bonds, or occasionally as a wealth replacement vehicle when giving something away, such as a philanthropic gift made to a charitable remainder trust.

A family insurance program is circumscribed only by the extent to which the members want to "self insure." Insurance is a many-faceted term for safeguarding what is materially and personally important to you. Even though all risks are not insurable, risk management is the function of insurance coverage. You can choose to avoid risk (virtually impossible), reduce risk (by loss prevention), assume risk (by size of deductibles), or transfer risk (with liability and disability insurance) by virtue of the level of insurance coverage. This chapter attempts to introduce the most common types of insurance and why you might consider their use. This helps you begin to investigate your options, the availability of product, and the value of using advisors to further assist you as your portfolio and needs grow and change over time.

You begin with a review of your personal, family, and business goals and objectives, and your list of things that might need protection for one reason or another, learning what types of insurance are available, what specialty advisors there are to help you, and who is best at it, using the suggested hiring techniques found in Chapter 7 and elsewhere in this chapter. Then set about having the necessary discussions to make your insurance decisions. Some of these decisions will be unilateral; others might involve the whole family or business partners, depending on who will be affected by the decision. The final step in the process is to review your insurance coverage and your documentation, or to have a staff member do it with your involved input, on a regular basis, sometimes annually, sometimes only every few years. In the latter instance, reappraising property to make sure that you are adequately covered can become costly and bothersome if done annually, but to maximize your protection, it should be done at least every five to seven years.

The two categories of insurance most relevant to wealthy families are personal protection and property insurance and life insurance. The category of business insurance is not addressed except to the extent that personal protection or business succession planning is specific to your business activities. Examples of these blended needs would be in the case of personal and business property protection requirements, liquidity needs for a business transition to protect an owner's family, and liability insurance for a family member serving as a director of a family or nonfamily entity.

PERSONAL PROTECTION AND PROPERTY INSURANCE

This overview of the most common types of insurance coverage used by very wealthy families introduces you to what others like you use in their risk management. Included with the actual policy types are other noninsurance tools employed for personal and family protection to complete your overall wealth stewardship planning in this area.

The specific details must be explored between the family and your advisors within the context of your overall planning needs. (Refer to Chapter 4 for a review of the planning process.) For example, in the case of personal property protection, flood insurance for a coastal property (if indeed it is available) may or may not be deemed essential by the owner. Crop insurance for the family farm, liability insurance for an investment asset, or an umbrella policy to protect a person of means from potentially harmful and frivolous lawsuits are valid and important considerations in wealth steward-ship. Begin with personal protection insurance.

Health Care and Disability

Regardless of the financial means to withstand the cost of long-term care or catastrophic illness, no one can anticipate the eventualities in store for them. Even a personality as successful and able as the actor Christopher Reeve can decimate his hard-earned fortune with the cost of long-term care. Most insurance policies have lifetime limits. With life spans increasing and medical costs rising, relying on your investments to protect you might be shortsighted or foolish. Most independent agencies have a medical insurance specialist that can review your options with you. At the very least, some form of cata-strophic insurance should be considered for every member of the family. Disability coverage for the self-employed should also be se-riously evaluated and considered. If your livelihood creates your wealth, disability coverage is a near imperative. If your family or business can be healthy without your day-to-day management, dis-ability insurance might be an unnecessary expense. The most effi-cient and cost-effective coverage is through a group policy that covers your business or family office and anyone who falls under that um-brella. Otherwise, individual coverage, a very individual require-ment, will be your alternative.

Kidnap and Ransom Insurance

Although not purchased frequently, as a commentary on our times, the inclusion of this topic bears witness to how fear and envy are sometimes associated with wealth. I suspect that no family or indi-vidual of exceptional means escapes threats to their loved ones. Con-sider a family security program. Depending on the level of fear that stalks a family, and the "profile" they carry, kidnap coverage is avail-able. The most common measures are to engage security services; to structure bank access through trustworthy officials for availabil-ity of some level of cash; and to place records in safe keeping that record all family members' vital statistics, fingerprints, photos, and so on. Each family must review their level for concern and proceed cautiously and thoughtfully. Over the generations, our family has not been immune to threats, stalking, and attempted kidnapping. As a result, the "gun-toting" ethic of the Wild West is alive and well with some of them. Sometimes experience evolves into a feeling that this response is justifiable.

Property and Casualty (Personal Liability)

Although there are countless combinations and options with which to build a meaningful protection package, only broad attention is paid to the most common insurance treatments. Wealthy families have peculiar and highly individualized insurance needs. Special focus areas might include artwork and unique property protection, depending on the specific interests and holdings of the family.

Property Protection (Replacement) Insurance

Property protection insurance should primarily focus on protecting against loss. You can choose to specify the perils you protect against (fire, wind, flood), or you can assume an all-risk coverage stance. Whichever you choose, make sure that it is enough to cover the value no matter what the cause of loss. Property insurance carriers don't give grace periods if premiums lapse the way life insurance carriers do. Therefore, regular appraisals and renewals are necessary to maintain seamless coverage. Always err on the side of excess and insure for a sufficient amount, whether it be for property value or liability levels.

Liability Coverage

Liability coverage is purchased for any private home, the operating business, and investment property. A comprehensive personal liability (umbrella) policy written into your homeowner's coverage is commonplace and includes the added protection that the insurance company will defend the insured in any suit covered by the policy. The umbrella does exclude certain coverage, including liability incurred in business or professional pursuits; the ownership and maintenance or use of automobiles, aircraft, and watercraft; and injury or damage caused intentionally by the insured. But separate policies for each (except for intentional damage) are available and advisable. Most states require liability coverage on automobiles and their owners. Location risk impacts cost and creates a greater necessity for coverage, such as in the case of boat moorage or vacation property in hurricane-prone areas.

Directors' and Officers' (D & O) Insurance

This type of insurance is recommended for any member of a wealthy family that serves as trustee on a corporate or not-for-profit board. Many companies and charities provide this coverage for their board members now as a matter of course (most new board members wisely won't serve if it is not a part of the organization's policy) to attract and retain effective and influential trustees. But having your own excess coverage is advisable. There is accelerated activity in the courts toward sizable monetary judgments against decision makers for "wrongful acts" and against board members and management for negligence stemming from their management decisions. This negative activity includes actions against not-for-profit boards such as pension funds and university investment boards, making this coverage invaluable. In any case, "gross negligence," whether corporate or personal, is never protected in any D & O coverage.

Investment Property and Liability Insurance

Investment property should have its own replacement coverage and liability protection due to potential injury to renters, workers, lessees, or even transients living on or traversing the property. The company or family office should also carry enveloping coverage over employees on company business. Also advisable from time to time is additional coverage for indemnity, which is useful to protect any perceived accountability an outside party would place on you when large events are held to which your name is prominently attached. This would be restricted to the event itself or to the time frame from planning through to completion. In the case of development real estate or farm and ranch land, other property insurance coverage should include liability for environmental damage mitigation.

Federal Flood Insurance

Although no longer provided to new coastal structures, federal flood insurance should be renewed with any purchase of a "grandfathered" property that has an effective policy. Insure that the coverage does not lapse with an ownership change. Once it does, it cannot be recovered and is no longer available. This is particularly important where storm surges occur near shoreline properties susceptible to hurricanes.

Specialty Personal Property Insurance

Over $10 billion worth of art is stolen annually, and the recovery rate is about 5 percent. Insuring your collection and the cost of doing so is all a part of the cost of amassing a collection. Itemized riders are advisable for valuable antiques, collectibles, luxury items of jewelry and furs, and art, and should be reviewed and updated on a regular basis every three to five years. The irony is that these lists become a documented inventory highlighting a value with potential tax consequences to the owner upon death. Thus, when cataloging protection needs, consider what the costs and consequences are for holding that protection. Each collection must be considered in its own unique way. If it will travel abroad, the coverage might have to be specialized for that purpose, but only when the item or object travels. To determine the best loss limit levels when several locations share a collection, pick the value in the one place at which the collection is represented in its highest concentration. Lightning shouldn't strike several places at once, and total loss limit may be too high to justify the policy costs.

Noninsurance Personal Protection Tools

These tools are an integral part of the insurance coverage you will use and are just as important to use and review along with your policy coverage.

  1. If you have been collecting extensively in one field, selecting an appraiser is easier than finding a specialist in a field unfamiliar to you. There are only a few, and with the exception of jewelry appraisers, the network is relatively small. A broad collection might be better appraised by an auction house with broad specialties or a generalist with auction house experience. Get three recommendations. Check the appraiser for experience and reputation. There is no certification process for personal property appraisers. There are two appraisers associations: The American Society of Appraisers and Appraisers Association of America. These associations teach good methodology, but they do not test for competency.[1]

  2. Valid appraisal characteristics should include understand-

able descriptions, including dimensions, color, and materials used; identification of maker/artist, date and period, and rarity and quality as compared to other works by the same artist; judgment by sight, not by photograph, videotape, or drawings; overall condition noted with prominent scars described; provenance, if available; the stated appraised value; and appraiser's credentials and signature.

3. Keeping a video and photographic inventory together with copies of policies and provenance documents in a safe, off-premises location is important. Qualified appraisals and sales slips are required for proofs of claim in the event of loss of any kind. Inventory, cataloging, and recovery technologies and services are available for collection owners and caretakers through the International Registry of Antiques and Fine Art. When formulating your inventory, review the discussion of appraising and valuing art and collectibles presented in Chapter 13.

4. Safekeeping methods such as bank safety-deposit boxes and jewelry and art vaults can protect your valuables and reduce the impact of policy cost through "in-vault" insurance. You only pay the higher cost when a single item is taken out of safekeeping. The average rate is $0.25 per $100 of value, although rates may be higher in California and Florida. Besides value and location, other factors that determine rates are availability of security and fire protection, the size of the collection, and the loss or claims history, and any limitations or additions to coverage, which might include off-premises and transit coverage, exhibition restrictions, restoration recovery, territorial limitations, and breakage.

5. Additional protection measures that supplement insurance include on-site, structural controls for valuable possessions: electronic and human security systems, fire protection systems, transportation of valuables protection, water damage controls, and heat and humidity controls.

Although the choices and decisions are many among available insurance products, none are more confusing or complicated than the ones you might consider about life insurance. It is a wholly different planning tool than those used for personal protection coverage.

LIFE INSURANCE

For persons with sizeable fortunes, life insurance is primarily valuable for wealth replacement (for what families anticipate relinquishing in estate taxes or in charitable gifting) or wealth enhancement. Life insurance decisions occur at the end of the estate and financial planning processes, to be used as tools, not as ends in themselves. You will undoubtedly learn that sophisticated life insurance policies are the most visibly marketed. Agents who sell them are on commission. In cases of extraordinary wealth, the cost effectiveness of protection might be nil when other types of lower-cost planning and investment techniques would suffice. We will first look at what insurance is available and used most often. We will then look at what other considerations are involved in making life and personal protection insurance decisions.

Types of Life Insurance

The array of life insurance products in the market today is confusing and incomprehensible in many ways. What follows are the most commonly considered policy structures in use today. As in any other investment, so much depends on how you define your family's missions and goals.

Term Insurance

When needed for only limited time periods, term insurance is the most economical coverage. It provides a death benefit without cash buildup. Because premiums increase with one's age, it is not a good choice if the needs will continue to an advanced age. However, if the client has limited cash available for a few years, term insurance available in 1-, 5-, 10-, 15-, and 20-year packages keeps the premium low and can later convert to a permanent plan. Choice is dependent on the length of time of the anticipated premium outlay as well as the desire to keep the first year's cost relatively low. Relevant considerations include how long the current premium rates are guaranteed, what the maximum premiums are that can be charged, how premiums compare with similar policies, length of renewable term, length of time the policy can be converted to a permanent or level premium plan, and if the current rates illustrated are based on required re-underwriting in the future.

Whole Life

Whole life is a permanent form of insurance, with coverage guaranteed for life and with a guaranteed amount payable at death. Premiums usually remain constant, and cash values are guaranteed unless the policy grows through dividends or available riders. The purchaser should know the range of plausible variations. Relevant considerations include (1) what the available alternatives are in the event of a *decrease* in interest rates, and (2) which policyholders benefit from interest rate changes.

Whole Life Base/Term Blend

This policy reduces whole life premiums by splitting the face amount between a whole life amount and a term rider. The premium is lower but is paid out over a longer term. A significantly higher death benefit internal rate of return (IRR) occurs in the earlier years. However, the longer the policy is in effect, the more the IRR on the cash value decreases because more premium dollars are paid into the pure insurance cost.

Universal Life

This type is most flexible, and it is the easiest to understand because expenses and the cost of insurance are identified separately in the policy. Lifetime coverage remains in effect if there is sufficient premium to cover the death benefit to life expectancy. Relevant considerations include the minimum premium necessary for life expectancy, number of years, if policy face amount can decrease, if policy face amount can increase (changes can usually be made as frequently as once per year after the first few years of coverage), if evidence of insurability is necessary for face amount increases, and if there are penalties on the surrender period.

Variable Life

Designed to satisfy permanent needs, variable life insurance can outperform traditional products due to segregated accounts invested in various funds. The results of chosen investment funds pass through to the policy and are reduced only by the expense loads. Actual investment strategy and performance are disclosed up front. There is less risk from potential carrier financial problems. Relevant considerations are what investment funds are available to the consumer, historical fund performance, what total return is used for illustrative purpose, which funds were chosen for illustration, and if the policy provides a minimum death benefit.

Second-to-Die Insurance (Joint and Survivorship Insurance)

I single this out as a special life insurance product because it, more than any other, is designed as a tool for wealth replacement or enhancement and is one of the most widely used tools in estate planning today. This policy type is highly cost effective because it pays a death benefit only upon the second death (the actuarial formulas allow the cost to be spread over two lives). Second-to-die insurance serves as an effective means of transferring value, tax free, to a spouse or partner at a lower premium cost than that available with twin policies. Ease of underwriting is another preferred feature. For split-dollar plans, there is a lower (often 10 times lower) economic benefit reportable as income.

Reliable components of a second-to-die policy include a whole life element with guaranteed premiums, cash values, available dividends, lump sum payment alternatives, a term element of nonguaranteed mortality charges, flexible premium design, a divorce clause, and provision for estate tax law changes.

Flexible components that need clarification before purchasing a second-to-die policy allow a blend of the permanent portion with the term insurance portion so that policy values hold up over time. Term insurance portions that don't endow over time can be extremely costly later. Often misleadingly labeled a *guaranteed* term premium, the policy premium can *increase* in order to maintain the initial death benefit. This flexible pricing structure must be explored if you are to consider this policy type.

The pricing structure for the permanent contract portion must be defined. Does it increase and, if so, at what level? What are the pricing structure and rates for the term portion (that guarantees the same benefit throughout the life of the contract)? Additional monies may be added to purchase paid-up additions of death benefits, replacement term insurance, or both. This must be clarified with the consultant as to whether additions can be made without evidence of insurability. The minimum protection required by the owner must be available in the policy at an acceptable pricing structure.

Contingencies in the event of changes over two lifetimes can determine your decision to choose a policy. If the company's dividend rates decline, will the premium of your preferred policy increase or will the death benefit decrease? Does the policy have an early warning system from the issuing company that forewarns of future problems for the insured? Does the divorce clause allow the parties to convert to separate policies without having to pass a health exam?

Second-to-Die as Liquidity and Estate-Planning Tool

In this case, the grantors make a gift to an irrevocable trust, thus removing the value from both estates. Annual gifts of $10,000 by each of the insureds (annual exclusion gifts or more if unified credit still applies) are made to the trust, which the trustees then use to purchase a second-to-die policy on the grantors' lives. At the death of the insureds, the trustees collect tax-free proceeds and purchase assets from the estate. The estate then uses the proceeds to pay transfer taxes.

Second-to-Die for Key Executives

This type of policy is written on the life of the key managers or owners, whose deaths would cause grave disruptions in the daily life of a business. It is very often used as loss-protection insurance for family members and others in the business who would be most affected by a key loss of this kind. This insurance is effective when two unrelated, key people are involved, such as in a managing partnership or other joint ownership. It also serves as reassurance in future succession issues for banking and supplier relationships and for outside limited partners.

Second-to-Die Insurance and Buy-Sell Planning

To help keep the business in the family, buy-sell agreements are common. This type policy can provide liquidity. For instance, two married couples each own 50 percent of a closely held business. At the death of one spouse, it is intended that the surviving spouse will receive the decedent's stock and continue participating in the business as a 50 percent shareholder. However, upon the death of the surviving spouse, the surviving married couple would want to purchase the decedent's stock, thus assuring control of the business. Each couple can own a joint life policy on the lives of the other couple. A split-dollar purchase allows for corporate funding of such a cross purchase to help preserve the viability of the business. The corporation can then recapture the premium outlay upon distribution from the insurance company.

Second-to-Die Insurance and Generation Skipping

In those instances where the client has adequate wealth and wishes to maximize the value left to grandchildren, second-to-die insurance is an ideal vehicle. Because of the tax-free nature of the proceeds (assuming an irrevocable generation-skipping trust (GST) is in place to receive the policy), the after-tax rate of return is usually superior to most alternative investments. Furthermore, in generation-skipping situations, there is a possibility for the ultimate beneficiaries to enjoy the proceeds at an earlier age.

Second-to-Die Insurance to Aid a Disabled Child

This insurance is specifically for a couple raising a child with physical and emotional disabilities. Both parents worry about the impact of the death of the second spouse on the care for the child given the likelihood of the child's continued dependence. A second-to-die policy can provide the funding for financial security and special needs. Careful planning with an attorney is essential. Proper drafting of trust clauses and appointment of guardians and trustees are crucial to protecting the legal rights of the disabled beneficiary. Putting the policy in trust also lessens the parental estate tax burden for the disabled child and his or her guardian and allows eligibility for public assistance if it is required for the dependent's care.

Second-to-Die as Charitable Gift Replacement

When a gift of appreciated property is given to a charitable remainder trust (CRT) (see Chapter 4, "Imperatives of Planning," and Chapter 8, "Philanthropy"), the lifetime income is received by the grantors. Establishing a separate irrevocable trust with a second-to-die policy effectively replaces the value of the charitable gift back to the family. The trust can either be funded with the income tax savings generated by the charitable gift or by the additional income available to the grantors by virtue of not having paid any income taxes and receiving income from the entire asset. If so designated, at the second death, the corpus of the CRT can pass to a family foundation whose trustees are the grantor's children.[2]

CHOOSING AND REVIEWING INSURANCE

To begin your involvement in risk and liquidity management use, the questions in Figure 14.1 to evaluate your needs. You will be much more likely to get the right people to advise you if you think about it first. If you need assistance from staff or insurance professionals in order to answer them, you should set about finding those individuals.

FIGURE 14.1

Evaluating Insurance Options

- Who (or what) is being insured?
- Why is the insurance necessary?
- What amount covers the concern?
- What is the cost?
- Who pays the premiums?
- Who owns the policy (in whose name is it held?) and why?
- Who collects the payments? (A trustee? Insurance company?)
- Who is the desired beneficiary?
- What is not covered by the policy and why?
- What is the length of the policy?
- How often should the decision be reviewed?
- Is the coverage relevant or necessary?
- Are valuations commensurate with coverage needs?

Choosing compatible, responsive, and professionally experi-enced agents or consultants and financially sound carriers is critical to the development of a comprehensive insurance program. Equally important is the extent of their practice in providing guidance and service to similarly situated families. Outside professionals will be either independent agents (agents who shop around for the best cov-erage among many suppliers), company-specific agents (with only one line of products from which to choose), or insurance consult-ants, who are generally a blend of the other two types but are found exclusively in the life insurance field or in some other specialty such as fine arts and collectibles insurance.

Some family offices hire insurance managers to design and monitor plans that include property and casualty, liability, health care and disability, employee fidelity bonding, kidnap and ransom, automobile, directors' and officers' (D&O), and business and life in-surance. Others rely on the office manager to perform this function. Some families might rely on high-quality, independent insurance agents or consultants who can "shop" around for individualized "best protection" service rather than hiring internal personnel for the task. Generally, life insurance is purchased from a separate spe-cialty agent.

Regardless of the type of professional advice you seek, familiar-ity with your circumstance or like circumstances, professionalism, availability, credibility, freedom from conflicts of interest, maintain-ing current oversight, and up-to-date and relevant protection are all attainable with the right advice. Choosing good people (see Chapter 7) is as important as choosing the best insurance company and the most appropriate coverage.

Life insurance professionals present products from companies that manage money, but they have not necessarily proven their effectiveness as money managers. They are investing your premium payments over time in order to be able to pay future claims to you and to other customers. If wealth replacement is your goal, money managers who are not in the insurance sales business but specifically concentrate on replacing and enhancing wealth through active portfolio management will better serve you. Specialty, personal insurance products for a very small number of extremely wealthy individuals who demand superior investment returns and wish to pay to get the protection they seek have only recently become available. Only the most sophisticated insurance consultants, working closely with money management firms can provide the valuable guidance for multigenerational family needs. The exercise of choosing personal protection insurance is simple. Life insurance choices are complex and can be bewildering.

If you have used the methods suggested in earlier chapters on forming mission statements, setting goals and objectives, and planning, and have evaluated your insurance needs using the questions in Figure 14.1, getting down to the specifics of what policy, if any, to purchase can best be accomplished by this recommended due diligence process, which is used by consultants guiding a family or individual to choose a company. The policy choice will come out of the larger planning and the work of hiring professional advice.

Due Diligence for Selecting Companies

Conducted by the insurance professional and/or family, due diligence involves review of the quality of the company, the product, and the advisor. The willingness of the advisor to put time and effort into due diligence insures a greater chance of successfully filling the family's specific needs. Your family's own investigation should begin with choosing an agent or consultant that you trust who has good ideas, has your best interests at heart, who has specific experience in serving a client base similar to yours, and who is most likely to give you good service during the process with the promise of consistent follow-up reviews. Any insurance professional you choose should be equipped and knowledgeable enough to explain the available options to you and to issue a number of diligence tests.

Financial Strength of the Insurance Company

What happens if lower interest rates result in lower cash accumulations, creating longer premium payment periods or increased premium payment demands? Will the company still be here when the policy matures? Within the company itself, are its dividend rates being credited today to new contracts different from those contracts issued in prior years in an attempt to attract new policies? Is the company illustrating its numbers on a "new money" (new policy sales) or "portfolio" (old and new policy investments) method? And although the prevailing rating systems do not measure the same qualities, one has to ask about the company's ratings in Best's, Moody's, and Standard and Poor's.[2]

Best's Best's assesses the financial strength and operating performance of over 1400 life insurance companies. A+ is their highest rating and is assigned to over 200 companies, making it generally unnecessary to do business with lesser-rated carriers. Best's also rates how companies' lapse mortality and expense ratios compare to the industry average. A high lapse ratio causes a company to set premiums high enough to recoup acquisition costs from a smaller base of existing policy owners.

Moody's Moody's rates the claims-paying ability of certain life insurance carriers and the companies' investments. Moody's concentrates on the industry's largest companies and rates most at Aaa to Aa3. Only a few receive the highest Aaa rating. Best's and Moody's lowest rating is a C.

Standard and Poor's Standard and Poor's (S&P) rates life insurance companies from a high of AAA through a low of D. Few companies request a rating by S&P. Of those that do, the majority are rated AAA.

Policy's Historical Performance

Ask for actual results, not projections. The focus should be on past performance and operating costs. Illustrations of current as opposed to future dividend rates, often used to attract new clients, pushes costs onto "old" policyholders to hide the true costs to the new policy buyer. These projections are thus bent to appear as if the dividend rates in the future will be high when, in fact, once your proceeds are folded into the old policy pool, the dividends will drop due to the costs allocated to the "old policy pool of capital."

Treatment of Policyholders

Talk to others who use them.

Compatibility

Ascertain how the carrier's market combines with a client's needs.

The Company's Product

If the dividend crediting drops by 1 or 2 percent, lower interest rates result in lower cash accumulations, possible longer premium payment periods, or increased premiums and decreased death benefits.

The Company's Illustration Assumptions

Is the mortality assumption underlying the illustration based on current experience, or does it include projected improvements in mortality? Are rates being illustrated that exceed the current rate actually being credited? Are in-force illustrations readily available?

After the due diligence is performed, policy decisions are then made and executed. Having sufficient coverage does not stop there. As in all other aspects of wealth management, the need for periodic review is equally important to insure that you are getting adequate protection, addressing your needs, and meeting your goals.

Periodic Review

Regular insurance company and broker reviews are as important as systematic reviews of wills and estate plans and other investment portfolios. Cost efficiency is an ongoing challenge. Internal safeguards of checks and balances, where valuable assets are exposed, should be monitored and reviewed within the purview of the risk manager for the family, or at least together with key advisors and the family group. Most insurance policies are cancelable at any time, although you should be particularly careful when canceling a life insurance policy that could retain the bulk of the capital you have invested.

Reviewing and updating property insurance coverage, more than any other type of insurance, tends to be ignored after the initial purchase. Property values are never static for long. An owner needs to keep sufficient coverage to meet at least 80 percent of the property's replacement cost (if new) and to be current with construction cost increases. Homeowner's coverage is only available for an owner-occupied dwelling. In determining the amount of coverage for investment property, however, the insurance may be written for actual-cash-value basis coverage, but cash value and fair market value may be different from each other and from replacement cost. Adding coverage to an existing policy is as simple as mailing a sales slip to your agent to have additional coverage placed on new purchases.

But property insurance isn't all you need to review regularly. Each year I review all of my insurance coverage with the counsel of an independent insurance agent, updating or eliminating as needed. My insurance coverage is reconfigured when my office changes locales, my family grows up and scatters, the office downsizes, property is sold or otherwise transferred to children, and when staff is pared. Each year I ask my agent/advisor where I can reevaluate and economize. Can I eliminate liability coverage at the office and retain a personal umbrella policy? His answer has always been an emphatic no until recently, when another office change allowed the change in policy. He insists that employees and contractors be separately covered when on a job for the business in case they are in an off-site accident. This would cushion the family from potential, especially spurious, legal action. Only when I turned over the office space to an outside contractor did the agent finally allow me to shrink the coverage. The value of this periodic review can be illustrated by my most recent experience.

My agent continually insists that I carry a minimum employee fidelity bond even though my staff shrank to one person several years ago. Then he agreed to carry a bare minimum (in his estimation) coverage for me, not allowing me to cancel it in a cost-cutting move. Six years after the last office shrinkage, a change in bookkeepers exposed irregularities, and I could only humble myself by thanking him for his insistent position with me. The "bare minimum" insurance he insisted on covered less than half the loss of funds my family suffered, but without it there would be little if any hope of even minor recovery of the loss. A theft loss claim on my income taxes, confined to the year of its discovery, was the only other ameliorating action I could take to make up for the loss.

Should such a thing happen to you, you might be surprised to find that you receive little sympathy from the general public. A very lenient restitution judgment against a bookkeeper for Anne Morrow

Lindbergh (an author and the widow of Charles Lindbergh) was handed down in which the judge accepted a plea for clemency by sentencing the embezzler to restore one-half of $250,000 taken from the invalid victim and no jail term, "because she (the victim) could afford to lose the money." Mrs. Lindbergh's family appealed the ruling. Had the woman stolen the money from a bank, I suspect that the judge's ruling would be quite different, even though the bank "could afford to lose the money." Sadly, this is a common attitude toward wealth that should suggest the use of fidelity bond insurance for transferring risk.

Conclusion

To the layperson, the insurance world may seem complex and unfathomable, but this is no reason to shy away from using it. It provides great benefits, particularly in complex situations that come with the benefits, opportunities, and responsibilities of wealth stewardship.

If you first examine your areas of need and determine what you want to protect, then get the best, most cost-effective advice and products from agents and consultants compatible with those objectives, then you can enjoy a sense of security from your position as a satisfied steward of your assets and your life.

Author's Note: I am grateful to Suzan Peterfriend and Howard Shapiro for providing the materials on which the life insurance segment of this chapter is based.

ENDNOTES

1. Richard S. Wolf, *Fine Art: Acquisition–Protection–Recovery*, The Second Annual Wealth Management Forum, Institute For International Research, New York, N.Y., September 1995. Richard S. Wolf is senior vice president of Sotheby's, Trust and Estate Services.
2. Suzan Peterfriend, and Howard Shapiro, DC Planning insurance consultancy, a compilation of presentation materials and narrative, Spring 1996.

Personal Asset Stewardship Questionnaire

1. What are your attitudes toward money? Where do they come from?

2. Have you ever thought of a financial plan for yourself?

3. Do you have a current will? Does your spouse? If yes, when was it last revised?

4. Do you know why you need a will?

5. Do you know what your spouse's will says? Do you know what you need to know to assist in planning your own will content?

6. Do you know where your wills are kept? Insurance policies? Other important papers? Do you know what should be on the "important papers " list?

7. Do you know what you own? What you will own? Who will be in control if you aren't? Is it a trustee? If yes, what kind? What is your knowledge of that person?

8. Do you and your spouse have a mission statement outlining what your financial future looks like if anything happens to either? If a femme sole, do you?

9. Do you have your own personal working relationship with a planner? Financial advisor? Accountant? Attorney? Insurance consultant? Banker? Trust officer? Do you know how to obtain or build one?

10. Do you know the questions to ask to learn what your financial rights and responsibilities are with respect to your future? Your family's future? Your spouse's business future? Your business future?

11. Do you know you have a right and a responsibility to ask these questions and get answers for yourself?

12. Do you have a retirement plan in place in the event that you are the surviving spouse?

13. Do you know what to do if you inherit an operating business?

14. Do you know what you need in order to feel financially secure? From where do your attitudes come?

15. When should you begin your financial survival planning?

16. Are you philanthropically inclined? Do you feel free to speak up for your desires in this regard if they differ from your spouse or other family members? Do you want to or know how to integrate them into your personal and family financial planning?

17. Do you know that you may be held legally and financially responsible for any indebtedness your spouse now carries? This can be the case if an owner signs personal guarantees that the spouse will be held directly responsible for the debt (including home mortgages, business loans, and taxes) if the owner is no longer alive?

18. Do you know what it means to you financially if you live in a city and/or state with income tax and/or community property laws? Are you prepared to move for financial reasons if your financial security needs and your realities are in conflict?

19. Are you prepared to go to work or resume a career if necessary? How?

20. Do you know how your children's financial welfare (including coverage of essentials— food, clothing, and shelter—and medical and education expenses) is prepared for? Do you know what it costs today and what it will cost in the future?

21. Do you balance your own checkbook? That of your household?

22. Do you know what a financial statement is? What it looks like? A balance sheet? Income statement? Cash flow projection?

23. What are your attitudes toward the family business or family office?

Financial Planning Outline

A. Analyze all factors and elements related to the individual or family, ideally based on consensus agreement among all affected parties.
   1. Review pertinent facts including changes in health, age, needs, cash flow, and so forth.
   2. Consider the disadvantages and advantages of your current situation.
   3. Determine what actions are required.
   4. Gather recommendations where appropriate.
B. Follow the process.
   1. Establish goals and objectives.
   2. Gather data.
   3. Analyze data.
   4. Develop a comprehensive financial plan.
   5. Implement the plan.
   6. Monitor, review, and adjust the plan, and then begin the cycle again.
C. Prepare a comprehensive financial plan.
   1. Personal data.
   2. Mission statements and goals and objectives statements.
   3. Identification of issues (such as age and cash flow requirements) and problems in the simplest terms (liquidity, dependency, etc.).
   4. Basic assumptions.
   5. Financial statements.
      a. Balance sheet (Assets – Liabilities = Net worth).
      b. Cash flow and budget information, including sources and uses of cash and running cash balances.
   6. Income and other tax projections.

      7. Risk management; addressing security and insurance needs.

      8. Listed investments (see balance sheet).

      9. Financial independence needs.

   10. Estate planning.

   11. Recommendations.

   12. Stated implementation plan.

D. Keep listed locations for all essential permanent records in a safe but accessible place such as with an attorney and/or a reliable relative.

- Updated list of family members' names, addresses, phone numbers, driver's license numbers and social security numbers.
- List of responsible people and their locations and contact numbers.
- Safe-deposit box location.
- Social security card and documentation, if you are older.
- Inventory of accounts (bank, investment, credit, property records, etc.) including numbers and locations.
- Birth certificates.
- Marriage certificate.
- Passports.
- Divorce decree and marital property agreement.
- Prenuptial agreement.
- Legal name change documentation.
- List of insurance policies (including names of agencies holding the policies with contact names and phone numbers).
- Updated will.
- Trust documents.
- Funeral instructions.
- Handwritten bequests.
- Revocable living trust.
- Durable power of attorney.

- Living will (advanced medical directive).
- Medical power of attorney (depending on the state in which you live).
- List of other beneficiary designations such as for IRAs and profit- and pension-sharing plans (to expedite filing for death benefits).
- Letter of instruction for distribution of special items not designated in the wills.
- Personal property inventory with photographs and narrated video and computer back-up (with hardcopy transcription).
- Tax records.
- Military records.
- Title papers (to homes, autos, and so forth).

Advisor Considerations

First, review Chapter 7 and gather the general information suggested below; then, review the specifics provided in the following section for the area of your current provider search.

General Considerations for Outside Advisors

- Integrity.
- Good, reliable character.
- Continuity in service personnel, especially in banks, trust departments, and accounting firms.
- Willingness and ability to bring excellent people into key leadership positions on your behalf.
- Personal chemistry; beware of promoters and slick operators.
- Style of management, advice, and surroundings; note how they spend the money they're given.
- Experience (including quality, quantity, and longevity) with like work and a similar client base.
- Conception of continuing communication. Are they proactive and do they expect you to keep them informed of your needs?
- Wants to walk the process at hand with you. Beware the advisor who thinks they should lead while you sit in the back seat. It is your process.
- Willingness to disclose philosophy on sensitive matters such as self trusteeships for living trusts, prenuptial agreements, and wealth management investment policy.
- Forthcoming with information—as much as you need. If the advisor discourages self education, find another advisor.
- Ability to work across disciplines with other advisors and retainers.
- Willingness to disagree with other advisors if they believe that the advisor's recommendations are not in a client's best interest.
- Willingness to give their opinion of their own strengths and weaknesses.
- Open disclosure of referral policy. Are they compensated? What do others say?
- Presence of insurance coverage including liability, malpractice, and, in the case of a managing partner or small operation, key executive insurance.
- Revealing and open compensation policies. How does the advisor charge? Are fees negotiable? Are any advance payments required? What is the billing cycle? Can the advisor provide the best estimate of the total cost of a project? Look for an open policy on revealing time sheets for senior and junior partner billings, and examine the style of broker (stock, insurance, etc.) compensation. (In short, whose best interest is being served?)
- Reliable and reputable client and professional firm references.
- Appropriateness of the advisor for the advice. For example, a friend is wise counsel in personal affairs but might be totally inexperienced in divining the legal work you require. Use your best judgment.

Investment (Money) Manager (See Chapters 5 and 9.)

A request for information (RIF) that includes many of the following elements is typically sent by investment consultants. This information will help you weed out inappropriate managers. You can create your own specific interview that addresses what you most need to know to further winnow your choices.

- Examine the firm structure (if applicable), including minimum account size, total amount under management, number of accounts, type of accounts (what percentage are taxable and/or institutional), how many accounts the firm has gained or lost in the last year and in the last three years, the average size of lost accounts, who to contact, and how much of their net worth is invested in their strategy. Request three references and phone numbers.
- Examine the style and investment philosophy. Does the manager show a willingness to change course, or is he or she always right? (Head for the exit if the answer is yes!)
- Determine the level of experience in market cycles, with previous employers, with similar clients, and with this strategy. Review the history of hiring, monitoring, and firing by outside consultants.
- Make an investment policy and performance measurement. This would include an examination of the upper and lower limits of accounts under management; number of positions per account; model portfolio characteristics; who makes policy and policy shift decisions; process of philosophy through to manager implementation; manager monitoring and compliance procedures; advantages, disadvantages, and risks of investment approach; trade execution policy; socially responsive investment criteria; taxable/nontaxable client policy differences; alternatives for clients with low-basis stock; and proprietary products and partnerships.
- Investigate the fee structure including the minimum fee, fee schedule per product, commission schedule, fee negotiation policy for larger accounts and taxable/nontaxable portfolios of like size, and policy on fees for multiple accounts.

- Make inquiries regarding personnel. This might include questions regarding the biographies of key personnel, size of staff, number of portfolio managers and numbers by type of analysts, and turnover in past year to three years. If the individual is not a registered financial or investment advisor, what the status is of his or her state licensing as a taxable client advisor.

- Examine research policies and practice, including sources, percentage from outside, stock rating system and process of investment opinion of a given issue, stock valuation approach, and technology applied to analysis. Also, inquire as to compensation (soft dollar) for outside research.

- Examine performance levels, including 10 years of quarterly returns, the number of accounts and total assets in the sample, total taxable assets, and tax-exempt assets in sample accounts.

- Evaluate the quality of communication, execution, and reporting. This might include questions regarding the relay of individual security changes, the timing and frequency of written reports, income and dividend collection, taxable account reporting capability, online linkage, average portfolio turnover rate, account custodian and insurance, directed brokerage policy, hedged products, any current litigation or arbitration, and National Association of Securities Dealers complaints.

- Make inquiries regarding what firms supply legal and accounting work; check them out, especially with alternative LPs and new money managers.

Commercial Bank (See Chapters 4 and 9.)

- Determine experience and policy with similar clients.
- Determine the bank's *current* reputation for personal banking relationships. (Regional banking consolidations all but eliminated these.)
- Examine lending policies for family mortgages, art lending, and small business lending.
- Determine the quality of service by interviewing current clients for satisfaction level.

- Investment management (not highly compensated as those in independent firms). (See Services, Investment (Money) Management above.)
- Make inquiries regarding niche services, such as trading of global bonds, international equities, structured balance sheet lending, and derivatives.
- Determine the bank's global and domestic custody capabilities. Make inquiries regarding efficiencies, security, costs, and quality of administrative and distributive procedures in execution, operations, reporting, technology, research, client service, financing, securities lending, cash management, cash protection, fee policies, and international transactions. Many wealthy families conduct complex multinational business transactions.

Note: A custodian who doesn't have the means to deliver these complex services is not worth retaining solely on the basis of "it has always been the family bank." Where global custody is at stake, knowledge and access to foreign markets, speed of tax reclamation, multicurrency accounting and reporting (daily), liquidity management, income and dividend collection, sub-agent management, timely customized client reports accessible through online linkage, and, most importantly, the capability to grasp the peculiarities of the taxable client by providing after-tax return analysis and reporting are absolute necessities.

Prime Broker (See Chapter 9.)

- Determine software capacities (critical to the family office trading operation).
- Examine pricing policies. Do they give taxable clients of like size the same treatment as nontaxable clients?
- Examine the ability to consolidate near the credit source and to manage cash.

Investment Banker

- Evaluate the levels of service and research (by choice, some grossly overpay for top-notch research), efficiency in execution on transactions, derivatives, custody, swaps, and use of different banks, depending on their specialty.

- Examine the fee structure. Are institution-like coverage and institutional pricing policies available?
- Determine reputation, including quality around difficult trades requiring special expertise and capital markets advisory.

Trust Company/Private Bank (See Chapters 4 and 9.)

- Check the institution's technical efficiencies. Ask for references of similar client families.
- Evaluate account responsibility and staff turnover in trust management.
- Determine availability and expertise level for philanthropic management.
- Evaluate loan policies. (See commercial bank requirements.)
- Investigate investment policy formation, implementation process, and performance. (See money management requirements.)
- Ascertain routine use of outside board of directors to manage an operating company or trust (if applicable).
- Determine level of expertise with management of like assets in trust.
- Examine the trust policy for those residing in a state where Third Restatement applies. Determine whether trustees qualify as investment advisors and what provision the bank makes to insure compliance in the case of unqualified named trustees. Investigate the policy on removal powers for trustees.
- Evaluate the institution's abilities as a trustee. For long-term trusts, is there flexibility and education of individual trustees (you can't teach a bank, and a trust officer can't teach a child about a family's business)? Emphasizing long-term safety issues makes an institutional trustee a compelling alternative.

Financial Planner

- Check for licensing (CFP), Investment Advisory certification (not an evenly trained or monitored profession), client base, experience, and disciplinary history.

- Examine the fee structure. Fee-based planning is preferable. Many product salespeople masquerade as CFPs but are compensated for wrap account and insurance sales, which are their primary goals.
- Evaluate client policy and determine the planner's perception of him- or herself as fiduciary. Does he or she fire clients?
- Determine the level of experience with like clients.

General Counsel (Attorney)

- Determine the nature of the practice. Is it tax and trust and estates driven, or is the focus general with underlying specialty? How long has the counsel been practicing in this area? Will the attorney work with others outside his or her firm on specific matters that are not in his or her area of expertise? Does he or she have the ability to use the interrelatedness of his or her expertise with others affecting the clients needs?
- Determine billing policy and willingness to disclose allocation of staff use and time.
- Evaluate the advisor's philosophy on important considerations in planning for the future, including "fairness" in a family estate plan; philanthropic bequests structure and implementation; marital property agreements; prenuptial agreements; trust structuring; investigate the counsel's estate and succession planning and experience with family wealth and family business planning issues.
- Investigate the counsel's client relations policy. Is there a willingness to establish client relationship, not just prepare documents? Is he or she proactive with the client? Is there reciprocity with the client? Does the individual generate periodic reviews? Is there formal client education? Is the counsel current with legal changes that might affect planning? Who has the responsibility for educating staff attorneys about your interests? What about staff turnover? Is there a policy on drawing on experts outside the counsel's field? Is there a reputation for remaining personally distant from the desired outcome (free from a personal agenda)?

Corporate Counsel

+ Determine the level of experience in dealing with families in business together. What percentage of the advisor's practice is comprised of this work?
+ Inquire as to the philosophy on periodically updating clients as a service.
+ Is there a return call policy? Will anyone else in the counsel's office be working on client affairs?
+ Inquire about the ability to assist with related legal business transactions, such as buy-sell agreements, succession transfer, shareholder buyouts, and stock restrictions. (See General Counsel.)

Accountant

+ Determine experience and depth of exposure to like clients.
+ Inquire about staff turnover. Who educates the new staff about your business? (Many expect the client to educate at client expense.)
+ Investigate account oversight, and documents and tax return preparation.
+ Determine the individual's role in estate planning. What is his or her philosophy on tax-driven decisions or belief in balance of business with personal planning priorities. What does he or she consider important in tax planning options, wealth transfer and business succession planning, and family compensation advisory for family businesses?
+ Evaluate the fee structure. Are fees negotiable? Are you charged for staff work rather than sophisticated tax advice?
+ Determine the communications policies regarding valuing your holdings and other concerns you might have. Determine what information your family should expect and understand. Does he or she have the ability to inform children about parental tax matters in simple terms? Does the advisor keep clients informed of changes affecting them?
+ Evaluate the audit and tax capabilities of the accountant if the family is in the business of buying and selling businesses and managing companies and liquid portfolios.

- Determine the accountant's ability to smoothly supplement the in-house accounting staff of a larger family office.

Note: Although technical in nature, the accounting function is more art than science.

Philanthropic Advisor (See Chapter 8.)

- Request references and a resumé of experience. The philanthropic advisor is highly personalized to the degree the client family has their own experience, focus, or lack of experience in the area of philanthropy.
- Does he or she have a defined mission? There is a difference between seeking advice for guidance in defining philanthropic focus and strategies from someone whom you hire to manage and administer the family foundation.
- Determine the level of familiarity with and service on not-for-profit boards and foundations. In what capacities has he or she served? Have he or she ever managed a not-for-profit entity or administered grant monies from public and private funding sources?
- Determine the advisor's qualifications for consulting in this area.
- Make inquiries regarding the advisor's personal philanthropic mission and policy.

Board of Advisors/Board of Directors

- The board of directors for an operating business is not an appropriate resource for financial or personal advice, but it can be a resource for referrals to those who *are* qualified to advise you in wealth management and to help identify advisor resources.
- Members of the board of advisors can be either paid or unpaid advisors. You will determine the value of each. An unpaid board is an important tool for setting goals and helping define mission statements and policy and for identifying other potential advisors.

Suggested Reading List

Diamond, Ann B. *Fear of Finance: The Women's Money Workbook for Achieving Financial Self-Confidence.*, New York, N.Y.: Harper Business, 1994.

Downes, John, and Jordan Elliot Goodman. *Dictionary of Finance and Investment Terms.* Hauppage, N.Y.: Barron's Educational Series, Inc., 1991.

Edie, John A. *First Steps in Starting a Foundation.* Washington, D.C.: Council on Foundations, 1993.

Ellis, Charles D. *Investment Policy: How to Win at the Loser's Game.* Burr Ridge, Ill.: Irwin Professional Publishing, 1993.

Friedman, Jack P.; Jack C. Harris; and J. Bruce Lindeman. *Dictionary of Real Estate Terms.* Hauppage, N.Y.: Barron's Educational Series, Inc., 1993.

Frishkoff, Patricia A. *Financial Smarts: Understanding Financial Statements: Business, Personal, and Estimated Estate Taxes.* Family Business Workbook. Eugene, Oreg.: Oregon State University, 1993.

Frishkoff, Patricia A., and Bonnie M. Brown. *Preparing . . . Just in Case.* A workbook. Eugene, Oreg.: Oregon State University, 1993.

Gersick, Kelin E., and Mildred Salganicoff, eds. "Women and Family Business," *Family Business Review* III, no. 2 (Summer 1990).

Gibson, Roger C. *Asset Allocation: Balancing Financial Risk.* Burr Ridge, Ill.: Irwin Professional Publishing, 1990.

Hausner, Lee. *Children of Paradise: Successful Parenting for Prosperous Parents.* New York: St. Martin's Press, 1990.

Lynch, Peter. *One Up On Wall Street.* New York: Simon & Shuster, 1989.

Lynch, Peter, and John Rothchild. *Learn to Earn: A Beginner's Guide to the Basics of Investing and Business.* New York: Fireside, 1996.

Magee, David S. *Everything Your Heirs Need to Know.* Chicago: Dearborn Financial Publishing, 1995.

Morris, Kenneth M., and Alan M. Siegel. *The Wall Street Journal Guide to Understanding Money and Investing.* New York: The Lightbulb Press, 1993.

Quinn, Jane Bryant. *Everyone's Money Book.* New York: Delacorte Press, 1979.

Quinn, Jane Bryant. *Making the Most of your Money.* New York: Simon & Schuster, 1991.

Rosenberg, Claude N., Jr. *Investing With the Best: What to Look for, What to Look Out for in Your Search for a Superior Investment Manager.* New York: Wiley, 1986.

Rosenberg, Claude N., Jr. *Wealthy and Wise.* New York: Little, Brown & Company, Limited, 1994.

Rosenberg, Claude N., Jr. *Stock Market Primer,* New York: Warner Books, 1981.

Scott, David L. *Wall Street Words.* Boston, Mass.: Houghton Mifflin, 1988.

Trone, Donald B.; William R. Allbright; and Philip R. Taylor. *The Management of Investment Decisions.* Burr Ridge, Ill.: Irwin Professional Publishing, 1995.

Zabel, William D. *The Rich Die Richer and You Can Too.* New York: William Morrow and Company, Inc., 1995.

Glossary

absorption rate (real estate)   The rate at which the available finished but vacant buildings can be filled, regardless of type (i.e., apartments, office, warehouse, retail spaces, etc.), based on projected demand in a specific location or region.

ADV (money management)   The annual filing required by the SEC of all registered investment advisors that reveals the background of key professionals, fees, and investment procedures.

ad valorem tax (planning)   A general property tax to a private owner based on the value of underlying real property such as real estate and minerals.

adjusted gross income (AGI) (planning)   The term most often associated with the calculation of Federal Income Tax (FIT) returns. The figure is calculated by subtracting from gross income any unreimbursed allowable business and other expenses such as some IRA and Keogh payments, statutory alimony, and disability income but *before* subtracting itemized deductions such as charitable contributions, medical expenses, state and local income taxes, and ad valorem tax computed under the Tax Reform Act of 1986 and its subsequent revisions.

AIMR performance presentation standards (money management)   Unenforceable standards defined by the Association for Investment Management and Research that include full disclosure and fair reporting representation of investment results as well as defined ethical principals for investment advisors and analysts.

alpha (money management)   A measure of a portfolio's return in excess of the market return adjusted for the risk in that same market. A positive alpha indicates a positive reward for the residual risk taken for that level of market exposure. *(CA)*

Note: *(CA)*   Definition provided by Trone, Albright and Taylor.
              (DC)   Definition provided by DC Planning.
              (K)   Definition provided by Donald Kozusko; Jones, Day, Reavis and Pogue.
              (P)   Definition provided by Pitcairn Trust Company.

alternative investments (money management)   Often used to define blind-pool, limited partnerships making investments in privately held companies, hedge funds, and other publicly traded derivatives-based strategies. *(CA)*

alternative minimum tax (AMT) (planning)   The tax imposed on every individual and corporation who thinks they have the perfect tax plan to minimize federal taxes. AMT is calculated by adding back certain "tax preference" items, including charitable contributions, to the normally calculated federal income tax (FIT). The AMT is payable only after applying the AMT tax rate of 21 percent to the newly calculated taxable income (AGI) if the resultant tax is higher than the tax computed under the regular method. The amount of AMT (if any) included on your tax return is the excess of the tax as computed by the alternative method (AMT) and that computed under the regular method (FIT).

annual exclusion (planning)   The annual $10,000 gift, tax-free, outright transfer of cash or other assets to family members or other persons often employed to reduce future death tax penalties on those same amounts. Currently there are no restrictions on the number of these gifts that can be given in any one year. Special kinds of trusts allow people to make gifts in trust and still qualify for the annual exclusion. See **Crummey trusts** and **2503(c) trusts**. In addition to the $10,000 annual exclusion, gifts can be made free of tax, and without using the $600,000 tax-free amount provided by the unified credit if the gift is made in the form of directly paying qualified educational expenses (tuition) or medical expenses for a person other than yourself. The exclusion is also available under the federal generation-skipping tax (GST) rules. Sometimes the exclusion is not available for gifts given to certain trusts. *(K)*

annual outlay (insurance)   Yearly computation of the life insurance premiums. *(DC)*

annuity   Set annual distribution or payment from a structured legal entity such as an insurance policy, trust, and so forth.

asset allocation (asset allocation, planning, money management)   The practice of spreading risk across a range of investment assets and styles of investment management to balance the effect of market forces and volatility in relationship to the risk level acceptable to the investor. According to modern portfolio theory, as much as 95 percent of the return of a diversified portfolio of assets is attributable to the distribution (allocation) and regular rebalancing of a range of investment classes and styles within those classes.

asset protection trust (creditor protection trust) A trust intended to protect the assets against the claims of the creditors of the grantor, and presumably of the beneficiaries. Such a trust is most often established in a jurisdiction that has specific legislation protecting trust assets from such future creditors. The term is sometimes used to refer to any trust that is specifically designed to protect assets from threats arising from expropriation claims by governments, monetary controls, kidnapping, and so forth.

balance sheet (B/S) (managing the process) A statistical statement of financial worth that lists assets and liabilities of the owner, the difference between which determines the net worth of the individual or corporation. Assets listed are usually listed at their original cost or tax basis, but they can be listed at market value for planning purposes. The liquid assets such as a managed market portfolio are listed at market value as of the preparation date of the B/S.

balanced account (money management) An investment strategy that combines equities (stocks) and debt (bonds) securities to obtain the highest return consistent with a low-risk strategy. Characteristics are a higher yield but a lower total return in a rising market and less volatility and downside risk in down markets than an all-equity strategy.

basis ("stepped up" and "carry over") (planning; real estate) Basis is used to track the cost of property for determining a gain or loss at the time of a later sale. The tax cost of the property received from a decedent at death is generally the fair market value of the property when it was inherited, regardless of its actual original cost, thus creating a "stepped-up" basis in appreciated property. The appreciation occurring prior to the decedent's death thus escapes income taxes upon a later sale. Different rules apply for gifted property. The original cost carries over after the gift (a so-called "carryover basis"). *(K)*

basis point (money management; asset allocation) 100 basis points equals 1 percent.

benchmark (money management) A chosen measurement such as an index like the S&P 500 against which to compare an investment manager's value added to the portfolio he or she manages. To be a true measure of value, the measurement should be as close to the same type investments and strategy as those of the manager.

beneficiary (general)   Person who receives financial benefits of an asset subject to certain conditions. Asset may be an insurance policy, pension plan benefit, IRS benefit, annuity, trust, and so forth. *(P)*

bequest (planning)   A transfer of personal property by a will. *(K)*

beta (money management)   A statistical measure of volatility of a security or portfolio in comparison to a corresponding market index. Beta equals the change in return of the security or portfolio per 1 percent change in the return on the market index (beta=1) being followed, usually the S&P 500. A portfolio with a beta of 1.1 is expected to move 10 percent more than the market when that index rises, and to fall 10 percent more than the market when that index is down.

bond (general)   A marketable-debt security issued by a borrower such as a corporation or government agency who pays interest to a buyer in return for the use of the borrowed funds. Bonds most often carry a face value in $1,000 increments and have a stated maturity date. If held to maturity, the face value of the bond plus any unpaid balance of the interest is returned to the investor. Taxes are payable on the interest from corporate and U.S. government bonds, but state government and municipal bonds are generally tax exempt.

bottom-up (money management)   An approach to valuing securities that involves first analyzing the companies, then the industry, and finally, the economy. *(CA)*

buying on margin (money management)   Also known as "leveraging," it is a regulated action taken by a customer in a brokerage account in which a level of equity must be maintained (varies by brokerage), the balance of which can be borrowed to buy more securities. When the prescribed level of equity is not met due to falling stock or bond values in the account, a customer must make up the difference—known as "meeting a margin call"—with cash or with eligible securities. Buying on margin is something you do when you think the market is only going up. The outsized returns that can be generated from investing with borrowed funds makes this strategy attractive to an investor.

capital gains/losses (general)   The results of an increase or diminution in the value of a capital asset between the day it is bought and the day it is sold. Capital assets are generally stocks, bonds and other assets held for investment. *(P)*

cash equivalent (money management)   Marketable instruments easily convertible to cash, such as money market fund shares and short-term government instruments.

cash sweep accounts (money management)   A money market fund kept at an investment institution into which all new contributions, stock dividend income, and bond interest income are placed (swept) for a period of time. At regular intervals, or when rebalancing is necessary, this cash is invested in the designated investment management accounts. *(CA)*

Certified Financial Planner (CFP) (planning; money management; getting good advice)   A designation granted by the Certified Financial Planner Board to individuals completing study and examinations in personal finance and retirement planning; CFPs are pledged to uphold an ethical and continuing education standard. *(CA)*

Chartered Financial Analyst (CFA) (money management; planning; getting good advice)   A designation granted by the Institute of Chartered Financial Analysts to persons who pass examinations in economics, financial accounting, portfolio management, security analysis, and standards of conduct. *(CA)*

contrarian (money management)   Term referring to investment managers that favor out-of-favor strategies or attempt to take advantage of anomalies in the marketplace by going against the grain. Value style managers are often referred to as contrarian.

coupon (money management)   Used interchangeably with the term "interest," it refers to the interest rate of a bond the issuer promises to pay to the holder until maturity. The coupon is expressed as an annual percentage of the bond's face value. *(CA)*

cumulative annual outlay (insurance)   Total of premiums paid over a given number of years. *(DC)*

current yield (money management)   The annual interest on a bond divided by the market price. See **yield**.

capital gains tax (planning; money management; real estate)   A personal investment tax paid at the time of sale of the asset on the appreciation in intrinsic value of that asset. Long-term growth (over one year) is taxed at the capital gains rate (28 percent in 1996), and short-term growth (less than one year) is taxed at the ordinary income tax rate (maximum of 39.6 percent in 1996).

cash flow projection (managing the process)   A printed statement that uses a running balance at the bottom of each monthly column to indicate the effect of income and expenditures on the cash available to the owner at any given time now and in the future based on actual information and projected estimates from best available predictions. Quarterly and annual reports are used for preparing budgets and for investment planning.

cash-on-cash return (general investments)   Expressed as a percentage of cash inflows against cash outflows for the investment (not considering appreciation in value or length of investment term).

"C" corporation (C corp) (planning)   The "regular" form of business corporation as defined by subchapter C of the Internal Revenue Service code. A C corporation can be owned by almost any number and any type of shareholders. The price for this flexibility makes the corporation an independent taxpayer subject to a complicated special set of rules that require that it pay tax on its income, even if that income is currently distributed to its shareholders in the form of taxable dividends to them (double taxation). Generally, a C corporation must also pay income tax on its realized and recognized gains from sales of assets, including the "deemed sale" that applies upon liquidation of the corporation, even when the property is not sold but is distributed in kind to the shareholders in the liquidation. Reduction of the corporate tax comes from allowable deductions, such as compensation paid to executives and employees (who may be shareholders also); by interest payments to creditors, rent, and other business expenses; and by depreciation deductions that are available on most capital assets. The subchapter S and limited liability corporations are taxed through their individual ownerships. See **subchapter S corporation** and **limited liability corporation**. *(K)*

charitable annuity (charitable gift annuity) (planning; philanthropy)   A tax-advantaged plan, without using a trust, by which a donor transfers property to charity in exchange for a specified current annual payment, with the charity retaining the funds after the annuity is paid. This has less flexibility than a CRT because the charity in question usually structures the terms of the annuity and manages the fund. See **charitable remainder trust**. *(K)*

charitable deduction (planning; philanthropy)   The ability to reduce income taxes by making charitable contributions. Also, the fact that a transfer of property to tax-qualified charities during one's lifetime or at death is not subject to wealth transfer tax if the transfer is properly planned. Tax-qualified charities include private foundations managed by the donor or the donor's family, as well as public foundations. See **501(c)(3)**. *(K)*

charitable lead trust (CLT) (planning; philanthropy)   A trust that allows the grantor (either living or at the time of death) to provide an income stream from designated assets to a qualified charity for a specified period of time, get a tax break, and retain ownership of the asset for the grantor's beneficiaries after that time expires. This results in reduced estate and gift taxes. Lead trusts are less common due to the very different set of tax rules that apply to each and the quite different nature of the potential tax benefits. However, the trust itself is not free from income tax, but instead receives an income tax deduction for the amounts paid to charity by reason of the "up front" annuity. If the trust fund produces better investment returns over time than the presumed rate of return used in valuing the present worth of the annuity, there should be more property "left over" for the beneficiaries after the annuity is paid than was subject to gift tax when the trust was first established. See **charitable remainder trust (CRT)**.

charitable remainder trust (CRT) (planning, philanthropy)   A trust that allows the grantor (donor) to leave assets to a qualified charity (either living or at the time of death), get a tax break, and retain income for the grantor or the grantor's family for a specified time. It provides thereafter that the property be distributed or held for the benefit of the charities. The grantor usually pays tax on the annuity as it is distributed. The charitable remainder may be deductible by the grantor as a charitable contribution at its present value against his or her federal income tax liability. It is usually established by a lifetime gift because that maximizes the tax benefits.

A charitable remainder annuity trust (CRAT) must receive a fixed annual amount of at least 5 percent of the value of the assets establishing the trust. A charitable remainder unitrust (CRUT) is required to calculate a fixed percentage of at least 5 percent of the net fair market value of the trust assets valued annually, creating a fluctuating annuity stream. See also **charitable lead trust (CLT)**.

closely held business (company)   A formally managed business, the interest in which is not available for purchase by the general public. The company is not required to disclose their financial condition either to the general public or to regulatory agencies for publicly traded companies.

community property (planning)   Community property varies by state, but generally, all property acquired by either spouse during the marriage while in a community property state is presumptively owned by both partners share and share alike. There are exceptions for inherited property, income on separate property, and property brought to the marriage, if such property is not commingled with community property. In general, a move to a noncommunity property state does not destroy the previous nature of community ownership. At death, the decedent's estate plan controls only an undivided 50 percent interest in the community property, and the surviving spouse continues to enjoy the other 50 percent interest.

convertible (money management)   A form of security that may, at the holder's option, be exchanged for another form of ownership, usually common stock. The issue produces higher income as an inducement to the holder and is used by some as a hedge against fluctuations in the value of the underlying stock.

corpus (planning; money management)   The term used interchangeably with principal as a trust term. It represents the assets (cash, real estate, securities, personal property, etc.) held in a trust. *(P)*

credit shelter (bypass) trust (planning)   Trust that bypasses the surviving spouse's estate in order to maximize use of the unified credit ($600,000) in the estate of each spouse. Without denying use of the deceased spouse's credit, it shelters the surviving spouse from estate tax on that amount. The bypass is usually established at death, although it can be established in one's lifetime.

Crummey power (planning)   A provision written into a trust instrument by which future interest gifts can regularly be transferred gift tax free ($10,000 exclusion amount) into an otherwise closed (irrevocable) trust, for example, to fund insurance premiums for an insurance trust.

Crummey trust (planning)   A "present interest" trust that allows the beneficiary to benefit from limited withdrawal (under $10,000) of property from the trust under a strict set of guidelines. When withdrawal rights expire, the property is held in trust on the terms specified in advance by the grantor. Crummey is the name of the key tax case that upheld this technique for wealth transfer. *(K)*

custodianship (planning)   In order to avoid legal and practical problems, gifts for minors are sometimes made to a "custodian" for the minor. The custodian will have certain powers and responsibilities as provided under the applicable state Uniform Gifts (or Transfers) to Minors Act. The grantor names the custodian responsible for investing the gift and using the funds for the minor's support, education, and benefit. When the minor attains the age of majority (18 or 21 according to state codes), the custodian must turn the property over to the minor. The custodianship avoids the more cumbersome court supervision of a guardianship, is less flexible than a trust, but can be enhanced during its lifetime when a trust can be technically closed to gifts from an outside grantor. *(K)*

death benefit (insurance)   Amount insurance company will pay out in the event of death. *(DC)*

declaratory judgment (planning; managing the process)   A judgment rendered by a court upon the introduction by affected parties of a request to settle or clarify a clouded point of law. Usually rendered in "friendly" lawsuits brought for clarification before a potential dispute arises.

defective trust (planning)   See **income tax defective trust**.

derivatives (money management)   Financial instruments whose value is derived from or linked to other underlying assets or liabilities. In their most common forms, derivatives help companies control financing costs in much the same way that caps on adjustable-rate mortgages do for homeowners. More complex derivatives are used as pure investment-return generators that carry inordinate risk in comparison to traditional investment strategies.

disclaimer (planning)   By a disclaimer, a person waives or surrenders all (or part of) a gift or bequest, including an interest in a trust, so that the disclaimed benefits then pass under an alternative plan. Disclaimers are used to allow property to pass to someone else, or to be held in trust on different terms, with a goal of a better estate planning result than is available at that time. The disclaimer is usually structured so as not to constitute a gift by the disclaimant who usually (but not always) must give up all rights in the disclaimed property or trust interest. *(K)*

discretionary account (money management)   An investment account giving a broker or advisor the right to trade securities without the client's consent, although broad guidelines set by the client can be defined.

dividend (insurance)   Distributable surplus of an insurance company as annually determined by mortality, expense, policy debt, and investment returns. *(DC)*

dividend (money management)   A cash, securities, or other property distribution made by the board of directors to the equity shareholders of a corporation. Also, a distribution of cash from net income made by a regulated investment company, such as a mutual fund, to an investor in that company.

dividend yield (money management)   The current annualized dividend paid on a share of common stock, expressed as a percentage of the stock's current market price. *(CA)*

Dow Jones Industrial Average (DJIA, the Dow)   The most widely quoted of all market indicators in the United States financial markets, this average reflects the price-weighted average of 30 actively traded, primarily industrial, blue chip stocks.

dynasty trust   See **GST exempt trust**.

EAFE index   See **MSCI EAFE index**.

employee benefits taxes   Federal and state "nanny" taxes—social security, disability, and workman's compensation for personal employees.

employee stock option plan (ESOP)   Used for closely held business continuity planning, ESOPs are trusts established for at least all full-time employees of the company. Although not advisable for all, weighing the legal and financial costs against the benefits might suggest an owner incorporate this as a planning tool to (1) use tax-deductible corporate cash contributions to buy out all or part of an owner's shares; (2) cause the ESOP to borrow to buy the shares and repay the loan with tax-deductible contributions to the plan equal to the loan payments; and (3) defer taxation on the gain from selling to the plan, if it owns at least 30 percent of the stock and the seller reinvests the funds in securities of other companies.

estate freeze (planning)   Class of transactions designed to "freeze" the asset values in the estate that are considered owned by an older generation so that the appreciation in those assets, or future income, can be shifted to younger generations in a manner that avoids the substantial estate and gift tax that would otherwise apply on such future appreciation and accumulated income. Joint purchase and the sale of a remainder are such transactions. (See **GRIT, GRAT, QRTP,** and **joint purchase**). *(K)*

estate tax   Tax on value of all property at death, with exception of the first $600,000 (as of 1996) given in one's lifetime to noncharitable recipients (exclusive of the $10,000, tax-exempt annual gifts).

excise tax   Sales taxes levied by the federal and some state governments, usually on commodities and some services, such as tobacco, slot machines, travel, cigarettes, and gasoline.

executor (planning)   An individual or institution named in a will and then appointed by the court to carry the will into effect. If a woman is appointed, she is legally referred to as an executrix. The principal duties are to safeguard estate assets, probate the will, assemble estate property, have appraisals made, manage the assets, settle claims and debts, settle taxes, account to the court, and distribute the net estate to the designated beneficiaries.

face amount (insurance)   Death benefit. *(DC)*

fair market value   What a willing buyer will pay a willing seller.

family limited partnership   See **partnership**.

fees and charges (money management; hiring professionals)

management fee   The quoted fees paid for money management (not including trading costs) based on the amount of money and type of account under management. These fees and costs will vary with the type and complexity of the account. Fixed-income accounts are easier and thus less costly to manage than are equity accounts. A standard fee for an equity portfolio might be 1 percent (100 basis points), for a bond portfolio ½–¾ percent, and for a balanced account somewhere in between. The fee percentage decreases as the portfolio size increases. Each firm has a schedule that defines the thresholds. In mutual fund parlance, the fee is referred to as a "load."

performance fee   Fee utilized by limited partnerships in addition to a management fee; it is annually calculated as a percentage of the gross gains of the partnership interest at the end of each year. It is important to ask a manager to give you a status report net of fees and taxes. The fee is not deductible as an investment expense against federal income taxes, and deductibility of other expenses are limited by law.

commissions   Fees charged by retail brokers for every transaction made for you. Unless an account is of institutional size ($20,000,000 and above can be the norm), retail brokerage commissions are the costliest fees in the industry. If a private account is sufficiently large to be individually managed, costs are defined as trading costs, which are a function of a calculation including commission costs of the broker executing the transaction and the actual execution cost at the time the trade is final. The variance in the impact the trading cost has on the portfolio can be significant.

custodial charges   Charges imposed by the keeper of the securities—a brokerage house or major bank serving as intermediary between manager and investor—that include custodial (instrument holding and dividend and interest gathering) fees, transaction (trading) charges, and cash management fees. Trust management fees, by comparison, provide low-cost management due to the conservative, low activity nature of trust management.

consulting fees   Administrative costs and fees charged by outside consultants hired to provide one or two specific functions related to portfolio management, such as a manager search. Typically, these can be $10,000 or more per manager and will not include the fee for monitoring of the hire. There can be associated termination costs. However, hiring or terminating a manager should never be based solely on fee levels. On the other hand, disclosure of all costs should be insisted upon by the client. See **hard dollars, soft dollars,** and **wrap fees.**

fiduciary (general)   Any person who handles property or transacts business for the benefit of another person in a relationship of special trust, such as a trustee and a beneficiary; a guardian and a minor child or legally incompetent adult; or an executor and the estate. *(K)*

501(c)(3) organization (philanthropy)   The Internal Revenue Service code provision describing qualifications for tax-exempt status for a charitable organization (foundation, institution, or agency). When reviewing the validity of an organization's receipt or request for funds, to insure that a contribution is treated as a tax-deductible gift, a 501(c)(3) form is often required as proof before a deduction can be taken.

fixed-income security   See **bond.**

fund of funds (general to all investments)   Usually in a limited partnership arrangement that pools investors' contributions and invests in other limited partnerships, most often those of hedge funds and other alternative money management styles and asset classes (venture capital and real estate).

generation-skipping tax (GST) (planning)   Draconian federal tax (55 percent) levied on transferred property (whether bequeathed or gifted, outright or in trust) after the first $1,000,000 in value (as of 1996), to a beneficiary one or two generations or more younger than the grantor. This tax is imposed in addition to any other applicable tax, including federal estate tax. This is a type of wealth transfer tax that is designed as a backstop to prevent "tax avoidance" by taxing gifts and bequests that "skip" a generation for tax purposes and thus avoid the regular estate and gift tax. See **GST exemption** and **GST exempt trust.**

generation-skipping tax exemption (planning)   A provision in the federal tax code that exempts the first $1,000,000 ($2,000,000 for a married couple) of property transferred to a line heir one or two generations younger than the grantor from the imposition of the generation-skipping tax. Any amount above that amount passing to a grandchild is taxable at the highest federal estate tax rate (55 percent). In the case of a trust shared by generations, the law is more complex.

generation-skipping tax (GST) exempt trust (planning)   Also referred to as a dynasty trust, it is designed to protect property from transfer taxes. This is the simplest vehicle with which to transfer the $1,000,000 (and more if executed and managed properly) of the generation-skipping tax exemption on to subsequent generations.

generation-skipping trust (planning)   A complex trust used to preserve the $1,000,000 generation-skipping tax exemption for both members of a couple. Putting smaller amounts into a trust and allowing them to grow can leverage the limitations of the exemption. See **credit shelter trust, generation-skipping tax**, and **generation-skipping tax exemption**.

gift tax (planning)   A transfer tax imposed by the federal government and some states on substantial lump sum gifts over $10,000 per noncharitable recipient. This tax is not levied on gifts between spouses.

grantor trust (planning)   A trust that, for virtually all tax purposes, is considered transparent and is "owned" by the grantor, making the grantor still taxable for the trust income. A trust would fall into this category when the grantor has retained certain powers or benefits over the trust, or assigned those powers or benefits to a related party or someone whose interest is not adverse to the grantor. The trust could also be a grantor. See **income tax defective trust**.

grantor retained annuity trust (GRAT) (planning)   An irrevocable trust used for making gifts while incurring little or no gift tax that minimizes the share of the trust enjoyed by the grantor and maximizes the share that is ultimately enjoyed by the grantor's intended beneficiaries, while minimizing the value assigned to the gift for gift tax purposes. The gift tax is minimized because the grantor transfers property to the GRAT but keeps the right to receive an annuity from the trust for a stated term. The property remaining in the GRAT after the term is intended to escape the grantor's estate tax, just like any other gift. A "zero GRAT" provides such a large annuity for the grantor that the tax cost of the gift of the remainder is extremely low, almost zero. The grantor must survive the specified term of years of the annuity, or all, or substantially all, of the gifted property is included in the grantor's estate and little or no estate tax saving occurs.

growth manager (money management)   A manager whose investment style is characterized by buying stocks of companies that are expected to have above-average long-term growth in earnings and profitability.

guaranteed cash value (insurance)   The mandatory reserve the company must maintain to fund the death benefit. *(DC)*

hard dollars (money management)   Specified fees paid in cash for services rendered. See **soft dollars**.

hedge fund   An investment fund, mutual fund, or limited partnership that uses various hedging techniques to take advantage of anomalies in the marketplace and to limit loss and maximize gains by investing in offsetting positions and securities-based instruments. See **hedging**.

hedging (money management)   An offsetting securities position that limits a loss caused by market uncertainties such as interest rate and currency fluctuations; volatility in investment returns; and price changes in commodities, inventories, and equipment. In a securities hedge fund, typically, common stocks are purchased (long position) or borrowed and sold to hold for later purchase at a lower price (short position). Other commonly used hedging instruments are referred to as derivatives. Companies, for example, use forwards and exchange-listed futures to protect against fluctuations in currency or commodity prices, thereby helping to manage import and raw materials costs. See **derivatives** and **hedge funds**.

income (general)   When income refers to gains from property ownership, it includes rents, interest, dividends, and so forth, and is distinguished from the "principal" or "corpus," which is the property that produces the income.

income beneficiary (planning)   The beneficiary of a trust who receives income for life, with the underlying remaining assets passing to other beneficiaries at the death of the income beneficiary.

income statement (managing the process)   A printed statement that lists income and expenses for a specific time period such as a month, quarter, or year.

income tax (general)   Federal, state, and local tax on earned (salary, working interest, and personal service) or unearned (dividends, royalties, and interest) income.

income tax defective trust (planning)   Irrevocable lifetime trust that constitutes a completed gift no longer includable in the grantor's estate for tax purposes under the gift and estate tax laws but that is still considered "owned" by the grantor under the federal income tax laws and is thereby known as a "grantor trust." This result can occur (deliberately or otherwise) because the income tax rules specify a broader range of circumstances under which a trust is considered taxable to the grantor for income tax purposes than the corresponding estate tax rules specifying when a trust is still considered owned by the grantor for estate and gift tax purposes. Such trusts are sometimes specifically used to gift property in which it is desirable to avoid changing the "income tax owners" from the grantor to the trust, such as in gifts of S corporation stock and partnerships.

index fund (money management)   A passively managed investment in a diversified portfolio of financial assets designed to mimic the performance of a specific market index. See **Dow Jones Industrial Average, S&P 500, Russell 2000,** and **Wiltshire 5000.** *(CA)*

insurance appraisal value (stewardship alternatives)   What it would cost you to replace with a minimum of effort a valuable personal object from loss or damage, regardless of the cause.

intestate (planning)   To die without a will so that property passes to heirs according to the court of the state of residence.

internal rate of return (IRR) (investments)   An inexact discount figured by measuring the best estimates of costs of the investment (cash outflows over time) and the projected returns (cash inflow over time). When these equal zero, the rate of discount used to reach zero is the IRR. When this is higher than the required target total return for the investment, then it is believed to be an acceptable investment risk.

internal rate of return (insurance)   The equivalent amount of interest that would have to be earned on the premiums invested over a given number of years to end up with the stated return. *(DC)*

inter vivos trust   See **living trust**.

irrevocable life insurance trust (insurance; planning)   A trust that serves as owner and beneficiary of a policy on the life of the client that effectively removes the death benefit of the policy from the taxable body of the giver/client's future estate. See **Crummey power**.

irrevocable trust (planning)   A trust that cannot be changed by the grantor; the surest way to remove an asset to be gifted from an estate to protect that asset from estate taxes. Special provisions can be included to use appointment and trustee powers to adjust the trust for changes in circumstances, but these require careful drafting to protect the irrevocability test that gives the trust its special tax protection status.

joint property (planning)   When joint property is held between spouses, the property will usually pass to the surviving spouse free of federal estate tax (and gift tax) because of the marital deduction. Sometimes having "too much" joint property can increase the total estate taxes to be paid by both estates, because property that escapes tax initially by using the marital deduction will typically be subject to tax upon the surviving spouse's death. See **joint tenancy** and **tenancy in common**.

joint purchase (planning)   A form of "estate freeze" that is designed to allow an older generation to retain the enjoyment of property for life or for an extended period of time, while shifting future appreciation to the younger generation. In the classic case, parent and child simultaneously purchase property, with the parent paying for the actuarial value of the life interest and the child simultaneously paying for the future remainder at its discounted present worth and later succeeding to the entire property free of wealth transfer tax. Joint purchases are still possible for purchases of a personal residence, but they are generally made very difficult and may therefore be structured differently. *(K)*

joint tenancy (planning)   Implies joint ownership of property by two or more persons who become owners at the same time by virtue of the same transfer and with the same "undivided interest" and possession. When a joint tenant dies, the surviving joint tenant(s) automatically then owns all of the property. The interest of the joint tenant who died does *not* pass to his heirs-at-law or those specified in his will. This *right of survivorship* is the principal characteristic of a joint tenancy. In a joint tenancy with right of survivorship (JTWROS), if one tenant transfers his interest to a third party, the right of survivorship is destroyed and the new tenant and the other original tenant(s) become "tenants in common." In the tenancy by the entirety (TBTE), which is a joint tenancy between a husband and wife, neither spouse is allowed to transfer his or her interest during their lifetime without the consent of the other spouse. Very few states have TBTE. See **joint property** and **tenancy in common**. *(K)*

K-1 partnership return (planning; money management)   The federal tax form that reports results of annual activities of a partnership and is sent to all investors in that partnership on which the investor's personal tax return bases investment gains and losses, and income and expenses per their partnership interest.

large cap stock (money management)   A colloquial term used to refer generally to the universe of large-sized companies whose individual market values range from $700 million to $1 billion on the lower end to $2 to $10 billion on the high end, although the median size held by a manager might be several billion dollars greater. In the case of the latter, companies valued at over $10 billion may be characterized as "super-cap" stocks. These larger companies generally enjoy higher trading volumes and thus are more liquid than small- and mid-cap stocks. See **mid-cap stocks** and **small-cap stocks**.

letter stock   An unregistered stock or bond that cannot be sold on the open market but is usually issued to early investors in a company. It can be sold directly by the issuer through a letter commitment (letter of intent/investment letter) and signed by the purchaser agreeing that it is not being bought for resale. If a sale is ultimately made after the period of restriction has lapsed, a 144 filing must be made with the SEC. See **144 filing**.

life estate (planning)   A property interest by which someone (life tenant) enjoys the property, and income from it, but that lasts only during his or her lifetime, or the lifetime of some other person or persons. After the life estate runs out, the life tenant has no rights and the property passes beyond his or her control unless the life tenant also has been given a power of appointment or sale.

life insurance trust (planning)   A life insurance policy put in an irrevocable trust for the benefit of spouse and/or children that keeps death benefit out of an estate. Additional gifts to the trust to pay the premiums for the policy allow further transfer of wealth down to the beneficiaries (if kept within the range of the annual exclusion gifts of $10,000) free of transfer tax. See **inter vivos trust, annual exclusion,** and **Crummey trust**.

lifetime exclusion   See **unified credit**.

limited liability corporation (LLC) (planning)   An LLC is a legal entity formed under state laws enacted specially for the purpose of protecting all of its owners from personal liability for the risks of the entity like a corporation, but that, like a partnership, does not pay the federal income tax at the entity level but only at the owner level. The single level of tax is a clear advantage over a regular C corporation, where there are two levels of income tax involved, and it is particularly important if significant or regular distributions of profits are going to be made to the owners, or if the entity may be liquidated or sold in the foreseeable future. See **C corporation, partnership,** and **S corporation**. *(K)*

limited partnerships   See **partnerships**.

liquidity   In general, liquidity refers to the ease with which a financial asset can be converted to cash. *(CA)*

living trust (planning)   Also known as the inter vivos trust, this is a trust created by a person during his or her lifetime.

load (money management)   The percentage commission or charge on a mutual fund or partnership. This includes both front-end and possibly ongoing (12(b)(1)) charges borne by an investment. *(CA)*

marital deduction (planning)   This is a tax "privilege" that allows certain gifts or bequests of property to pass between spouses free of wealth transfer tax. Assuming the spouse is a U.S. citizen, there is no limit on the amount that can be so transferred during life or at death free of the tax. "Bypass trusts" use the unified credit of the first spouse to die and avoids qualifying these trusts for the marital deduction, even though the spouse benefits from them, thus partially protecting the "second to die" from federal estate taxes on what was inherited tax free from the first spouse. Different rules apply to gifts and bequests to spouses who are not U. S. citizens. See **credit shelter trust**. *(K)*

market value (planning; investments)   Price at which a buyer and seller are willing to exchange an asset. Value is based on best available information and competitive forces of supply and demand in a free and open marketplace. See **fair market value**. *(P)*

mid-cap stock (money management)   A colloquial term used to refer generally to the universe of "mid-sized" companies whose stock price suggests their market capitalization value is in a range from $200 to $500 million on the lower end, and up to $700 million to $2 billion on the higher side. Small- and mid-cap companies are generally more volatile in nature (they go up farther and fall farther faster) and are more thinly traded than large companies because large blocks of their stock are more likely to be owned by only a few shareholders. See **large-cap stock** and **small-cap stock**.

minority discount (planning)   A "discount" that is applied in order to arrive at a value for an asset transfer when the preliminary asset valuation has been determined by supporting financial data on controlling interests and the asset in question is a noncontrolling interest, such as a small block of stock in a closely held company. The extent of the discount is a matter of judgment based upon the application of various objective financial data that indicates the value that buyers tend to place on the ability, or inability, to control a business or investment position. Under existing wealth transfer tax law, the minority discount can be applied even if the minority position being transferred is an ownership interest in a company, business, or real estate property, that is in fact controlled by related parties who presumably cooperate with each other. *(K)*

modern portfolio theory (money management; asset allocation)   A theoretical approach to investment decisions that attempts to measure and control both the kind and amount of expected risk and return of an overall portfolio of mixed investments. It relies primarily on the statistical relationships among the individual securities in the total portfolio.

money markets (money management)   Financial markets in which financial assets with a maturity of less than one year are traded. *(CA)*

MSCI EAFE index (money management)   The Morgan Stanley Capital Index of approximately 1000 securities representing stock exchanges in Europe, Australia-New Zealand, and the Far East. It is represented in U. S dollars and is the benchmark most commonly used to measure results from investments in financial markets outside the United States, just as the S&P 500 or Dow Jones Industrial Average is used to measure results of the large capitalization financial markets in the United States.

net cash value (insurance)   Total cash value for internal calculation purposes equaling the sum of guaranteed cash value, the cash value of additions, and the cash value of any paid-up additions riders to a life insurance policy. *(DC)*

net income (planning)   All ordinary income and capital gains net of income taxes. *(P)*

nonsimple will (planning)   A longer, more carefully constructed will prepared by specialized attorneys that is designed for wealthier clients to both minimize taxes and arrange for more involved distributions of property. In most situations, it provides for the creation of one or more trusts at the client's death.

144 filing (money management)   Refers to an SEC requirement of holders of restricted securities to file an intent to sell their letter stock in a company. Closely watched by some as indication of the belief that a company's stock value might be at or near a peak, prompting the "insiders" who hold the original letter stock to lessen their exposure to a possible downturn in value. The filer does not have to sell, and a restricted stockholder might merely be exercising the option because the restriction period has lapsed. Caution should be used when using this as a future stock price indicator. See **letter stock**.

opportunity cost   A term used in business planning and investment evaluation that measures the highest rate of return achieved by an alternative investment; that is, opportunity cost is what it costs you to choose one investment over another if the one not chosen does better over the same period of time.

option (money management)   A financial instrument or contract that gives the holder the right to buy or sell property (stocks, etc.) that is granted in exchange for an agreed-upon price. If the option is not exercised within a specified period, the option expires and the buyer gives up the money.

ordinary income/loss (planning)   The difference between normal, recurring income (earned income, portfolio, or trust) and your fixed and controllable expenses. It excludes capital gains and losses, acquisition or disposition of assets, and any loan activity or extraordinary items. Positive ordinary income gives a general indication of living within one's means. Conversely, an ordinary loss is indicative of spending in excess of available income, resulting in the diminution of principal assets or corpus of a trust. *(P)*

owner (insurance)   The person or entity owning the policy. *(DC)*

paid-up additions (insurance)   Dividends and extra premiums used to purchase additional life insurance to increase the policy's cash value. A paid-up policy is one that generates its own dividends and cash values, thus increasing its ultimate cash value. *(DC)*

payer (insurance)   The person or entity responsible for premium payments. *(DC)*

partition (planning)   A form of legal proceeding in which an owner of an undivided interest in real estate, usually as a tenant in common, petitions the local court to equitably divide the real estate among the owners in satisfaction of their fractional interests or, failing any other alternative, to require a sale of the property and a division of the net sale proceeds among the owners. Such a forced division of the property is generally not available to an owner of an undivided interest in any other type of property, such as jewelry, boats, and other tangible personal property. The availability of a partition action, and the associated delays and costs, is usually taken into account in valuing a fractional interest in real estate because it is relevant to the discount for lack of marketability and for a minority interest. See **undivided interest** and **minority discount**. *(K)*

partnership (family limited partnership) (planning)   A legal form for holding assets (an operating business or more passive financial assets) that is significantly different from a corporation, especially a C corporation, and particularly suitable for closely held businesses and other assets involved in family estate planning. Because a partnership is not a separate taxable entity for U. S. income tax purposes, only its owners and not the entity itself pay income tax on profits and gains, much like a subchapter S corporation or LLC, and unlike a C corporation. Unlike a general partnership, the limited (not the managing) partners in an FLP and other types of private limited partnerships are protected from liability of partnership activities. A limited partnership interest of an FLP is generally entitled to discounts in valuation, such as for lack of marketability. The valuation of gifts of family limited partnership interests is a matter of some complexity under the estate freeze rules. See **estate freeze**. *(K)*

per stirpes (planning)   "By the roots"—distribution of property made so that persons take equal portions of the share that their deceased ancestor would have taken if living. For example, if a grandfather leaves a distribution to his descendants "per stirpes," and he is survived by a son and two granddaughters of a daughter who predeceased him, the son will receive one-half and the granddaughters will each receive one-fourth (sharing the one-half their mother would have received had she survived). Under a "per capita" ("by the head") distribution, in which each then living descendant takes an equal share, in the above example, the son and two granddaughters would each receive one-third. *(K)*

pour-over trust (planning)   A trust designed to receive assets from other trusts (insurance, retirement accounts) to avoid probate.

power of attorney (planning)   An instrument authorizing another to act as the principal's agent or attorney (called the attorney-in-fact, as distinguished from attorney-at-law). A general power of attorney authorizes the attorney-in-fact to act for the principal in all matters, while a special power of attorney is limited to certain specified matters. A "durable" power of attorney remains in effect even if the principal becomes incapacitated, but until then it can be revoked at any time.

prenuptial agreement (planning; wealth is more than money; maintaining personal control)   A legal agreement used when it is desirable to limit the rights of one party to the other party's property or to limit other claims of one or the other. These are generally used when there is substantial disparity in the assets of one of the parties, particularly when a family business is at issue.

private annuity (planning)   Involves the sale of an asset, usually to a family member, in exchange for the right to an annuity for life. Used in specific and highly specialized circumstances, such as when transferring voting shares of a closely held company to minor children and retaining income and voting rights in the parent for the life of the parent or until some other specified time.

private equity swap (planning)   A customized transaction designed and executed by an institution between owners of securities to minimize the effects of diversifying out of large blocks of low-basis stock.

present interest (planning)   To qualify a gift for the annual exclusion, the gift must be of a "present interest" in property. Most gifts in trust, however, are gifts of a future interest. Crummey trusts and 2503(c) trusts represent exceptions. Gifts to such trusts qualify as present interests. *(K)*

probate (planning)   The process or act of "proving" a will before the appropriate court; also, the court-related proceedings in the administration of a decedent's or incompetent's estate. *(K)*

pro forma (investments)   "A matter of form"; a Latin word used for a partially fictitious financial statement based on assumptions before the facts and used to evaluate the efficacy of investment decisions. A term often used in real estate and venture capital investing.

property tax (planning)   State and local (ad valorem) real property owner tax used by local authorities to underwrite local services such as schools. Mineral royalties, investment real estate, personal property and residences and family limited partnership values are subject to this tax.

prospectus (investments)   A formal written offer to a potential investor containing facts used by an investor to make an informed decision. These facts include the history, management profiles, investment objectives, risk level of the investment, financial statement, and other pertinent data submitted by limited partnerships in securities, real estate, oil and gas, and venture capital, and by mutual funds.

Prudent Investor Rule (money management; planning)   The rule defining the duty owed by a trustee to the beneficiary in making "prudent investment" decisions for the beneficiary's benefit. All that was initially required were actions taken as though the trustee were a man of prudence, discretion, and intelligence. That 1830 statute has been revised over the years and is now commonly referred to as The Third Restatement of the Prudent Man Rule. See **third restatement**.

qualified personal residence trust (QPRT)   See **residence trust**.

qualified terminable interest property trust (QTIP) (planning)   A trust that allows an individual to obtain a marital deduction for the full value of assets transferred to the trust even though the spouse has only limited rights in the trust (essentially, the right to income) and the trust terms control the ultimate disposition of the property. Taxable in the spouse's estate, it will also be subject to gift tax if the spouse disposes of all or even a part of his or her interest during life. *(K)*

rate of return (investments)   A percentage used to measure investment interest and capital growth earned. *(P)*

real rate of return (asset allocation)   The nominal rate of return less inflation annually over the life of the investment or for a specified term such as annually.

remainderman (planning)   Used to refer to someone who holds an interest that follows after a prior term of years held by someone else, this term refers to a trust beneficiary or a legal owner of a partial interest in property. The remainderman does not have a present interest in property, either through the trust or in outright ownership, because the life beneficiary (in the case of a trust) or the life tenant (in the case of divided legal ownership) has the current interest in the property. *(K)*

residence trust (GRIT) (planning)   Sometimes used to refer to a QPRT (qualified personal residence trust), the GRIT reduces estate taxes by allowing the grantor to transfer the future value of the grantor's personal residence out of his or her taxable estate at a greatly discounted value. The grantor retains the right to live in the residence rent-free for a specified period of time. Estate tax savings is achieved if and when the grantor survives the time period because the property is expected to be in the beneficiary's hands, thus excluding it from the grantor's ownership.

revocable trust (revocable living trust) (planning)   A trust that can be revoked or changed by the person creating the trust. It can be used to hold property for management purposes during life, thereby avoiding a guardianship and providing a more comprehensive solution than a power of attorney in the event of incapacity. It can also be used to avoid probate at death and to manage property after death (unlike property managed under a power of attorney). At death, the trust would become irrevocable, because the grantor has died, although occasionally a trust will provide that it can be revoked by someone other than the grantor. A revocable trust can specify how the property will pass at the death, but it affords no estate tax advantages as compared to a will. *(K)*

Russell 2000 index (money management)   An index for measuring the stock price performance of the top 2000 small companies whose stocks trade in the United States tracked by Frank Russell & Company.

Securities and Exchange Commission (SEC)   The federal agency that has prime regulatory responsibility over the securities industry.

security (money management)   An instrument, usually freely transferable, that evidences ownership (stock) or creditorship (bond) in a corporation, a federal or state government, an agency thereof, or a legal trust. *(P)*

short-against-the-box (planning)   A planning strategy by which an investor borrows securities that are identical to their low-basis stock and then sells the borrowed shares. This is a nontaxable event. Using a series of steps, the investor uses up to 95 percent of the proceeds from the sale of the borrowed stock to invest in a diversified portfolio. This strategy is used to push payment of capital gains taxes into the future while effectively diversifying a stock portfolio. The strategy is currently under intense scrutiny by Congress and the Internal Revenue Service.

short sale (money management)   Betting that a stock's price will fall, an investor will borrow stock and sell it hoping to replace it (cover a short) at lower prices later, pocketing the difference.

small business investment companies (SBIC)   Privately managed venture capital structures funded with favorable borrowings from the Small Business Administration (SBA) to support independent small companies.

small-cap stock (money management)   A colloquial term used to refer generally to the universe of the smallest-sized companies whose market values range from less than $100 million to $200 million, although the median size held by a manager might be several million dollars lower. In the case of the latter, they may be characterized as micro-cap stocks. The stock in these companies is generally thinly traded (low volume) and may have a majority of its shares controlled by only a few shareholders, which increases their volatility and lowers their liquidity or marketability. See **large-cap stocks** and **mid-cap stocks**.

soft dollars (money management)   Referring to fees paid to brokerage firms and money managers in forms other than cash for services rendered. They are a form of commission that include directed brokerage arrangements (steering business to a specific brokerage house) and research agreements (trading business for research the manager might otherwise buy in hard dollars). In LPs, the partnership agreements should disclose any soft-dollar arrangements that exist in their fee structures. See **hard dollars**.

spendthrift trust and clause (planning)   A clause inserted in a trust to protect the beneficiary's interest from the beneficiary's creditors that is generally not available to a beneficiary who also funded the trust.

split-dollar (insurance)   An arrangement in a life insurance policy that divides the payment of premiums as well as the receipt of death benefit and/or cash values. Benefits may be divided between an employer, employee, the insured, spouse, trust, business partner, or children. Certain tax benefits derive to both an employer and the employee. *(DC)*

Standard and Poor's 500 (S&P 500) index (money management)   A measure of the value movement of 500 widely held common stocks. It is considered as a measurement of average stock market performance of 400 industrial and 100 other issues: 20 transportation, 40 financial, and 40 public utilities. *(P)*

standard deviation (money management)   A measure of portfolio risk (volatility) based on how wide a particular investment deviates from a mean average. It measures how much a series of monthly returns, measured individually, vary from the arithmetic average return. The wider the typical range of returns of the portfolio, the higher the standard deviation and the higher the portfolio risk.

standby trust (planning)   Trust that provides for control and management of a person's assets should physical or mental disability occur.

stepped-up basis   See **basis**.

stocks (money management)   Financial instruments issued by corporations in exchange for money. Stocks represent individual ownership in a corporation entitling the owner to certain rights such as the right to vote on certain corporate issues and to participate in any dividends paid.

structured equity shelf (money management; planning)   A transaction structured by a money management firm for a private client involving a large block of "market moving," publicly traded stock, by which that stock can be moved into the market over a period of time to lessen the impact of the sale of such a large block on the broader market value for that stock. Primarily used to lower "concentration" risk, this can be more effectively used in conjunction with a charitable remainder trust to minimize the tax impact on the owners of large blocks of low-cost-basis stock.

subchapter S corporation (planning)   This is a tax-advantaged form of corporation that is governed by subchapter S of the tax code. These corporations are established under the same state corporate statutes as C corporations, but in order to qualify for their special federal income tax status, certain tax code requirements regarding stock ownership must be met, including limited numbers and types of shareholders and limited classes of stock. The company's profits and gains are passed out to its shareholders, more or less automatically, and the income tax is paid only at that level. No owner of a corporation is liable for the risks of the entity if the corporation was properly operated, whereas a partnership (even a limited partnership) has to have at least one partner who is liable for the debts and obligations of the entity if the entity's net worth is insufficient to cover them. However, this limited liability for all owners is now also available through an LLC. See **C corporation**, **LLC**, and **partnership**. *(K)*

tenancy in common (planning)   A common form of co-ownership in which there is no right of survivorship and each co-tenant is entirely free to dispose of his interest without the approval of his co-owners. Since there is no right of survivorship, the interest of a tenant who dies passes to his or her heirs-at-law. See **joint tenancy**. *(K)*

third restatement (investments; planning)   Revision of the Prudent Man (Investor) Rule that is currently being reviewed and adopted by various states. It defines much broader guidelines for investment policy standards for fiduciaries, including diversification, total portfolio policy direction, support, monitoring, readjusting, justification of expense, and documentation of investment policy and decisions. It allows delegation of investment management duties to advisors with special skills not present in the fiduciary. See **Prudent Investor Rule**.

time horizon (money management; asset allocation) The period of time for holding an investment strategy or viewpoint. One of many factors weighed when making investment decisions.

top-down investment approach (money management)   Before making investment decisions, looking first at general economic trends, selecting industries, and then identifying companies within those industries most likely to benefit from the trends.

total return; (money management)   Standard measure of performance that includes capital appreciation/depreciation and realized gains/losses and income.

trading costs (money management)   After investment management fees, the second highest cost to the investor. Trading costs are usually quoted in cents per share and vary from volume discount, institutional rates of 5–7¢, up to retail customer rates of whatever the market will bear, such as 15–30¢ per share.

transfer tax (planning)   Any tax imposed on the transfer of assets from one person to another, which include gift, generation-skipping, and estate taxes. In New York, when combining federal and state death taxes, the penalty in 1996 on estates valued at over $1,000,000 equaled 63 percent of the estate value.

trust (planning)   A legal agreement by which a fiduciary (a trustee) agrees to manage property contributed by a grantor for the benefit of one or more persons, known as beneficiaries. *(K)*

2503(C) trust (planning)   A special trust for making "annual exclusion" gifts to beneficiaries under 21 years of age. If a large amount of property could accumulate in the trust by the time it must be distributed (21 years of age), the Crummey trust provides an attractive alternative. *(K)*

undivided interest (planning)   A percentage ownership share in a single property (real estate, jewelry, artwork, etc.) that may or may not be readily divisible. For wealth transfer tax purposes, gifts and bequests of such fractional interests are usually valued at a discount attributable to the lower price that an unrelated third party would pay for such an interest, reflecting the fact that a third-party purchaser could not acquire control over the property and could not resell the interest without the cooperation of the other owners or without a division of the property. See **joint tenancy** and **tenancy in common**. *(K)*

unified credit (planning)   A dollar-for-dollar reduction in taxes due, it can be viewed as an exemption of a certain amount of property from gift and estate taxes—up to $600,000 worth of property (as of 1996) can be transferred tax-free to non-spousal beneficiaries during life or at death (exclusive of the $10,000 annual per-person exemption) before a gift or estate tax is levied on the balance. Charitable beneficiaries are treated outside this provision.

Uniform Gift to Minors Act (UGMA)   See **custodianship**.

value manager (money management)   Managers who invest in companies believed to be undervalued or possessing lower-than-average price/earnings ratios, based on their potential for capital appreciation. *(CA)*

wash-sale rule (money management)   Rule designed to prevent an investor from buying the same security issue (stock, bond, or mutual fund) sold within 30 days of the former transaction. When swaps and short-against-the-box are used, timing to avoid this penalty is important. If it is deemed a wash sale, the investor cannot deduct the loss incurred.

Wiltshire 5000 index (money management)   Prepared by Wiltshire Associates, this index is the broadest measure of value in billions of dollars of all stocks listed on the New York Stock Exchange (NYSE), American Stock Exchange (AMEX), and over-the-counter (NASDAQ) stocks for which stock quotes are available.

wrap account (money management)   A form of investment product offered by investment consultants, money management professionals, and mutual fund companies that generally have a limited time horizon (3–5 years) in an attempt to simplify investment procedures while minimizing fees. Services usually included in traditional wrap accounts include consulting (asset allocation), custodial services, quarterly performance monitors, discretionary money management services, and consolidated 1099 (income statements for federal tax reporting purposes) reporting. Mutual Fund wrap accounts are available for lower minimum investment amounts and lower fees (brokerage fees are eliminated), and the personal involve-ment with the money management professionals is removed.

yield (money management)   Percentage return on a security invest-ment. *(P)*

Contributors and Collaborators

CONTRIBUTORS

Sally S. Kleberg (New York, New York, and San Antonio, Texas) Author and editor of *The Stewardship of Private Wealth: Managing Personal & Family Financial Assets.* Sally Kleberg is manager of Kleberg Asset Stewardship Education (K.A.S.E.) Study, customized advisory services for family businesses and offices and their service providers emphasizing financial literacy and education with the integration of family and business goals regarding ownership, management, and wealth, particularly the inclusion of women, the younger generation, and philanthropy into the education and management process. A former senior vice president of Bankers Trust, New York, in Owner-Managed Business Advisory Services, she also manages a family office in Texas, overseeing a diversified portfolio, trust management, business interests, and family philanthropic education and implementation. She served for 10 years on the board of directors of her family's company, King Ranch, Inc. She studied at Duke University and the University of Texas at Austin, with further graduate studies at the Institute of Latin American Studies at the University of Texas at Austin. After serving many years in varied management, development, and strategic-planning functions for the not-for-profit community, Ms. Kleberg currently serves on several not-for-profit boards and major gifts committees of educational and environmental institutions in New York, North Carolina, Virginia, and Texas.

Bryant Cushing (Santa Monica, California) Author of *Picking People and Choosing Professional Resources.* Bryant Cushing is a lecturer and author on the fine art of picking people, working for such organizations as Harvard Business School, YPO, National Venture Capital Association, *The Wall Street Journal, The Practical Lawyer,* and others. Mr. Cushing is chairman of Cushing & Cushing, Inc. Consultants, specializing in appraising emerging entrepreneurs and reshaping management for venture capital firms (Bessemer Trust, Warburg Pincus, the Rockefeller family). Mr. Cushing trained under William Allen of Boeing in the post-war rebuilding of that company; he then worked with Norton Simon while Mr. Simon acquired and restructured Hunt Foods & Industries, later Norton Simon, Inc. He is a graduate of Yale University and Boston University.

Lee Hausner, Ph.D. (Burbank, California) Author of *The Silence of Money*, and *Maintaining Personal Control: Communicating About Wealth.* Dr. Hausner is an internationally recognized clinical psychologist and business consultant specializing in the unique issues confronting individuals involved in family business and high-net-worth families. Dr. Hausner appears on network and public television and speaks before corporations and professional groups. She was senior psychologist for the Beverly Hills Unified School District for 19 years and currently has two books in print: *Homework without Tears* and *Children of Paradise: Successful Parenting for Prosperous Parents.* A third book in the field of family business is in progress.

Graeme W. Henderson (Pasadena, California) Author of *Venture Investing.* Mr. Henderson is a board member of Dallas-headquartered Capital Southwest Corp., an early SBIC prototype, now the largest publicly held venture capital investment company in the United States. He served on the management team for seven years and then became president of Source Capital, Inc., a publicly held VC fund ranked best-performing fund in 1977 of 146 funds of equal size. Mr. Henderson's current personal focus is on developing private companies, technology transfers, and leveraged acquisitions. Mr. Henderson was educated at Andover, Princeton, and Harvard Business School.

Thomas B. Henderson, Jr. (Corpus Christi, Texas) Author of *Oil & Gas Investing and Other Minerals, Too.* Mr. Henderson is a geologist trained at Duke University and the University of Texas at Austin. For many years a Humble Oil (now Exxon) petroleum geologist, Mr. Henderson is general partner in an oil and gas company and is an independent geologist with broad interests and involvement in natural sciences, community service, and the broader business of geology, including discoveries of minable oil and gas fields, lignite, and uranium deposits. He has extensive experience as a consultant to banks and wealthy families, defining and estimating mineral reserve values for estate valuation purposes.

Louis Leeburg (Phoenix, Arizona) Author of *The Imperatives of Planning—Financial* and *Asset Allocation and Investment Policy*. Mr. Leeburg is treasurer and cotrustee of the John E. Fetzer Memorial Trust, and financial consultant to the Fetzer Institute. Following a career in public accounting and corporate financial management, Mr. Leeburg has served as investment counselor and financial services advisor to individuals and families for many years.

Jane Gregory Rubin, Esq. (New York, New York) Author of *The Imperatives of Planning—Philanthropy*. Ms. Rubin is currently a counsel with Lankenau, Kovner & Kurtz, in New York. She was formerly with Coudert Brothers, specializing in trust and estates law, not-for-profit charitable entities, and multiple-jurisdictional issues especially involving asset and estate planning for artists with significant bodies of work. Ms. Rubin serves as executive director of "InterAmericas," a project of the New York Foundation for the Arts. Ms. Rubin serves as an advisor to and is an active member of numerous not-for-profit boards and organizations. She was educated at Vassar College, Columbia University School of Law, and New York University Taxation Institute.

COLLABORATORS

Gerald Freund (New York, New York) Mr. Freund is the primary interviewee in the text *Philanthropy*. Mr. Freund is president of both Private Funding Associates and Pro Bono Ventures, Inc., and he has a long history of consulting to individuals and foundations. He is currently director of the Whiting Writer's Awards, New York. Mr. Freund is the past director of the Prize Fellows Program for the John D. and Catherine T. MacArthur Foundation in Chicago; in addition, he was an officer of the Rockefeller Foundation, New York, and Dean of the Humanities and the Arts of Hunter College. He consults to major private foundations, national and state councils for the arts, and the Center for Effective Philanthropy, and he serves on several New York arts, education, and medical institution boards. Mr. Freund has broad research and teaching credentials in foreign policy relations, history, and advanced studies; he is a member of the Council on Foreign Relations and has written or contributed to several books and articles on philanthropy, arts education and programming, world history, and foreign relations. His most recent work is entitled *Narcissism and Philanthropy: Ideas and Talent Denied*. He completed his Ph. D. as a Fulbright, Oxford, Carnegie, and Rockefeller Foundation Fellow at Oxford University.

James E. Hughes, Jr., Esq. (New York, New York) Mr. Hughes is the primary interviewee for the text *The Imperatives of Planning—Tax and Legal*. Formerly a trust and estates partner with Coudert Brothers, and then Jones, Day, Reavis & Pogue, Mr. Hughes is a tax attorney in private practice specializing in domestic and international private client activities and in closely controlled corporate entities managed through trust vehicles. He serves as a consultant to Jones, Day, Reavis & Pogue and to trust companies. He also lectures frequently at professional meetings on international trust and estate matters and related tax issues. He serves in board and committee capacities to the New York State Bar Association, International Academy of Trusts & Estates, Brown Brothers Harriman Trust Company, and the Albert and Mary Lasker Foundation.

Suzan Peterfriend and **Howard Shapiro** (Westwood, New Jersey) Ms. Peterfriend and Mr. Shapiro served as the primary resource for the text, *Security and Insurance—Life Insurance*. Partners in D.C. Planning, a life insurance consultancy specializing in private-label recommendations for estate planning solutions for high-net-worth individuals and families, Ms. Peterfriend and Mr. Shapiro maintain strategic consulting arrangements with Brown Brothers Harriman, Bankers Trust, and U.S. Trust Company. Ms. Peterfriend is a Johns Hopkins graduate, and Mr. Shapiro is a Syracuse graduate. They coauthored the book, *Survivorship Life Insurance*.

INDEX